THE LANDSCAPE OF UTOPIA

A collect ia,
philosop py
academi

Explo lic
life, taste he
book pro es
landscap le
and plac to
wilderne

With rs,
this is a rk
discussic ch
as COV

Tim Wa ol
of Archit d,
taste, pla al,
political

"This collection, like all Tim Waterman's work, is a delight. He combines reflections on the relationship between place, space and social process with a drive towards imagining better lives and the conditions that might generate them – thus towards utopia. The varied pieces, written with elegance and grace, are thought-provoking, engaging and at times deeply moving."

— Ruth Levitas, author, Utopia as Method, *Professor Emerita, School of Sociology, Politics and International Studies, University of Bristol, UK*

"*The Landscape of Utopia* delivers a rich new contribution to utopian theory and lively reflections and meditations on what it means to think and practice better ways of living and being in very particular places. Tim finds utopian promise and provocation in practice and imagination; what is and what might be; the ordinary and the fantastic. With its extensive range of reference, sociological curiosity, agile thinking and inviting prose, the book returns us refreshed to familiar landscapes and invites us to keep hold of transgressive hope for changing them."

— Lisa Garforth, author, Green Utopias, *Senior Lecturer in Sociology, Newcastle University, UK*

"Intelligent and perceptive, Waterman draws on local stories from a wide range of places and times, weaving the narrative in and out of the subject, landscape, with insight and humour. The book is timely because it comes at a point when the discourse on 'landscape' is expanding, gaining interest by scholars and professionals across disciplines to address global concerns, climate change, cultural heritage, food security and issues of identity. Many of these concerns are addressed in the 26 chapters, some a single paragraph and others several pages, a statement, a reflection and food for thought. Waterman keeps his citation to a minimum, introducing key landscape scholars in an offhand manner to pique the reader and avoid the 'stuffiness' of academic writing. The fresh narrative of 'landscape' will be of interest to non-academics, architects and landscape architects, anyone interested in the environment, culture and shifting world politics and how they affect popular taste and ordinary citizens."

— Jala Makhzoumi, editor of The Right to Landscape, *Adjunct Professor of Landscape Architecture, American University of Beirut, President, Lebanese Landscape Association, Lebanon*

THE LANDSCAPE OF UTOPIA

Writings on Everyday Life, Taste, Democracy, and Design

Tim Waterman

Routledge
Taylor & Francis Group

LONDON AND NEW YORK

First published 2022
by Routledge
4 Park Square, Milton Park, Abingdon, Oxon OX14 4RN

and by Routledge
605 Third Avenue, New York, NY 10158

Routledge is an imprint of the Taylor & Francis Group, an informa business

British Library Cataloguing-in-Publication Data
A catalogue record for this book is available from the British Library

Library of Congress Cataloging-in-Publication Data
Names: Waterman, Tim, author.
Title: The landscape of utopia : writings on everyday life, taste, democracy, and design/Tim Waterman.
Description: Abingdon, Oxon; New York, NY: Routledge, 2022. | Includes bibliographical references and index.
Identifiers: LCCN 2021042111 (print) | LCCN 2021042112 (ebook) | ISBN 9780367759209 (hardback) | ISBN 9780367759155 (paperback) | ISBN 9781003164593 (ebook)
Subjects: LCSH: Social ecology. | Manners and customs. | Political sociology. | Landscape architecture–Philosophy. | Eating (Philosophy) | Utopias.
Classification: LCC HM861 .W38 2022 (print) | LCC HM861 (ebook) | DDC 304.2–dc23/eng/20211109
LC record available at https://lccn.loc.gov/2021042111
LC ebook record available at https://lccn.loc.gov/2021042112

ISBN: 978-0-367-75920-9 (hbk)
ISBN: 978-0-367-75915-5 (pbk)
ISBN: 978-1-003-16459-3 (ebk)

DOI: 10.4324/9781003164593

Typeset in Bembo
by Newgen Publishing UK

CONTENTS

FIGURES

FOREWORD

By Tom Moylan

> stay together
> learn the flowers
> go light
>
> —Gary Snyder, "For the Children," *Turtle Island*,
> New York: New Directions, 1969, 86.

> It is inconceivable to me that an ethical relation to land can exist without love, respect, and admiration for land, and a high regard for its value. By value, I of course mean something far broader than mere economic value; I mean value in the philosophical sense.
>
> —Aldo Leopold, "The Land Ethic," *A Sand County Almanac*,
> New York: Ballantine, 1966 [1949], 261.

Tim Waterman is a utopian in all aspects of his life and work. As a friend, a collaborator, and a fellow member of the party of utopia, I am honoured to have this opportunity to write a foreword for this wonderful collection.

It's important to stress that, for Tim and me and many people around the globe in all our intersectional being, utopia is not simply the name for an object of study (though it is usefully studied as text and practice and theory). Rather, it evokes a *project*, more precisely a *praxis*, of radical critique and totalizing betterment of reality for all of humanity, all of nature, all of the planet. Utopia therefore incorporates the *problematic* of theoretical categories by which the world can be interpreted and re-envisioned, the *method* of negation of what is and positive movement towards the horizon of a radically better reality, and the *way of being* that brings this hopeful dynamic into all aspects of life. Utopia calls forth a process of *becoming utopian*: of breaking with official normativity, seeing the world with new eyes, and contributing politically and artistically, day by day, year by year, to recasting that world in the name of all life and not a privileged few.

This utopian project involves a totalizing understanding and vision of the world, a transgressive (what Tim would also term *insurgent*) break with existing structures of power and privilege, and an ongoing transformative engagement. As a holistic undertaking, utopian energy can be brought to bear on entire social systems even as it subversively works its way through the intricacies of body and mind in everyday life. Utopian practice is undertaken by scholars and intellectuals, artists and scientists, teachers and organizers, and citizens of all ages. In all these efforts, the utopian vocation is embraced with the sober wisdom that such work is fragile and co-optable but also with the militant hope that the impulse to negate the bad old world and build the better new one can carry on in ways that we yearn for but can not yet conceive given the harsh conditions of the present. As it does so, the utopian journey is experienced not only in drained and often defeated affect but also in joyful camaraderie as people, in all their diversity, live and strive together towards the horizon of a fulfilled reality that none of us yet know.

As I said, Tim is immersed in a utopian way of being in his very life, with his vitality and creativity, his righteous anger against injustice, and his inclusive production in an array of undertakings to create not only a more just world but also a convivial one, for all. As an intellectual, an architect, a teacher, a collaborator, a citizen, a friend, a genuinely warm and open person in all areas of life (including music and gastronomy), Tim embodies the utopian virtues of compassion and cooperation, of hope and love. And he never gives up doing so, not only because the world won't let him, but because his own driving spirit carries him forward.

It is this situated utopian standpoint, this radical energy, this devouring and creating self, that Tim brings to this wonderful collection of essays. In *The Landscape of Utopia*, he gives us twenty-six short pieces that individually and collectively map our present landscape (understood as a contested one in which the repressive and destructive structures and practices of a planet governed by privilege and greed, hatred and violence, are negated, permeated, and superseded by insurgent possibilities already enacted yet reaching further for a critical mass of transformative change). In this work, he brings re-energized life to our lived landscape (from the scenic to the devastated to the promising) as well as our semiotic one (in film, theatre, design, policy). However, this is also an embodied landscape within which everyday life continues, in eating and drinking, discovering and designing, as well as engaging in political insurgence. Importantly, this is a refunctioned landscape wherein utopian being works with a double consciousness of knowing the horror of our dark times but also of making new cracks of light that open to the fullness of the better horizon—and indeed, a dual temporality in which the utopian radical is both struggling to overcome current problems even while living by the terms and conditions of that anticipated better world as it informs the theory and practice of that struggle. Consequently, this appropriately radical utopian political praxis is robustly rooted in specific challenges to present conditions, as well as in prefigurations that are ultimately more healing and fulfilling.

For me, this collection resonates in content, method, and form with the writing of the great utopian philosopher Ernst Bloch, who, with his Marxist hermeneutic of hope, read all the world, throughout history, around the globe, and into the future diagnostically to chart the long red line, as he put it, of humanity's efforts to produce that better world against the mendacity and meanness of their existing one, to discover its defeated possibilities and revive them as a surplus of not yet achieved promises that can engender new and more radical agency (see *The Principle of Hope*). In delivering this great project of deep interpretation, one of Bloch's favourite forms was the very brief reflection, or *spuren* (trace): short pieces that discovered in the "small things of life" the figuration of a utopian hope that reaches from the immediate, the micro, the local to the totality of reality, not only in the provincial present but in the unfolding future.

As with Bloch's, Tim Waterman's traces (developed via his own deep interpretive method which abjures the disciplining enclosures of the surface realism and empiricism which serves the reinforcement of the world as it is and as it is ruled) bring us a fresh new way of looking at and being in the world, rising above tiredness and stasis, summoning creative vision and practice, in all areas of our life. These works are infused with a utopian, overtly anarchist, imaginary that is deeply rooted in a *sense of place* (as the natural historian John Muir spoke of it), that's embodied with the demands of a *land ethic* (as Aldo Leopold termed it) that puts material flesh on the bones of theoretical totality, and that is always committed to what poet Gary Snyder termed "the real work" of radical democratic transformation infused by justice and beauty (see "I Went Into the Maverick Bar").

And so, I will end by encouraging you, the reader, to enjoy this book, to be disturbed by it, to be transformed by it. Like a good music album, the book invites an overall experience but then opens itself to an open-ended, partial absorption of this trace or that, exploring riffs on landscape or food or political indignation or militant hope (doing so with or without music, but I think the author might appreciate your choice of soundtrack). This book will, I sincerely hope, remain within your reach for this reason, for it can be consulted, enjoyed, and learned from, again and again. As well it should.

Tom Moylan
Ralahine Centre for Utopian Studies
Annacotty, Ireland
May 2021

PREFACE

The landscape(s) of utopia(s)

All the topics in this book are subjects commonly dismissed with a wave of the hand, or worse, derision and stern or even violent refusal: landscape, utopias, taste, anarchy. There is a readily available language of dismissal: "There's no accounting for taste"; "That's impossibly utopian"; "But that would just be anarchy." Once, in the Architecture Association bar someone simply turned on their heel and walked away from me when I said I studied landscape, saying "That is *such* a meaningless word!" This book, and, indeed, every sinew of my being, insists that each of these words is of profound importance. What these realms of ideas do is not so much define and pigeonhole and as smash down the silo walls and force a confrontation with radical openness, contingency, and relationality. Everything is connected, everything is inseparable, everything can have different meanings and purposes in different contexts, and that is good and useful. Taste, in particular, is important. The human is a discerning, sentient animal that makes distinctions based upon sense(s) and sensibility, and this is enshrined in the name Carl Linnaeus gave to our species: *Homo sapiens*. To be sapient is to taste and be wise.

Design is also central to this book, and in the fullest sense. When I write about design it is not just about the creation of alluring objects, it is also about design as an active (and activist) practice that is scenario-making, future-orientated, and attuned to lessons and forms from the past and to the intricacies of context. It is also political. It is impossible to design for the *polis* without engaging in *poli*tics.

The title of this book is imperfect. Its intention is to grab the reader, of course, and I make a false promise to be your guide around the landscape of a singular utopia. There are, of course, *many* utopias (and many dystopias) and each one of them employs a different place or world for critique and for testing ideas and scenarios. There are also *many* landscapes, and smaller landscapes nested into larger ones. And while utopias cannot, by definition, exist *in toto*, many of the forms, buildings, and landscapes that people occupy and interact with on a daily basis are the result of utopian thinking (or dystopian critique) and its influence on design. Humans live surrounded by glorious fragments of past utopias.

So, this book is unusual for its insistence upon woolliness, open-endedness, all-at-onceness, and infinite interrelation. This book is also unusual for an academic title as it draws from a decade's worth of my writing which is not all strictly academic. Much of the material is journalism, in particular from the pages of *Landscape*, the journal of the Landscape Institute and from *Landscape Architecture Magazine*, both with professional readerships. I hope this mix enlivens the texture of the book, as chapter lengths vary widely from 600 words or so to around 10,000. Readers can 'snack' on the shorter pieces or tuck into the longer ones for a fuller meal. The book is not divided into sections, but each essay flows into the next. The book may thus be read from cover to cover or sampled at will. Sprinkled throughout are titbits of the column I wrote for *Landscape* for six years, 'A Word… .' I hope, too, that it is possible to see the ways in which I have developed ideas and themes in different tones of voice and different settings. I am committed to the idea that theory *is in the world*, and that ideas and places and people and readerships all generate different narratives. Hence, too, the centrality of imaginaries in my work. Sometimes the places people inhabit are different from the ones they imagine, and always places are called into existence over time and through shifting imaginaries.

In addition to the previously published work, there are three new chapters—the introductory chapter, 'Taste, democracy, and everyday life in landscape imaginaries' and the concluding chapter, 'The tasty city.' Then the chapter 'On astronauts, LSD, and landscape architecture' has been developed from a talk I have given to students and other audiences for many years and in many settings, but which has never before been written up as an essay.

My approaches and methods, I believe, provide different tools for thinking from standard academic fare, and I hope that my radical utopian framings help others towards new tools as well. The many crises and challenges we face in the future cannot be faced with the 'common sense' that has created these crises. The world so many of us inhabit is built by racism (hetero)patriarchy, capitalism, colonialism and imperialism, nationalism, competitive individualism, and now neoliberalism, and that world, quite simply, is coming to an end. I'm confident, though, that as this world ends we can build a new one. To do so we need to imagine this world, and to do so we must become utopian. Though Tom Moylan has already contributed many bracing ideas in his foreword, there are a few more of his words I'd like to add that say better than I can what must be done, and these are that "the human person (and by extension human community)" is, and could be, and should be, "engaged in the process of becoming utopian." What we are concerned with "is not an abstract model or a disembodied study; rather, if utopia is to matter,"—and mattering happens in the material world—"it has to be regarded as knowledge and action, of utopian praxis" (2021: 191).

1

INTRODUCTION

Taste, democracy, and everyday life in landscape imaginaries

A project takes place

Human being and human becoming should be directed towards betterment. Our task as humans, as a sentient species, is to overcome our worst instincts and drives and to strive towards an ethical and customary relationship with each other and the world. In the last century revolutionary geographer and polymath Peter Kropotkin elaborated this idea as 'mutual aid' (1987 [1902]). In recent years the study of evolution and cultural evolution as both an evolutionary principle and a human value has both vindicated and renewed interest in Kropotkin's work. Human life, from the scale of the individual to family, community, and planet, is, for a species that makes and builds consciously, a *project*, and conviviality defines it. All the wars and aggressions of the human past are mere moments—aberrations, even—in the many long stories of people making peaceful lives together in and with landscapes.

History, it is said, *takes place*. But even before the Enlightenment sense of history came into being, cultures have told their stories through words, songs, painting and drawing, weaving and pottery, dancing; through journeys, through rites, through the contact between human bodies and the interaction between those bodies and with lived landscapes (see Abram, 1996; Dissanayake, 1992; Ong, 1982). All modes in which human stories are transmitted *take place*. It is useful to speak of stories rather than History (with a capital H), for another valuable habit is to move from capitalized singulars in study to lower-case plurals. History is certainly not, or shouldn't be, one Western, imperial story. Knowledge, too, is not a monolith, but there are many ways of knowing; many knowledges. And for [A]rchitecture, the formulation 'architectures' or 'the architectures' poses work(s) of educating, building, making, designing, developing as a platform for creation and becoming, instead of a rigid structure or an inexorable logic. Even the oft-repeated anarchist slogan 'another world is possible' benefits from this treatment, as other (life)worlds are

DOI: 10.4324/9781003164593-1

not only possible, but already exist to be learned from. Other lifeworlds are indeed possible: in fact, many are tangibly present and available as material from which future worlds may be imagined. The place of the body and the imagination in the world are most closely addressed in Chapter 14: 'Making meaning: Utopian method for minds, bodies, and media in architectural design,' and it explains how the full, sensate 'mind's body' (not merely the mind's eye) may be employed in the propositional imagination, simulations, and scenarios to better engage designers both with practices of dwelling in everyday life and with human and planetary betterment.

The essays in this book explore modes of making and building, dwelling, educating, the construction of professions, politics, and cultures (also *epistemic* cultures: see Knorr-Cetina, 1999). What underlies this range of subjects and gives cohesion to the whole is the question of how individual and collective imaginaries are created and employed in each process, and how taste, democracy, and a utopian horizon are imperative to them. People inhabit their lifeworlds as much through the direct experience of the senses as they do through the imaginary constructs that they, as individuals and members of collectives and cultures, project into those worlds. At a time of environmental crisis, when altering lifeworlds and life practices everywhere across the planet is crucial to the continued flourishing of our species and all others, it is vital to question the ways in which practices have been imagined. As Donna Haraway writes, "It matters what worlds world worlds," (2016: 35) and it is the realm of the imaginary and the epistemological at the root which must be understood in order to change the systems, processes, and forces through which our physical and cultural worlds are constructed, what stories people tell each other about them, and what lives they lead as a result.

Imaginaries may be very quotidian, a vision of the next meal and all its multisensual delights, perhaps; they may be very complex and far-reaching, from total, paracosmic worlds created in literature (Middle Earth, perhaps), to filmic utopias or dystopias from *Metropolis* to *The Truman Show*; or they may be ways in which collectives have envisioned the whole ordering of human life, from the building of nations to the operation of political economies. To understand imaginaries, we must understand how they frame questions, more than examine the answers arising from them. In the words of the philosopher of science Isabelle Stengers, "we must begin by reinventing questions wherever we have been converted to believing in the power of answers" (2010: 83). The dialogue between the fantastic and the ordinary consists in the posing and framing of questions in scenarios, and importantly, these "allow us to test potentially dangerous scenarios without endangering actual subjects" (see Chapter 14). And Kathleen Stewart frames the interpenetration of questions and practices and feelings in an appropriately kaleidoscopic way in the following passage from *Ordinary Affects*, worth quoting at length:

> The ordinary is a shifting assemblage of practices and practical knowledges, a scene of both liveness and exhaustion, a dream of escape or of the simple life. Ordinary affects are the varied, surging capacities to affect and to be affected that give everyday life the quality of a continual motion of relations, scenes,

contingencies, and emergences. They're things that happen. They happen in impulses, sensations, expectations, daydreams, encounters, and habits of relating, in strategies and their failures, in forms of persuasion, contagion, and compulsion, in modes of attention, attachment, and agency, and in publics and social worlds of all kinds that catch people up in something that feels like *some*thing.

(Stewart, 2007: 1–2)

At the very heart of my work is a founding opposition, or oppositional imaginaries, which again must be understood in order to provide for future human and planetary flourishing. Both comprise a dialogue between the mundane and the fantastic in the propositional imagination, and in the projection of expectations that may be considered to be utopian. On the one hand is the whole range of ideas and practices which, in modernity, produced the structures of state that spawned capitalism, colonialism, imperialism, heteropatriarchy, white supremacy, and their more recent evolution in neoliberalism and competitive individualism in postmodernity (see Bauman, 2000; Curtis, 2013; Gilbert, 2014; Harvey, 2005; hooks, 2000; Linebaugh, 2014; Linebaugh and Rediker, 2000; Makdisi, 1998; Mbembe, 2019; Scott, 1998; Toulmin, 1990). On the other hand is the burgeoning body of thought which, countering the modern conception of mind–body duality in which thought precedes action, proposes that thought and action, sense and emotion, are simultaneous, relational, and inseparable. This embroilment of mind and body in world (and ecology of mind or ecological thinking), is at the heart of the study of situated and embodied knowledges and the emerging and related field of practice theory (see Barnes, 2001; Haraway, 1991, 2016; Johnson, 2007; Ortner, 2006; Schatzki, 1996; Schatzki et al., 2000; Warde, 2016). In this ground are all the relational practices that are constitutive of place and the institution of the social: democracy, publicity and propriety (and, by extension, trespass and transgression), representation (all senses of this word), spatial justice, landscape/architecture, design, ecology, rurality and urbanity, the commons, pedagogy/education.

It is difficult for me not to see the entirety of the first, high state modern construct as largely dystopian, and the precondition or pretext for war, dispossession, inequality, and terror. And in the second relational construct I see whole worlds of both utopian possibility alongside the possibility to learn from the construction of landscapes as works over time (the Lefebvrean *oeuvre*: see Lefebvre, 2008 [1947]: 131–135) and the construction of cultures (including those of various indigenous peoples whose modes of knowing and being are discarded or erased by colonialism) as constructions of culture in timespace (see Bhabha, 1994; Casid, 2005; Gardiner, 2000; Lefebvre, 2008 [1947], 2005 [1981], 2002 [1961], 2000 [1968]; Soja, 1996; Stanek, 2011; and on decolonialism and indigenous studies Driskill et al., 2011; Smith, 2012). The first is a dystopia arrived at from the projection of a totalizing capitalist utopia, whereas the second is conditional, relational, composed of fragments and constellations of ideas, places, forms, and possibilities.

Though seemingly less significant, the study of taste (both gustatory and psycho-social/cultural) is worthy of far more research than it receives, as it shapes the socio-cultural, political, and affective interactions between people and place. Aesthetic taste functions in metaphoric and analogical ways that mirror the metaphoric construction of human cognition (see Johnson, 2007; Lakoff and Johnson, 1999). Combined with utopianism and striving, taste centres upon an understanding of fulfilment, human and planetary flourishing, good lives, and the paths through which these might be (at least partially) achieved. In design terms, utopianism employed as method allows for the propositional imagination to be exercised in acts of estrangement, transgression, supposition and simulation, prototyping, and narrative. An anarchist approach[1] here provides a radically different starting point (and thus different answers) from much other research and theory in this area, asking first the question: "How are people to help each other to govern themselves and avoid domination, compliance, and control?"

In the next pages, all of these themes will be elaborated and related to the body of work presented in this book, with reference to the contemporary idea of land-scape, the study of everyday life (in particular the study of taste and foodways), uto-pianism, anarchism, and the use of the propositional imagination in design, fiction, and politics.

Landscape, philosophy, cognition

The contemporary philosophy of cognition shows how thought does not pre-cede action, but rather is concurrent with it, and further how thought and action take place in a continual dialogue with space. The geographer and philosopher Theodore Schatzki (2010) calls this "activity timespace," and this relates to other framings such as sociologist Jean-Pierre Poulain's (2017) "food social space" and economic anthropologist Stephen Gudeman's (2001) "reason-in-action" (see Waterman, 2018). Useful comparisons may also be made with Mikhail Bakhtin's work on the literary and dialogic imagination, in particular in his "Forms of Time and of the Chronotope in the Novel" (1981: 84–258). The gustatory (and ultimately the sensate in general as well as all the particular senses) and the psy-chosocial and cultural construction of taste are all projecting individual and col-lective hopes and expectations (as well as fears and limitations) which inflect the timespace of human activity. The all-at-onceness of such thinking is also reflected in theorizations and conceptions of landscape. Landscape relations are practised in everyday life in customary ways that allow complex imaginaries or scenarios to be used from historical and sociospatial example to work through ethical questions for the present and future. The European Landscape Convention provides a useful if imperfect frame, defining landscape as "an area whose character is the result of the action and interaction of natural and/or human factors" (Council of Europe, 2000: n.p.), and Kenneth Olwig's work (Olwig, 2019, 2011, 2005, 2002, 1996; see also

---

1 One needn't *be* an anarchist in order to use an anarchist approach in research, analysis, evaluation, or design, just as one needn't be, for example, a sociologist to use a sociological approach.

Olwig and Mitchell, 2009) (both through his writing and my long-standing friendship and correspondence with him) has also provided a deepening and broadening of this frame by philological methods to describe land-*scape* as not merely the shape of land, but a land*ship*, and that the two suffixes are etymologically linked (Olwig, 2019: 25–26). A landship/landscape thus describes not only the condition or constitution of a place, but the nature of the relations through which it is created and constituted; relations between people and between people and the organic and inorganic milieus they inhabit; and the hopes, fears, expectations, and limitations people project (as imaginaries) and encounter there. And, finally, landship/landscape also describes the place itself and/or the view of that place.

The work of Chiara Bottici reminds us, too, that the ethical is also political and that the imaginal acts upon the lived world's mutual construction and inhabitation: "The fact that politics has always been imaginal is perhaps a banality that immediately appears if we consider that images are consubstantial with our being in the world, because there could be neither a world for us nor a subject for the world without them. Politics is imaginal because it needs a world in order to be in the first place" (2014: 104). When Bottici speaks of 'being in the world' it is useful to remember that this being is processual, performed, and enacted in space—what Theodore Schatzki calls "activity timespace" (2010: passim) and through what economic anthropologist Stephen Gudeman refers to as "reason-in-action" (2001: passim). Bottici draws a strong distinction between the imaginary, which she sees as purely occupying the fantastic: the imaginary "primarily means what exists only in fancy and has no real existence and is opposed to *real* or *actual*" (2014: 7), and the imaginal, which is composed of images. In tune with the relational qualities of my work, I find such firm distinctions to be at best unnecessary and at worst inhibiting. Bottici's narrow definition of the imaginary is created to give strength to the idea of the imaginal, which is, for Bottici, "that which is made of images" (ibid.: 5). This leaves too little room for forms of the imagination or imaginaries which might be constructed of not only images, but emotions, senses, stories (moral tales and more), and which might be *re*constructions of possible pasts, presents, and futures. Such complex sociospatial imaginaries are also particularly of interest when 'what exists in fancy' acts upon the real or actual, and vice versa.

Imaginaries

Imagination
creates the situation
and, then, the situation
creates imagination.

It may, of course,
be the other way around:
Columbus was discovered
by what he found.
　　　—James Baldwin,
　　　　"Imagination"

James Baldwin (2014), in a particularly delightful way here, hits upon a fundamental truth of how imagination is simultaneously and reflexively constituted
in the spatial and the social (the 'situation'), and how it is also the province, as
Cornelius Castoriadis (1987 [1975]) notes elsewhere, of both the individual and
the collective (Columbus, in his own head and in the imagination of 'what he
found'). Humour in this poem, as it so often does elsewhere, opens up a new
way of thinking. Baldwin imagines other frames from which to imagine worlds.
What so much of Baldwin's work does is to point out the flawed and dangerous
thinking that underlies much of Western life. This poem for me is emblematic of
the quest to find new ways to think: better worlds from which to world new
worlds. This quest in my work focuses upon the examination and understanding
of *imaginaries*: sociospatial, political, moral, and design imaginaries as well as literary
and filmic imaginaries. This includes understanding the way in which imaginaries
carry cultural meanings, significations, and narratives into reality and, again simultaneously and reflexively, reality acts upon cultural meanings, significations, and
narratives conveyed in imaginaries.

There are important links between these forms of imaginaries and the cognitive theory of pretence and the propositional imagination as found in the work of
Shaun Nichols and Stephen Stich (2000), and of Peter Carruthers, who writes of
practices of supposition as the acting out of pretence; supposition "can't be reduced
to believing, or to desiring, or to any combination thereof (nor can it be reduced
to any sort of planning or intending). It therefore needs to be assigned its own 'box'
within a functional boxology of the human mind" (2006: 90; and see Chapter 14).
It is this interpenetration of the real and the virtual and imaginary in supposition, or
perhaps of the insurgent irruption of ideas of practices of equality into the real, into
lived landscape, that illustrates an ecology, not just of mind, but of scenario-making
and world-making. Imaginaries are also employed in the work of design, in the acts
of prototyping, scenario-making, and supposition that happen in the studio, which
are fictional works that act in real ways upon built futures. Jens Beckert writes,
following Paul Ricoeur,

> Fiction can 'change reality' in the sense that fiction invents its own reality:
> fictions 'do not refer in a "reproductive" way to reality as already given,
> they may refer in a 'productive' way to reality' (Ricoeur 1979: 126). Quite
> aptly, Paul Ricoeur speaks of fiction as increasing reality. Fictions have the
> capacity to open and unfold new dimensions of reality, thus adding new
> layers to it.
>
> *(2016: 63–64)*

Imaginaries and landscapes (and propositional situations and scenarios and fictions)
are multiscalar. One of the key principles of landscape, and a key part of its useful-
ness as a term, is its applicability to multiple scales simultaneously: North Africa, for
example, is a landscape, as is the Maghreb, as are the Mediterranean and Saharan

Maghreb, as is the Mediterranean steppe, as is Marrakesh, as is a street or square in Marrakesh and so on—and all of these are places or bioregions to which a person or a community could conceive themselves as belonging (for more on this see Waterman et al., *Landscape Citizenships*, 2021). Not only does landscape exist at multiple simultaneous scales, but each scale slides in and out of the other in a relational and ecological way: a conversation between people, practices, imaginaries, and bioregion that is mutually constitutive. Arjun Appadurai has undertaken to show this, and if not from an explicitly landscape perspective, it is pertinent to it.

> [T]he imagination has become an organized field of social practices, a form of work (in the sense of both labor and culturally organized practice), and a form of negotiation between sites of agency (individuals) and globally defined fields of possibility. ... The imagination is now central to all forms of agency, is itself a social fact, and is the key component of the new global order.
>
> *(1996: 31)*

Appadurai's framing reflects not just the work of Castoriadis, but also of Henri Lefebvre and his great interpreter Edward Soja, whose concept of 'thirdspace' echoes the idea of landscape, and Soja's commitment is to always look for not a dialectic of 'either/or,' but a 'trialectic' consisting of 'both… and' (ibid.: passim).

> *Everything* comes together in Thirdspace: subjectivity and objectivity, the abstract and the concrete, the real and the imagined, the knowable and the unimaginable, the repetitive and the differential, structure and agency, mind and body, consciousness and the unconscious, the disciplined and the transdisciplinary, everyday life and unending history. Anything which fragments Thirdspace into separate knowledge or exclusive domains—even on the pretext of handling its infinite complexity—destroys its meaning and openness.
>
> *(Ibid.: 56)*

That such a conception uses an ecology of mind to encounter relationality in everyday life and to the supererogatory forms which embellish it—dreams, desires, hopes, fictions—also admits and necessitates a utopian horizon (as does Lefebvre) that inflects and impels the political as a drive. Also important here is that the political consists not of incontrovertible or inalienable rights, benefits, or obligations, or indeed of intractable positions, ideologies, or 'party lines,' but of practices, imaginaries, and ethics that are enacted and performed in (social) space. Jacques Rancière, speaking via his muse, the late eighteenth-century French revolutionary educator Joseph Jacotot, the titular *Ignorant Schoolmaster*, writes that "equality is neither given nor claimed, it is practiced, it is *verified*" (1991: 137), and likewise emancipation is a process and a practice that must be verified. The ideal must simultaneously exist as an imaginary in order for the mental image to be fitted to the practices at hand. The ideal is also a utopian horizon, as no perfect state of equality or emancipation can here be imagined as actually existing and permanent: however, the impossible drives the possible and the actual. Emancipation, equality, and democracy are practices, projects of sensible bodies in substantive landscapes. As also in Castoriadis (1987 [1975]), society and social practices are not something given, but rather are the result of collective imaginings. Social psychologist Angela Arruda, following Castoriadis, writes "The imaginary may be considered as the mental activity of producing iconic or linguistic images. The social imaginary, on the other hand, refers to a network of significations, collectively shared, that each society makes use of to think about itself" (2015: 128) Kristin Ross, to complete my productive oscillation between Castoriadis and Rancière, writes in her radiant introduction to *The Ignorant Schoolmaster*, that it

> forces us to confront what any number of nihilistic, neo-liberal philosophies would have us avoid: the founding term of our political modernity, *equality*. And in the face of systematic attacks on the very idea, powerful ideologies that would relegate it to the dustbin of history or to some dimly radiant future, Rancière places equality—*virtually*—in the present. Against the seamless science of the hidden, Jacotot's story reminds us that equality turns on another, very different logic: in division rather than consensus, in a multiplicity of concrete acts and actual moments and situations, situations that erupt into the fiction of inegalitarian society without themselves becoming institutions.
>
> *(1991: xxiii)*

Ross provides an astute and corrective reminder that the existing sociopolitical and spatial order is itself driven by an imaginary (dystopian or utopian or both) and that insurgent subaltern imaginaries may project themselves upon and into the(se) hegemonic vision(s) (see my essay 'Publicity and Propriety' (Waterman, 2017) for a discussion of how bodily and societal imaginaries are deployed in the space of the street). Lefebvre, in *The Production of Space* (1991 [1974]: passim) provides the canonical trialectic (to use Soja's term) of conceived, perceived, and lived space and de Certeau elucidates the key for navigating it in *The Practice of Everyday Life*, and it is a slight but productive oversimplification to say that the Certeauian *strategy* is the product of the totalizing hegemonic imaginary, whereas the *tactic* is the insurgent practice of the subaltern within, against, or despite that totalizing order (1984: 91–110).

Imaginaries are forms of knowledge and narratives that are both individual and shared and collective. At the smallest scale a utopian narrative in a film or a novel may compose an imaginary. At another scale a group, such as a community, may have a conception of itself that involves stories it tells about itself, and about whom it includes and excludes and why. At yet another scale, imaginaries can include the idea of nations and nationhood, of movements of resistance, or frameworks of knowledge out of which worlds are constructed, such as the idea of 'the West,' 'the New World,' or 'modernity' and 'modernization.' Benedict Anderson in *Imagined Communities* (1991 [1983]), for example, has shown how print media allow for widespread nationalist sentiment and simplified and standardized forms of belonging and fellow-feeling to be propagated, while Stephen Toulmin in his *Cosmopolis* (1990) defines the "hidden agenda of modernity" as residing in a rationalist quest for certainty and an insatiable urge to wipe the slate clean and start again from a neutral 'scratch line.' He tracks changes in the structure of thinking in modernity and since the Renaissance "from the oral to the written"; "from the particular to the universal"; "from the local to the general"; and "from the timely to the timeless" (ibid.: 30–33), and he shows these changes as aligning to a (utopian) *telos*:

> The beliefs that shape our historical foresight represent (as German philosophers put it) our *Erwartungshorizonten*, or 'horizons of expectation.' Those horizons mark limits to the field of action in which, at the moment, we see it as possible or feasible to change human affairs, and to decide which of our most cherished practical goals can be realized in fact.
>
> *(Ibid.: 1)*

Finally, James C. Scott in *Seeing Like a State* diagnoses the predispositions of the nation-state as the need "to make a society legible, to arrange the population in ways that simplified the classic state functions of taxation, conscription, and prevention of rebellion" and further that legibility is "a central problem in statecraft" (1998: 2). The power of the processes of simplification and legibility led to no less than

> the creation of permanent last names, the standardization of weights and measures, the establishment of cadastral surveys and population registers, the invention of freehold tenure, the standardization of language and legal discourse, the design of cities, and the organization of transportation.
>
> *(Ibid.: 2)*

The "administrative ordering of nature and society" (ibid.: 4) had a profound and steadily accelerating effect on landscapes throughout modernity, from the introduction of scientific forestry to collectivized farming to 'rationalized' human settlements. Scott holds all this together in "high-modernist ideology" with its ironclad narratives of

> scientific and technical progress, the expansions of production, the growing satisfaction of human needs, the mastery of nature (including human nature), and, above all, the rational design of social order commensurate with the scientific understanding of natural laws. It originated, of course, in the West, as a by-product of unprecedented progress in science and industry.
>
> *(Ibid.: 4)*

Thus can be defined and understood the immense power of the high-modernist *Erwartungshorizonten*—the shaping of the actual by the expected through ideological imaginaries of a clarified, simplified world.

It is not enough, however, to understand modernity, but also to see how the idea of 'The West' is constituted. Stuart Hall, the founder of cultural studies, provides a useful breakdown of how the imaginary of 'the West' is constituted, from which it becomes plain how imaginaries are inextricably tied to the real and the actual. Linda Tuhiwai Smith explains that, in his work, 'The West,' "is an idea or concept, a language for imagining a set of complex stories, ideas, historical events and social relationships" (Smith, 2012: 44). Hall himself explains that this concept functions in the following ways:

1. It *categorizes, characterizes*, and *classifies*; i.e. 'Western' vs. 'non-Western.' It is a tool for thinking which allows the operation of particular structures of thought and knowledge.
2. It is a *system of representation*, in which images, sets of images, and language are employed to concentrate and simplify complex people, culture, and landscapes.
3. It provides a standard *model of comparison*, allowing for *difference* to be articulated.
4. It provides *criteria of evaluation* through which other societies may be ranked, and around which powerful negative and positive associations are formed.

(Hall, 1992: 277)

I cannot resist here but to point out how similar these frames are to the function of taste distinctions (also see Bourdieu, 1979). The imaginary of 'the West' and 'the Rest' is immense and far-reaching and it has had substantial agency to shape knowledges and to shape the world in its physical forms and its attitudes, from how landscapes are built to how they are destroyed and/or exploited, and whether they are loved or loathed (often according to taste). Imaginaries also have a strong mythic element. All these narratives, despite their immense agency to shape the world, are losing their power, and understanding what new (or what rediscovered) epistemologies might next shape the world is the greatest task of our generation, as so much depends upon it—from the lives of our own and other species, to the preservation of lifeworlds and landscapes people hold dear. These ructions in late modernity and late capitalism are often defined as postmodernity, neoliberalism, and post-Fordism, but sociologist Zygmunt Bauman's idea of 'liquid modernity' helps to hold all of these framings together.

Liquid modernity

Zygmunt Bauman's definitions of solid and liquid modernity have proven to be immensely useful for elaborating theories that attempt the all-at-onceness encountered when bringing practice theory and new materialism to mapping the currents of change in late twentieth and early twenty-first-century life. His account of how forms of culture, society, and power have changed in the transition from high state capitalist modernity to late capitalist neoliberal postmodernity is a brilliant and wide-ranging synthesis. Bauman (2003: 11–12) defines 'solid modernity' as a settlement between those forces that sought to calculate earthly value only via financial metrics, characterized by the bourgeoisie, industrialists, and robber-barons operating a rentier economy and those who put sociality, good living, and human rights and dignity first, characterized by unionism, syndicalism, and humanism as a warm stream nourishing the working and middle classes. During the time of this uneasy settlement, wealth was measured in labour and its products, in often immovable material artefacts such as factories, and in land. In liquid modernity, on the other hand, power moves in flows, and often power's prime tool is escape and slippage—its constant threat of flowing away (ibid.: 15). This power may be able to extract from land and labour and resources, but it is extraterritorial in nature. Thus, Bauman argues, there is a growing divide between those who are bound in the social and political realities of substantive landscapes, and those in power "who do not apparently belong to the place they inhabit. Their concerns lie (or rather float) elsewhere" (ibid.: 16). Bauman cites Manuel Castells to explain the problem of this divide, of "increasingly local politics in a world structured by increasingly global processes" (Castells, 1997: 61) and diagnoses that local politics and urban politics are overstretched and overloaded. They are "expected to mitigate the consequences of the out-of-control globalisation with means and resources that the selfsame global-isation rendered pitifully inadequate" (Bauman, 2003: 20). The fundamental conflict is between spaces of flows and spaces of places. The two are not incommensurable, but their interaction is lopsided and fraught, as local politics depend upon the power held in the flows, but it cannot grasp enough of the wealth and power from those flows for its own sustenance. The power of the local is also consciously held in check, and, as Bauman notes elsewhere,

> [t]he ease of movement of the elite in the planetary 'space of flows' … depends to a great extent on the inability or unwillingness of the 'natives' (or people fixed by contrast in a 'space of localities') to act with soli-darity. The more discordant their relationships and the more dispersed the natives, the more numerous and slimmer their warring factions, the more passion they invest in fighting their equally weak opponents from the neigh-bourhood, the smaller is the chance that they will ever bring themselves to unite and close ranks.
>
> *(2011: 43)*

Awareness of the construction of liquid modernity and of the need to claw power back from the space of flows and into the spaces of places (landscapes) is key to my research; and it is the projection of landscape imaginaries through both design and philosophy that seeks to re-emplace power in substantive landscapes that is my goal.

Resistance is, more often than not, enacted by human bodies in physical places (see Chapter 16). The new epistemologies made available through the study of everyday life, practice theory, and new materialism (and also, by extension, queer theory and eco- and intersectional feminism), are in themselves more 'liquid,' flowing across simplistically legible boundaries and categories, and the modes of thought available through these theories have allowed my work to expand in ways that are relational and contingent. Casting oneself adrift from the certainties of rationalism, dualism, and high-modernist ideology is initially disorientating, but then once it is possible to see the interplay of ecologies and social ecologies, such fields of study that have previously been exiled to the margins become instead very central: and for me these are the study of the construction of gustatory and psychosocial/cultural taste, the study of landscape, and the study of the action of the utopian imagination in these categories and in political and cultural life. To return to Henri Lefebvre, whose life-span from 1900 to 1991 and immense scholarly output documented the transitional period between solid modernity and liquid modernity (though those terms are not his, I think he might have welcomed them and used them), again his writing has profound resonance:

> The fields we are concerned with are, first, the *physical*—nature, the Cosmos; secondly, the *mental*, including logical and formal abstractions; and thirdly the *social*. In other words, we are concerned with logico-epistemological space, the space of social practice, the space occupied by sensory phenomena, including products of the imagination such as projects and projections, symbols, and utopias.
>
> *(Lefebvre, 1991 [1974]: 11–12)*

These fields all have a future orientation through the projection because of the human aspirations and appetites tied to them: "Hope," I have written elsewhere, "through the action of utopia employed as a method using the propositional imagination for scenario-making, is essential to teach for, design, and build a future that is substantively better and permanently geared toward further betterment" (Waterman, 2019: 10).

The utopian and transgressive imagination

When Stuart Hall writes about the concept of The West as a construct which categorizes, characterizes, and classifies; as a system of representation; as a model of comparison; and the basis for criteria of evaluation, he is describing not merely the operation of an ideology or set of ideologies, but he is identifying the tools, fixtures, and methods of construction of a complete world-making assemblage. In the same way, so does Henri Lefebvre apprehend a complete world-making assemblage that stretches across the physical, the mental, and the social, and which is projected and which becomes a project in 'logico-epistemo-logical' sociospatial worlds. Neither Hall nor Lefebvre are at all bashful about their debt to utopian thought or their desire to employ its methods to change whole human lifeworlds: "We are all utopians," says Henri Lefebvre, "so soon as we wish for something different" (2000 [1968]: 75); and Stuart Hall describes utopianism as "future-becoming," a work which is "not just an empty projection but is grounded in experiences that we can already have, and is seen as an incubation of prototypical relationships—trying to embed them as alternatives within an existing structure" (2007: 126). This also is important to the propositional imagination in design, covered below. Both writers, too, were at the centre of a new mode of utopian thinking that formed from a particular moment in the late 1960s and 1970s in which a backlash against the suppression and trivialization of utopian modes of thought required a fresh opposition to the hegemony of (and boredom within) the traditional capitalist utopia and all of the forms of dystopianism ranged around it and arising within it. Tom Moylan identifies what he calls the 'critical utopia.'

> 'Critical' in the Enlightenment sense of *critique*—that is expressions of oppositional thought, unveiling, debunking, of both the genre itself and the historical situation. As well as 'critical' in the nuclear sense of the *critical mass* required to make the necessary explosive reactions.
>
> *(1986: 10)*

The sense here, when applying Moylan's model for the use of the imagination in literary utopian world-making to concrete sociopolitical world-making, is that these critical totalities have power—in the nuclear sense—to change human lifeworlds fundamentally and for the better.

That the human imagination acts in and on the world is evident in Moylan's foundational definition of utopia:

> Utopian writing in its many manifestations is complex and contradictory. It is, at heart, rooted in the unfulfilled needs and wants of specific classes, groups, and individuals in their unique historical contexts. Produced through the fantasizing powers of the imagination, utopia opposes the affirmative culture maintained by dominant ideology. Utopia negates the contradictions in a social system by forging visions of what is not yet realized either in theory or practice. In generating such figures of hope, utopia contributes to the open space of opposition.
>
> *(Ibid.: 1–2)*

By way of clarification here, utopian theorist Lucy Sargisson provides us with convenient bullet points to articulate how utopian thought works:

- It issues from political dissatisfaction and offers political critique.
- It articulates estrangement and offers an alternative perspective, from an alien (or new) space.

- It is creative and imaginative and often fictional.
- It has subversive and transformative potential.

(2000: 3)

Sargisson's further elaboration of transgressive utopian thought is a foundation the work in this book rests upon, and again she provides bullet points with great clarity:

- It breaks rules and confronts boundaries.
- It challenges paradigms.
- It creates new conceptual and political space.

(Ibid.: 4)

Transgression has great (critical) transformative power through action and imagination. When confronting such complete and powerful framings of lifeworlds and possibilities found in Stuart Hall's definition of the idea of 'The West,' or of Scott's and Toulmin's simple, legible models of high modern state ideology, it is utterly crucial that the utopian critique and resistance must offer the power, in the sense of critical mass, to blast received wisdom and entrenched practices from their foundations. This goes not merely for the collective, but for the individual too, or perhaps individuals embedded in scenes or in the intelligent and intellectual collectives I call, after Brian Eno, 'scenius' (see Chapter 14), and for all the processes of creating new intellectual and prefigurative worlds in design or fiction or political action. To be aware of oneself as a product of a 'scene' or 'scenius' also helps the individual to perceive themselves as having agency beyond the merely individual in a dog-eat-dog world. People, through education and making, can know and envision their place in a world of knowledge and action; as Jacques Rancière says: "To emancipate someone else, one must be emancipated oneself. One must know oneself to be a voyager of the mind, similar to all other voyagers: an intellectual subject participating in the power common to intellectual beings" (1991: 33).

Rancière shows us that the agency of the educator or the maker is rooted in a conception and perception of the lived world (again the Lefebvrean trialectic), but also that the agency is found in practices, in particular of emancipation and of equality (practised, verified), and finally in a projection into the future. Mutualist anarchists call these practices, particularly when they are seeking to demonstrate how lifeworlds might be differently practised in acts of public protest, 'prefigurative politics.' The student and the educator, or the protesters, enact a situation in which equality is performed and emancipation is enacted, thus constantly and repeatedly ushering them into existence. In prefigurative politics, such as that found in the Occupy! movement, no specific demands were issued by the protesters; rather, their exhortation was that they should be watched and emulated, as they were performing another better way to live beyond the bounds of capitalism and competitive individualism (see Graeber, 2013; and Chapter 16). To employ prefigurative politics is to show that 'another world is possible' and that a utopian horizon may be glimpsed in the here and now. Ruth Levitas writes:

Above all, we need to understand utopia as a method rather than a goal, and therefore as a process which is necessarily provisional, reflexive, and dialogic. It is always suspended between the present and the future, always under revision, at the meeting point of the darkness of the lived moment and the flickering light of a better world, for the moment accessible only through an act of imagination.

(2013: 149)

The power of new ideas, collectively held and acted upon, had been shown through movements such as the student protests of May 1968, but this power had also been abundantly evident in movements to radically shift the public view of built landscape and urban forms, particularly in the American conservation movement, which saw a pragmatic, perspicacious intellectual like Jane Jacobs pitted against a powerful, ruthless, and single-minded high modernist like Robert Moses. These two were not merely strong figures in themselves, but represented bodies of ideas collectively held on either side of a great divide between two visions—*Erwartungshorizonten*—for what the city could be and ought to be. Marshall Berman, a keen observer of these processes, in light of the modern mind wrote,

What stopped Robert Moses in his tracks was a great wave of collective learning. Americans came to see their cities could not be taken for granted— they were mortal and vulnerable, they needed to be nurtured and cared for, and ordinary people had the capacity to grasp the idea and act it out.

(2010 [1982]: 351)

Jacobs did not see herself as an anarchist—by any stretch of the imagination— she was a classical liberal who believed in the power of democracy to move the state. However, many of the ingredients of the 'scenius' that Jacobs was bolstered by had grown within a movement for humanistic planning and design that grew from proto-environmentalist conversations—in a time before mid-century political schisms had hardened—between early anarchists and socialists such as Peter Kropotkin, Ebenezer Howard, William Morris, and that flourished in the twentieth century, carried forward in the writings of talented polymaths such as Patrick Geddes and Lewis Mumford. This early fluidity of left politics provides a model of how a *new* polymorphous left could and should find ways to unite and close ranks against (disembodied, disemplaced) power's tendency to flow away.

Anarchism as method

When Miguel Abensour pronounces, in the preface, 'Of Insurgent Democracy,' to the French edition of *Democracy Against the State*, that "[d]emocracy is anti-statist or else it is not" (2011 xxxiii), he is referring to a democracy that is, as Rancière's equality, neither given nor claimed, but one in which the institution of the social in a politicized civil society enacts insurgency as a practice of non-domination "outside the state and against it" (ibid.: xxxix). It is precisely in this insurgency that democracy is found—"the live source of true democracy" which unites the social and the political to expose that the political is not found only in the state, and that the state "is not the last word of the political, its accomplishment. On the contrary, it is only its systematic and destructive form of *all ones* in the name of the One" (ibid.: xli). Here anarchism is clearly identified not as a political reality to be claimed and enacted with immediacy, but rather a set of practices—a method—and a set of tools for thinking about many things, but in particular the institution of democracy and the resistance to governmental forms of domination, control, and compliance. (Mutualist) anarchism often understands that its ends are utopian and impossible, but that only in striving for perfect mutualism, communalism, equality, emancipations, and democracy—asking for, *demanding* the impossible—can anything approaching a better world be brought into existence. This is not revolutionary so much as it is insurgent, a 'surging up' of change that is based in new understandings of what is of value and what is to be rejected. Revolution itself has been co-opted or subsumed into a constantly 'revolutionary' and restructuring neoliberal world, constantly erasing and rewriting so that cultural memories and forms are impossible to maintain. Now, holding systems and places together so as not to lose what is good in them while they are transformed is as crucial as the act of resistance in itself.

Anarchism's distant utopian horizon can be glimpsed from within the most mundane circumstances, however, and the great philosophical anarchist, the 'gentle' anarchist Colin Ward, points out that anarchism is also "a description of a mode of human organisation, rooted in the experience of everyday life, which operates side by side with, and in spite of, the dominant authoritarian trends of our society" (1982 [1973]: 18). It is practised, unknowingly, by people in all sorts of forms of organization from barn-raising to potlucks to cosmopolitan planetary initiatives such as the activist art of the Hyperbolic Crochet Coral Reef (Figure 1.1), a distributed work of stupendous creativity and beauty. Ward shows that these emancipatory institutions of the social are ubiquitous, and "once you begin to look at human society from an anarchist point of view you discover that the alternatives are already there, in the interstices of the dominant power structure. If you want to build a free society, the parts are all at hand" (ibid.: 20). "Anarchists," Ward tells us, "are people who make a social and political philosophy out of the natural and spontaneous tendency of humans to associate together for their mutual benefit" (ibid.: 19). Put this way, the insurgency is instituted in the homeliest of ways: in Marion von Osten's words, this is "the vernacular as didactic model" (2009: n.p.). Resistance to the hegemonic imaginaries that construct the contemporary world, from neoliberal capitalism to modernity to the forms of nation-states, can be found in everyday practices. Anarchism, then, following from Abensour and Ward, may be described as

- a theory of organization,
- an art of living,

FIGURE 1.1 The Hyperbolic Crochet Coral Reef on display at the Royal Festival Hall in London. It is composed of myriad pieces of hand-crafted coral contributed by artisans around the world. Credit: Tim Waterman.

- a model for thinking,
- an orientation against the state, and
- a utopian horizon.

Not only does anarchism as a tool for thinking temper my research, it also shapes my approach to working within higher education. One of the great problems of all scholarship is the fact that most research and writing takes place within an existing institutional, disciplinary, or professional structure, the erection and maintenance of which is arduous and all-consuming. Thus it is easy for many to make the dangerous assumption that when one has excavated down to the foundations of a field of thought, that one is beginning from the first principles of *all* fields of thought. These universalizing tendencies might be found amongst those studying political science, for example, where it is possible, indeed common, to define all questions in terms of existing models of state government. Questions framed from such a perspective might assume their first principles are "How shall we govern well?" or "How shall we legislate to overcome inequality?" Further, thinking of any deep and constructive nature is usually obviated by the necessity for close attention to the bureaucratic demands of the institution rather than the material, lived world from which theory arises and in which research is undertaken.

My approach to theory arises from a constant attempt to escape from such structures and find the right questions to ask from the examination of the lived world. This approach is anarchistic if not fully anarchist—engaging with the study of humans, human communities, and their vernacular lifeworlds, which are embroiled with other species in substantive landscapes. An anarchist method seeks to ask questions that are truly fundamental. Instead of asking how people are to be governed, it seeks first to understand how people take care of themselves in their situations, in the institution of the social, *without being governed* to minimize if not eliminate government. It seeks to describe how equality and freedom are continually practised and individually and mutually assured, and how human and planetary flourishing may be achieved without coercion, domination, or exploitation. Indeed, it is an approach that insists that such flourishing may only come close to being achieved when we have most fully removed the influences of coercion, domination, and exploitation. Such an approach must necessarily eschew the postmodern distrust of grand narratives—for this is certainly a grand narrative—and also embrace the idea that human becoming might follow the pull of a utopian *telos* (or, better, a set of situationally adjusted *telē*).

My attraction to philosophical anarchism began in my teenage years, when a North American strain of political punk alerted me to alternative possible worlds. Not only did I listen to the music of bands like the Dead Kennedys and Black Flag, but I followed their references to historical figures and ideas. I was about fifteen years old when I read the two-volume autobiography by Emma Goldman, *Living My Life* (1931). Her ideas of sexual freedom and her early understanding of ecology were abundantly appealing to a queer kid with an interest in the world and a healthy anger at the wrong-headedness of the prevailing common sense. More recently, a maxim from the work of Henri Lefebvre has guided me—and Lefebvre represents a strain of Marxian thought which is directed towards an anarchistic and utopian *telos*. "To penetrate ever more deeply into the content of life, to seize it in its shifting reality, to be ever more lucid about the lessons it has to teach us—this is the essential precept of research" (2008 [1947]: 182). Lefebvre was a Marxist, but argued that Marxism's goals should be 'the withering away of the state' and *autogestion* (which translates roughly as 'self-management'); thus there was an anarchist horizon to his work that often alienated state and doctrinaire communists. This helps remind me that critique about the landscape *is to be found in landscapes*, and that activism does not merely put ideas into action, but is itself a mode of critique.

Decentralization, cooperation, and mutual aid are emphasized in anarchism as first local qualities, and then larger decision-making and organization relies upon negotiated forms of federalism. The simultaneous focus on the local and the universal is unique to anarchism. It is also a form of thinking particular to landscape and to practice theory, as I have shown above. Such preoccupations were visible in anarchism's earliest incarnations and allowed the earliest manifestations of ecological consciousness to emerge in political thought. These foundations are to be found particularly in the work of two early theorists of anarchism, Peter Kropotkin and Élisée Reclus. Kropotkin is probably the most influential anarchist writer of all time, and his great work *Mutual Aid* significantly enriched the Darwinian study of evolution by asserting that mutations served evolution across whole species and in the interrelations between species (for a beautifully written account of this, see Stephen Jay Gould's 'Kropotkin was no Crackpot' (1997)). These theories reinforced mutualism's scientific as well as social claims, and had a strong influence early in the emergence of the field of sociology. Further, Kropotkin's important work *Fields, Factories and Workshops Tomorrow* (1985 [1912]) shows his rigorous engagement with the social and geographic forms of labour in his time, and draws conclusions about better models for political and social organization based in a clear observation of what actually works for people in actual places rather than elaborating upon any ideological preconceptions about the organization of labour. Peter Ryley, in his important study of early ecological thought in anarchism *Making Another World Possible*, writes,

> For Kropotkin, human institutions are not the product of any social contract but an emanation of human nature itself [...] he abandoned revolutionary rhetoric and began to examine human history through his particular expertise, the natural sciences. In doing so he established a small tradition of the geographer/scientist anarchist, in which he was followed by Élisée Reclus and Patrick Geddes.
>
> *(2013: 35)*

Élisée Reclus was just as widely travelled and his powers and energies of observation were just as keen and indefatigable. He survived the Paris Commune to write the monumental *L'Homme et la Terre*, and the memorable inscription in its frontispiece quite handily sums up its approach and its conclusions across all six volumes: "*L'homme est la nature prenant conscience d'elle même*"—"Humanity is nature becoming conscious of itself" (Figure 1.2). This sentiment expresses the very contemporary sense of embodiment, embeddedness, and situated knowledges found in new materialism while it implies a necessity for local and planetary stewardship based in perspicacious study of local landscapes, knowledges, and practices. Both Kropotkin and Reclus treated questions of human agency in physical landscapes— and the agency of those landscapes upon the lives of humans and the other species with which they are embroiled—as fundamental. Their ideas were also not merely transmitted through their writings, but with active engagement across a constellation of emerging left political fields. Kropotkin was a friend to, and influence upon, such great shapers of twentieth-century landscapes and ideas as William Morris, Ebenezer Howard, and Patrick Geddes. Reclus travelled to Scotland to work with Geddes, whose work is mostly explicitly anarchist in all but name. As Peter Ryley explains, "Geddes was neither an advocate of revolutionary violence nor of class struggle, yet still he claimed Reclus as his mentor. The phrase he used to describe the ideas of both Kropotkin and Reclus was 'constructive anarchism'" (2013: 158).

L' HOMME EST LA NATURE
PRENANT CONSCIENCE D' ELLE-MÊME

FIGURE 1.2 The monumental L'Homme et la Terre, and the memorable inscription in its frontispiece quite handily sums up its approach and its conclusions across all six volumes: "L'homme est la nature prenant conscience d'elle même"—"Humanity is nature becoming conscious of itself." Français: Illustration de "L'Homme et la Terre" d'Élisée Reclus. Gravures de Deloche et de František Kupka (1905). Credit: František Kupka (★23.9.1871 Opočno, Bohemia, Austrian-Ungarn Monarchy [now Czech Republic]; +24.6.1957, Puteaux, France).

Through Morris, Howard, and Geddes in particular it is possible to trace a clear, though often subterranean influence of those powerful ideas forged in early anarchism, right through twentieth-century landscape planning history through Lewis Mumford to Colin Ward and obliquely to Jane Jacobs (as discussed above). Even the most marketized and neoliberal of planning approaches in many ways are still rooted in these theories, for example the localism and desire for street-level human engagement expressed in the work of contemporary urbanists such as Jan Gehl, Andres Duany, and Elizabeth Plater-Zyberk. Needless to say, some cognitive dissonance emerges in the applications here. (Also perhaps some libertarian strains of competitive individualism or neoliberalism manifested as anarchocapitalism—both Colin Ward and the anarchocapitalist architect Patrik Schumacher stand against social housing, for example—Ward from a radical municipalist perspective, though, whereas Schumacher is merely toadying to the new aristocracy who are his clients.) Despite these confusions, the use of anarchism as a method and a tool for thinking has informed and impelled my research and my approaches, as it has generations of thinkers in the architectures, and whether hidden or subterranean or overt, it is continually insurgent.

Conclusion

My work is rooted in the study of everyday life and, more recently, in practice theory, which usefully extends that discipline; then, to what ends everyday practices are bent to, what narratives are told about them, and how prefiguration of better futures takes place as part of them; embodiment, embeddedness, and situated knowledges, intercorporeal human connectedness; and how the commons are created both in the landscape and in digital/virtual realms. The idea that landscape and virtual realms might be mutually constituted (which I have developed with the digital arts collective Furtherfield, resulting in the term the "situated digital"; see Chapter 10) also points to other realms which I see to be similarly embedded, and this includes the urban and the rural, and all the dimensions of landscape studies and food studies. It is impossible to conceive of the ecological interconnectivity of such approaches without a relational understanding of body and mind, morals, and human–environment interaction. Temporality is also an important part of this relational frame, with the idea of the landscape and the city as *oeuvre*, drawn particularly from Henri Lefebvre, and a utopian drawing of the best qualities and artefacts of the past into the future. Altogether this is a utopian framing of what Murray Bookchin calls 'social ecology' and 'the ecology of freedom' (2005). In 2013, Ed Wall and I framed this in terms of a 'landscape conversation' which, though it did not explicitly state it as such, was reaching beyond the idea of the dialectic to expand the sense to something more dialogic, conversational, relational, ecological, and evolutionary (in Kropotkin's sense, but also in the sense of cultural evolution as developed, in particular in the work of Michael Tomasello (1999)). Earlier yet, around a decade ago, I began to rough out a theory of taste, in an anarchist and utopian sense of the transformation of *what is* into *what ought to be*, which resulted in the study that became the book chapter "The flavour of the place" (Chapter 4). All together some of the grand narratives in my work are about the commons and their creation, fostering, and nurturing; the idea that conviviality is humanity's great project; that our freedoms are mutually assured and equality and emancipation are practices we share; and that each of these facts ties us to the landscapes in which we dwell, and to each other and all the other species in our lifeworlds. Democracy is consistently presented as both a goal and a practice (and it is also foundational in anarchism). Finally, a drive or set of drives is consistently presented. I prefer the term 'insurgency' to 'revolution,' in that I perceive that, in what Zygmunt Bauman calls 'liquid modernity' (2011, 2010, 2006, 2000), society has entered into a state of permanent revolution, and that the task of insurgency, rather, includes not only positive transformation into the future, but a holding together and a transmission of what is of value from the past. Thus, insurgency is a rising up within, not an overthrowing from without. A key part of this insurgency is radical storytelling—the creation of narratives, fictions, suppositions—which, for the architectures, takes place in design. Again, utopian qualities become evident in the power of the suppositional imagination to project alternative futures into spaces in the present. The anarchist slogan that pertains here is "another world is possible," and the other key anarchist formulation that applies is that of 'prefigurative politics,' in particular as it is practised in embodied and situated ways in the Occupy! movement (see Graeber, 2013).

It's important that an overall sense of striving and purpose are seen to be collective, and that the moral tales and narratives that generate or arise from shared landscape imaginaries become shapers for different forms of the commons. Make-believe is a practice that has agency in fiction, in sociopolitical imaginaries, and in scenario-making for design. An emphasis that is pervasive throughout my work is that democracy, equality, emancipation, and propriety are all relational spatial practices that are performed and enacted by human bodies in landscape space. The public, interpersonal, and intercorporeal dimensions of such spatial practices are guided by ideals and qualities that gain scant attention in much contemporary academic discourse. These are often known as the 'little virtues'—manners, grace, frugality, propriety—and they are constitutive of larger moral frameworks for human existence and social ecology that, together, have as much weight as the 'higher' moral values such as promise-keeping or abstaining from murder. All of this comes together with much higher purpose, proposing equality, emancipation, and democracy as practised and verified continually and collectively in everyday life, towards a utopian horizon.

2

THAILAND, HIGHLAND, AND SECRET ISLAND

Landscape and power in Bond films

Two indelible and endlessly reproduced scenes from James Bond films focus on a certain type of striptease in which the body of the subject of visual delectation is progressively revealed, not through a sequence of enticing disrobing, but rather as they emerge from the ocean, from the veil of the waves. In the first instance, in *Dr. No*, Ursula Andress (as Honeychile Ryder) steps onto the beach into the male gaze of Sean Connery's Bond—as well as the gaze of a largely male audience. Specific male desire for a specific female body is projected onto a slightly less specific landscape, though it is a particular generic type. The white sand, palm trees, lagoon, and waterfall of the setting represent a tropical Arcadia that audiences in the 1960s would immediately have recognized from lyrical tourist literature fuelled by the burgeoning international tourist trade of the time (and constantly reflected in and reinforced by Hollywood). "I must go there," audience members would have thought. "Come fly with me," crooned Sinatra, in a song popular at the time. Carefully and decisively the complex of sea, sand, and sex were bolted together, powered by the engines of (male) desire, and given wings by the Bond franchise. The second striptease, in *Casino Royale*, is differently gendered in an age when sexual objectification is becoming universal—a debased form of equality, perhaps. Daniel Craig as Bond is shown rising from tropical water, but there is less of an attempt to elaborate the landscape. The camera's eye in this case follows the female gaze of Caterina Murino as Solange, though, of course, as in Dr. No, it also represents a more generalized audience, in this case including the female or homoerotic gaze. The task of situating the viewer in the Caribbean is accomplished by the colour of the water, white sand, and the presence of an assortment of smiling, running black children (the children included as uncritical emblems of empire and colony). This convenient shorthand, made possible by an audience well-acclimatized to the bait offered by advertising, allows the camera full licence to linger on Bond's physical assets.

DOI: 10.4324/9781003164593-2

What interests me about Bond films is not so much what the characters, script, or the bodies of the actors themselves say about the content of the films and their political subtexts, but rather what the *backgrounds* communicate. The landscapes of Bond films may be read not so much as subtexts, but as propagandistic allegories and situating narratives that inform and represent both the overarching goals and the explicit practices and representations, initially of state capitalism and colonialism, and more recently neoliberal capitalism and its more veiled but equal or even greater spatially extensive ambitions. I will seek to clarify and expand upon the conundrum that W.J.T. Mitchell articulates so well: "Like money, landscape is a social hieroglyph that conceals the actual basis of its value. It does so by naturalizing its conventions and conventionalizing its nature" (2002 [1994]: 5).

Landscape

Landscape, for the lay observer, is often taken to refer to a particular scene, often specifically framed, and the association between the creation of picturesque landscapes and the painting of pictorial landscapes is one that seems a simple binary in history, with famous patrician landscapes such as Stowe and Stourhead drawing inspiration from the landscape paintings of Claude Lorrain and Nicolas Poussin. This was not, however, such a simple cause-and-effect relationship, but rather one in which the representational landscape informed representations of landscape ... which inspired representational landscapes which spawned representations of landscape, and so on in an endless, ever-magnifying loop: the "dialectical process whereby the painting of landscape scenery distances the viewer from the natural, while simultaneously making possible the perception of the land as nature" (Olwig, 2005: 32). This construction tended to valorize vaunted landscapes over quotidian ones, thus with every replaying of the loop, great landscapes became ever more rarefied and abstracted from lived experience and production, while everyday landscapes became ever more abandoned as sites for aesthetic satisfaction and ever more vulnerable to exploitation and despoliation. Such simulacra—to employ Baudrillard's term, "roughly defined as an exact copy of something that may never have existed" (Soja, 2010a: 379)—as those produced by the English landscape style in concert with picturesque and romantic painting are commonly seen as postmodern phenomena, but the dialectical processes occurring between eighteenth-century landscapes and landscape paintings and their ends are precisely the processes of reification and commodification that became evident in late twentieth-century hyperreality:

> With this expansive blurring of the difference between the real and the imagined, there is what Baudrillard defines as 'a precession of simulacra', a situation in which simulations increasingly take precedence over the realities they are simulating. Our lives have always been shaped by these hyper-realities and by the specialised manufactories that produce them, from religious institutions to Hollywood and Disneyland.
>
> *(Ibid.: 379–380)*

With these seemingly postmodern processes creating fantasy landscapes as far back as the eighteenth century, it was thus possible for Raymond Williams, in the late capitalist 1970s, to write that a "working country is hardly ever a landscape. The very idea of landscape implies separation and observation" (2011 [1973]: 120) and up until the time of that writing, this was largely true—it was impossible to conceive of a landscape of practice.[1] Since that time, however, and very much influenced by Williams' book, amongst others, the city and the country have come to be seen not as static, symbolic settings, but as a web of social, cultural, ecologic, and economic interdependencies, and we have even come to conceive of 'wilderness' as a space shaped by, as often as not, our urban conceptions and perceptions. Landscape is now seen as dialogic, not dialectic: the dialogic nature of landscape resists the closure sought by dialectics. Of course, philosophical conceptions of landscape are still at odds with entrenched totalizing concepts of a pastoral ideal, but the emerging clarity on relational concepts of landscape should, in time, begin to emerge in popular thought, as it is in political speech. "'Landscape' means an area, as perceived by people, whose [sic] character is the result of the action and interaction of natural and/or human factors" (Council of Europe, 2000: n.p.). This geographical definition of landscape, from the Council of Europe's *European Landscape Convention*, has now been adopted by the majority of European countries and there is now a significant movement towards an International Landscape Convention. At its core is the intention to foster international recognition that *all* landscapes are valuable for the human and other species that dwell in them, and that all landscapes are culturally constructed from a dialogue between people and place that is as constitutive of the character of those people who live there as it is of the landscape itself. And when I speak of all landscapes I am referring to all spaces "perceived by people" from cityscape to countryside to wilderness and everywhere in between: in the words of D.W. Meinig, "any landscape is composed not only of what lies before our eyes but what lies within our heads" (1979: 34).

Landscapes, as they are pictured in Bond films, are probably *not* intended to show this kind of subtlety and interaction. They are featured as symbolic backdrops, which, if they serve any physical function, is primarily to provide a challenging setting for a gunfight or a pursuit. Usually, they do both. For the trained eye, however, the landscapes selected as settings for Bond are as revealing as the action that takes place in them. Landscapes track large shifts across the twentieth and twenty-first centuries that are geopolitical, and in which sweeping changes in the construction of the nation-state and its relationship with industry and media can be read. These geopolitical shifts are not merely abstract (though certainly they have their roots in the abstraction of ideologies), but they are social, political, and cultural, and can be read in the inflection of local landscapes—something we might call not geopolitics, but *topopolitics*—local expressions of both real and symbolic forces which

---

1 This observation by Williams is often taken at face value, but as the book's arguments progress it becomes clear that Williams is working with a shifting and evolving notion of landscape that more and more allows the admission of 'working country' into its definition.

may be understood across a range of landscape scales. Where working landscapes are figured in Bond films, they are usually pictured as a backdrop against which to contrast the superior technology and gadgetry of the British Empire, or to provide an atmosphere of threat, as when the Istanbul chase scene in *Skyfall* takes a darker turn. Bond's fellow spy (Naomie Harris as Eve/Miss Moneypenny) loses track of Bond just as he enters an industrial rail yard, and here is where the landscape provides the cue that he is in trouble.

Where Bond meets disaster is along the railway lines in a wild landscape, and wilderness, particularly sublime wilderness, is as common a feature in the films as the manicured fantasy landscape. The idea of unclaimed or virgin land, codified in law as the doctrine of *terra nullius*, both provided a convenient logic for colonialism as it sought to lay claim to land, resources, and labour for exploitation and a foundation for a romanticization of wild landscapes. This supported (and continues to support) this logic as well as providing simple and legible mythologies that help to gloss over the violence of wresting lands from indigenous peoples. The appreciation of wild landscapes is a cultural construct, and its construction is seen in paintings such as Edwin Landseer's *Monarch of the Glen* of 1851.[2] The noble stag depicted against sublime Highland crags was symbolic not of a timeless Scotland, but of an image that was emerging as the population of the Highlands was dispossessed and displaced through eviction, forced and voluntary emigration, famine, resettlement on marginal (often coastal) lands and in meagre sub-subsistence crofting settlements, and all the violence and misery that accompanied the process of the Highland Clearances.

Rosalyn Deutsche speaks powerfully of the action that such visual images have in their reproduction and dissemination as companions to ideology; that they "can only be rescued from idealist doctrines and seen as social in the first instance if, released from the grip of determinism, they are recognized, as other cultural objects have been, as representations. Neither autonomous in the aestheticist sense—embodiments of transcendental aesthetic ideas—nor social because they are produced by external society, representations are not objects at all but social relations, themselves productive of meaning and subjectivity" (1991: 18). Thus it is the landscape, which, while represented (seemingly innocently) as object or backdrop in the Bond films, this chapter seeks to illuminate as a field of charged social relations bound into a mesh of official ideology and structures of race, class, gender, bureaucratic, military, and other such hierarchies. In the Bond films, wild landscapes

2 I like to think of the stag in the *Monarch of the Glen* as 'the face that launched a thousand biscuit tins.' Amusing, yes, but the durability of the image points not just to the symbolic force of the representation, but also to the political necessity of distributing such images. Its proliferation in the mid-1800s and after towards the end of the Highland Clearances is analogous to the proliferation of the admonition to 'keep calm and carry on' on posters, mugs, and other merchandise at a time when Britain's politics demanded action: in 2008, when markets and the existing political order had clearly failed utterly and criminally, and when that slogan was suddenly reproduced everywhere, the *last* things that were in order were calm and the maintenance of the status quo. In both cases uncomfortable realities were simply wallpapered over with propaganda.

appear as both idealized sublime nature, which *appears* wild, but which is in fact tamed or subdued (such as the prolific appearance of skiing landscapes), and as terrifying sublimity, which, as in the case of the Turkish landscape in which Bond meets disaster, has proven resistant to pacification (or which has not yet been pacified). The contradictions evident in these constructions cannot be reconciled, only recognized. Bond is presented in contrasting relationships to wild landscapes: either his urbanity and his gadgetry provide him with mastery, in which, after a strenuous struggle and the deployment of cutting-edge weapons technology, Bond dusts himself off and straightens his tie, or the presence of wilderness indicates be-*wilder*-ment, threat, and an overall darkening of tone.

Capitalism and imperialism

Dialogues between people and place, while always in existence in some form or another, are in themselves neither timeless nor immortal, and human conflicts over space have disrupted, rewritten, overwritten, or redirected these narratives through time reaching back into prehistory. Arcadia has never existed, and it must be assumed that if it ever came close to springing into being, or if an unspoilt corner of the world beckoned as such, that there was probably a covetous neighbour nearby to ensure that burgeoning earthly perfection met with violence and conquest. This urge for conquest, enclosure, and expropriation is tangible in this exchange between Auric Goldfinger and Pussy Galore in *Goldfinger*:

Auric Goldfinger: Your share of Operation Grand Slam will make you a very rich woman, my dear.
Pussy Galore: Why else would I be in it, Mr. Goldfinger?
Auric Goldfinger: You'll retire to England, I suppose?
Pussy Galore: I spotted a little island in the Bahamas. I'll hang up a sign: 'No Trespassing'. And go back to nature.

(Goldfinger, 1964)

Pussy Galore's desire for a secluded island—and the desire to enclose it and privatize it—are historic attitudes towards land that have been transported whole and largely unchanged from early modern capitalism to the present day. The assumption of *terra nullius* is what allows Pussy 'right of access' to what is conceptually virgin land.

Imperialism made extensive use of the doctrine of *terra nullius*—extensive in the sense of 'much,' but also in the sense of spatial extension. The grid, as an emblem of Enlightenment rationality, allowed for land to be mapped, plotted, and commodified. Its roots lay in the classical world, where the grid had been employed as an urban language of conquest, wherein the layout of new cities expressed efficiency and geometric purity. The Jeffersonian grid, extended across the whole of the emerging USA, provided a convenient vehicle for rapid expansion and the conceptual equalization of all landscape as virgin, extending the original colonizing impulse from early British imperialism to a new American imperialism that was later to become manifest destiny. The Jeffersonian grid was also seen to be democratic and egalitarian, even though its formal roots lay in classical conquest. Native populations, inconveniently, were distributed across this grid and would require clearance, extermination, or, failing that, concentration and isolation. The grid provides a clear illustration of how landscape "naturalizes its conventions and conventionalizes its nature." Some landscapes, however, were allowed to stand free of the equalizing grid, to become exceptional and emblematic, their imagery recruited as part of the state nationalist project. Whether wildernesses, private Valhallas, or picturesque urbanism, the image of these places was conflated with national myths of abundance. The New World was not alone in such celebration of landscape as image of the nation-state. The old world was just as busy painting pictures of its ideal self, both at home and in the colonies abroad (Barrell, 1980; Bermingham, 1987; Cosgrove, 1998 [1984]; Daniels, 1993; Olwig, 2002).

By the time of the rise of the Bond phenomenon in post-war, post-Suez Britain, it was no longer possible to maintain the mirage of empire, thus it is necessary to see Bond not as simple propaganda for British imperialism, but rather as a nostalgic, ironic, and self-mocking trope which becomes acceptable propaganda for a reactionary view of empire through its adoption of parody. What begins as light parody in the early Connery films develops into fully fledged lampoon in the later Roger Moore films. Bond is ostensibly poking fun, but the self-deprecation is a veil behind which an image of British mastery provides comforting illusions for the British public. Cynthia Baron captures these tensions capably:

> While 007's humour and 'masterful' style have consistently reassured the First World of its hegemonic position, and have provided a nostalgic bandage for England's wounded pride in the 'post-colonial' era, the Bond phenomenon also illuminates aspects of a 'modern' British identity that emerged in opposition to 'colonial' Others who had come to England to find a home. Bond's relationship to this 'new' identity invites us to re-examine British strategies of self-definition in the 'post-colonial' era, for 007's exploits remain steeped in the discourse of 'Orientalism' which had positioned the East as mysterious, incomprehensible, and pathologised in order to justify Western imperialism.
>
> *(2009: 153)*

Throughout the Bond films, until 2002's *Die Another Day* (when the liquid modern phase of neoliberal capitalism is becoming fully realized) Bond remained a more or less fixed caricature of the imperial Englishman, moving implacably through the Cold War. As Thatcherism gained ascendancy, his figure seemed perhaps more relevant against the backdrop of the war in the Falklands, but also oddly irrelevant and out of step with the yuppies and spivs who were the new 'masters of the universe,' no matter how much product placement identified Bond with conspicuous consumption. The film that exemplifies this uncomfortable mapping of Bond onto a neoliberal world is *A View to a Kill* of 1985—also an exemplar of the late lampoon (even low camp) phase of the Bond films. The film's overall aesthetic is certainly of its time, reflecting the post–Fordist realms of flexible labour that created the atmosphere in which it was plausible for Duran Duran to appear on a yacht in Antigua dressed like corporate wide-boys in suits and ties (in their 1983 video for the song 'Rio,' Duran Duran, of course, were also pressed into service to provide the film's theme tune).The uncomfortable fit of Bond to this particular world is accentuated by Roger Moore's advanced age in the role at this point, which coupled with his characteristically wooden performance, makes both his action scenes and any sexual athleticism improbable, even laughable.Add to this a weak script, and even the titanic presences of Christopher Walken (as Max Zorin) and Grace Jones (as May Day) fail to save the film from abject mediocrity. Perhaps to compensate for this, however, the views in *A View to a Kill* work especially hard, and several exemplars of the symbolic use of landscape in Bond are visible here. It is worthwhile tracing their succession in the film, as they are classic examples of particular landscape tropes in Bond films.

The film opens with a helicopter chasing Bond through an Arctic wilderness (the scenes were shot in Iceland—Figure 2.1). Bond vanquishes his foes and brings down the helicopter. The fireball created by the helicopter as it explodes accentuates both the sublimity of the landscape and of violence—a particularly fine bit of camera work. Bond then makes his escape in a motorized iceberg, the entry hatch of which is emblazoned with the union flag.The superiority of British skill and technology over its enemies, and also the implied dominion over the spaces of wilderness, this Arctic *terra nullius*, are classic expressions of supremacy, whether

FIGURE 2.1 Jökulsárlón glacier lake,Vatnajökull National Park, Iceland, through which Bond piloted his luxurious stealth submarine in *A View to a Kill*. Credit:Teddi Viscious/Shutterstock.

Bond's or English nationalism's. A brief scene in Whitehall at Horse Guards reflects the relationship between neoclassical buildings and streetscapes and the earthly power of the state, and situates Bond's life–work relationships at the epicentre of traditional urbanism—far from architectural modernism's whiff of either socialism or totalitarianism—all three often conflated in the conservative mythosphere, and indeed in Bond films. From there, Bond encounters the story's villains disporting themselves at Ascot. Ascot is both an equine emblem of Englishness and an arena of consumerist sport, a particular type of leisure landscape well identified by Michael Denning: "The sports represented are not the public school cricket pitch, nor the aristocratic blood sports and yachting, nor the working-class spectator sport of football: they are the consumer sports of golf, skiing, and casino gambling. They have the glamor of being the sports of the wealthy, the sports of the holiday on the Continent, yet are relatively free from traditional class connotations. Like Bond's vodka martinis, they are neither port nor a pint at the pub" (1987: 218).

From Ascot, the action moves to Paris, along the Seine, where a car chase strategically brings the Eiffel Tower into the frame, and where the urban peasantry manning souvenir booths are forced to flee from the paths of the speeding vehicles. Again, what is displayed is Bond's superior skill and technology, and forcing the working class of the city to scatter is intended both to employ *schadenfreude* to get a laugh and to belittle. The audience, naturally, will identify with Bond, even if after the film they will return to run their very own small shop or market stall. Chase scenes such as those that scatter market stalls and upturn displays of fruits and vegetables while making laughing stocks of the working class or peasantry are such stock imagery in Bond films as to have become necessary clichés, recognizable tropes, but which are also insidious reinforcements of the superciliousness and sadism of a persistently colonial English mindset.

Outside Paris in Picardy, Bond, posing as a wealthy playboy in a vintage Rolls Royce, approaches the Château de Chantilly (Figure 2.2), which here stands in as the stud farm of the villain Max Zorin. The landscape of Chantilly contains elements of the French Baroque style, which expresses a strong sense of the dominion of humanity (particularly wealthy humanity) over nature, bending it to a geometric will, and elements of the English landscape style, which developed during the dispossessions of the enclosures, clearances, emparkments, and 'improvements.' The implausibility of employing Chantilly's *ancien régime* excess as villain's lair is also characteristic of the self-conscious lampoon at work in *A View to a Kill*. Max Zorin and May Day assassinate Bond's companion and attempt to kill Bond by submerging his Rolls in one of the tranquil water bodies on the estate. Throughout the scenes at Chantilly, Zorin and May Day are characterized, confusingly, in an early liquid modern way, as communists, KGB agents, double agents, mobsters, crooked entrepreneurs, and aspiring totalitarians.

Both Zorin's mad totalitarian ambitions and his entrepreneurial goals are emphasized in a scene over the California landscape in his dirigible in which he addresses an airborne boardroom full of his investors. The long table opens down the centre to reveal a model of Silicon Valley, which Zorin intends to flood, in the

FIGURE 2.2 The Musée Vivant de Cheval at the Château de Chantilly, which doubled as Max Zorin's stable in *A View to a Kill*. Credit: Thomas Barrat/Shutterstock.

expectation that he will then be able to corner the market in silicon chips. The airship and the model serve to highlight the miniaturizing (and thus belittling and simplifying) view of the city that a model provides and to make the equation of power with altitude: the altitude of an airship or a skyscraper provides a totalizing 'god's-eye' view of the landscape below.

Bond, meanwhile, is on the ground in San Francisco, in various locations including the suburban mansion of the 'Bond girl' protagonist, in this case the geologist Stacey Sutton (played by Tanya Roberts). Despite being in the American west, her grand home is in the Palladian style of a southern plantation: white, pedimented and with a broad verandah. The sweeps of lawn evoke the English landscape style, but drooping vegetation adds to the southern atmosphere, as if to evoke a draping of Spanish moss. The plantation style is composed of these layers of symbolism: a clean white neoclassical (hence 'democratic') façade against an English landscape. It is an even more nakedly jarring juxtaposition of idealized styles with the realities of expropriation, exploitation, and brutality that the economy of the slave states were founded upon, along with the underpinnings of transatlantic capitalism. Another relic of maritime capitalism featured in the film is Fisherman's Wharf, once a working-class landscape now made boutique by regeneration investment for the purposes of tourism and real estate development.

The denouement of *A View to a Kill* takes place high in the cables of the Golden Gate Bridge. An armed struggle between Zorin, Stacey Sutton, and the nearly sexagenarian Bond at vertiginous height is intended to be gripping, but between the ridiculous improbability of the scene and Roger Moore's gurning at the camera trying to express grittiness and determination, it is merely funny. However, it does manage to scaffold another typical Bond/landscape relationship between the film's action and totemic infrastructure, signifying technical and engineering skill in overcoming natural forces, then recruiting them into the Bond mystique.

A View to a Kill provides views—and the ways of viewing particular to Bond and to capitalism and colonialism—into almost all of the landscape types that appear in all the Bond films in various combinations: Valhallas/playgrounds of the wealthy, tourist meccas (from the island paradise to the seedy sex-tourism district), sublime wilderness, totemic infrastructure, the synoptic/god's-eye view, and, to be put to ridicule, markets and other types of entry-level and working-class spaces of commerce and labour. Conspicuous in their absence from *A View to a Kill* are the sleepy colonial backwater with its country club (as Jamaica is pictured in *Dr. No*, for example), and agricultural fields and villages, which are often employed as objects of ridicule just as are markets. Also missing, amazingly, as it is so very common throughout the films, is any depiction of modernist architecture and landscapes as representative of totalitarianism, high organized crime, and socialism all at once.

Tourism, class, and labour

Landscapes do double duty in Bond, reinforcing the association between Baroque and English landscape styles, for example, with wealth and power, but they also express constructions of power that emerge and impress themselves upon landscapes over the years of the Bond franchise. Bond moves in a way that is apparently classless through these landscapes, and this is part of his appeal to a mass audience. His frictionless circulation is made possible, conceptually, by a long history of landscape access amongst the middle and upper classes, dating back to the late eighteenth century. At this time, these well-heeled tourists would have travelled largely to private estates, exhibited by their owners to this genteel crowd.

> Guides, guidebooks, hours of admission, and all the familiar structures of tourism were already in place. Drawings and paintings of such sights, initially commissioned by owners for their own viewing, developed into a business in its own right. By the early nineteenth century, books reproducing views of England's landscape sights addressed an audience of potential or vicarious tourists.
>
> *(Helsinger, 2002: 104–105)*

Possessing the representations of these landscapes would have provided visual access, and also a sense of ownership (by the elites) of a national aesthetic landscape. This commodification and packaging of such landscapes for tourism began with the itinerary of the Grand Tour, the educational rite of passage undertaken by upperclass men from the late 1600s to the early 1800s. The collection of visual imagery, such as the purchase of Canaletto's (tourist) views of Venice, or the maintenance of a sketchbook were *de rigueur*, and echoes of these practices can still be witnessed in the 'gap year' travels undertaken by the teenage children of the British middle and upper classes, which are now documented rigorously on Instagram and other social media. In the Bond films the tourist gaze is made explicit, not just through the representation of idealized and commodified landscapes, but also often reinforced by the picturing of tourists gazing at, consuming, and photographing the landscapes within the Bond films themselves. In *A View to a Kill*, this relationship is set up at least twice. First, Horse Guards in London is shown (Figure 2.3), and the camera pans from a mounted guard against the neoclassical background of Whitehall to a double-decker open-topped tourist bus from which spectators are snapping photos. Then, further reinforcement comes at Fisherman's Wharf in San Francisco, where Bond is shown stepping from a streetcar (such a common image that the streetcar is a synecdoche of the city). Another explicit example is a scene in *The Man with the Golden Gun*, in which Roger Moore as James Bond is pictured in the canals (the khlongs) of Bangkok.

In the scene, Bond commandeers a small, open motorboat, to make good an escape along the canals. In the background are picturesque villages and tour boats filled with tourists and their cameras. Bond's motor stutters to a stop, and his boat is boarded by a young, nearly naked boy, seeking to sell him a carving of an elephant. Bond declines, refusing to haggle, but the boy is persistent. Bond instead offers to reward him handsomely if he can restart the boat's engine so that he may continue his flight from pursuit. The streetwise boy sees that the fuel stopcock is off, and turns it on. It would seem that the boy's skill and savvy have shown up Bond's superiority,

FIGURE 2.3 Horse Guards, Whitehall London, with its typical throng of tourists. Credit: Ian Stewart/Shutterstock.

but, in a display of force gratifying to any mundane bully's sense of supremacy, as he accelerates out of the scene, he throws the boy bodily from the boat without recompense, presumably to gales of audience laughter. You can't best Bond!

Liquid modern Bond

Throughout the 1990s, with Pierce Brosnan playing James Bond, the films sought increasingly to adapt themselves to a changing global politics, in which certainties once peddled by the nation-states were fast disappearing, and the neoliberal project had flowered into the common sense of the age. Zygmunt Bauman coined the term 'liquid modernity' as a way of defining these changes: "The prime technique of power is now escape, slippage, elision and avoidance, the effective rejection of any territorial confinement with its cumbersome corollaries of order-building, order-maintenance and the responsibility for the consequences of it all as well as of the necessity to bear the costs" (2000: 11). Early in the decade, Bauman had described the order that was emerging: "With the state ethical monopoly (and indeed, the state's desire for monopoly) in abeyance, and the supply of ethical rules by and large privatized and abandoned to the care of the marketplace, the tyranny of choice returns, though this time it taxes not so much the moral competence, as the shopping skills of the actor" (1994: 5). In one sense this presented a particular challenge to the Bond franchise: that Englishness as embodied by the state had lost its centrality in the official narratives, as well as any loose ethical validation this might have provided to Bond's career as a spy and an assassin. The erosions of the certainties of the old solid modernity, and with any pretensions to moral responsibility, were accomplished by the supplanting of morality with a belief in a self-regulating market, with its 'invisible hand.' This helped to remove some of the agony of moral responsibility; that of having to choose between relative good and evil, and replace it with the power of the purchase. When financial might is considered a hallmark of goodness, then careful purchases and their display become guarantors of virtue: Rolex as stigmata, Aston Martin as heavenly chariot. In this sense the Bond franchise benefits, as it is so clearly a marketing engine for both places and products. The uncertainty of liquid modernity and the thick smoke of contemporary agnotology provide a shifting, obscure world of constant threat—a place where Bond can thrive—and where salvation can be purchased. As M, played by Judi Dench, pronounces ominously: "Our world is not more transparent now" (*Skyfall*, 2012). The sense of light parody evident in the early Bond films, and the outright lampoon of later Bond films has now clouded into irony.

Daub and Kronengold, in their superb and insightful book *The James Bond Songs*, quote Joan Robinson's maxim (1971) that "modern capitalism has no purpose except to keep the show going," and they say, "As the West has transitioned from making things to consuming them, and accumulating debt to pay for them, the show and keeping it going have become far more important than any actual product. Our labor now goes into putting on the show: it is a labor of stirring, maintaining, and circulating affect" (2015: 22).

The processes of obscuring the real labour behind actual landscapes—landscapes of practice—was, in Britain, accomplished almost completely in early capitalism, and has largely escaped documentation. This allows for the mystification of these landscapes to be almost total. Few traces of the underlying lived landscapes that preceded the fantasy landscape remain, and the fantasy landscape is then open to being marketed as the authentic original. These landscapes are 'putting on the show,' and it is in the film *Skyfall* that the landscapes so abundantly illustrate this fact. The film reaches a major crisis point when the headquarters of MI6 is bombed by cyberterrorists. The building itself is not an imaginary MI6 headquarters, but is in fact the present-day offices of the intelligence and surveillance organization, designed by architect Terry Farrell in a postmodern style (and in which the details are intended to evoke the forms of English hedges and topiary) (Figure 2.4). The explosion of the MI6 headquarters in the film, in fact, marks a moment as important for postmodern architecture as the destruction of the Pruitt-Igoe housing estate was for modern architecture in its sweeping symbolism of the end of an era. The bombing of MI6 in *Skyfall* is a powerful symbol of the end of architectural postmodernism. The building, still clinging too much to solid modernity and its need for visible institutions, is a clear target. In the film, MI6 is then relocated to the undercroft of Smithfield Market in working-class London's historic heart. Instead of 'pomo' flash, the agency is now put up in shabby-chic digs, with stained exposed brick and chipped glazed brick. Add a few exposed-filament lightbulbs, and it could just as easily be a burger restaurant for East End hipsters. Q, in fact, appears

FIGURE 2.4 'Our world is not more transparent now...' MI6 headquarters on the Thames, vividly destroyed by cyberterrorists and a marker of the 'end of architectural postmodernism' in *Skyfall*. Credit: Alexander Chaikin/Shutterstock.

as precisely that: an East End hacker-hipster played by the winsome and urbane Ben Whishaw who exemplifies the precarious-flexible entrepreneurial spirit of the nomadic liquid modern as, now, does Bond.

Bond has solid modern and high colonial and capitalist roots, however, and *Skyfall* forces him into some soul searching—it puts him on the couch, in fact—and sends him back to the Scottish Highlands and his upbringing as a member of the petty landed gentry. For Bond to live up to his role as classless nomad in the new neoliberal Britain, he must forsake these roots. As a result, his estate, Skyfall, is demolished completely in a pitched battle with his foes. The fact that the script is forced into convulsions to make this particular action take place in Scotland speaks of the importance to contemporary narratives of nomadism versus place and belonging. To complicate the scenario further, however, the final scene of the film has Bond pictured on rooftops above Whitehall with union flags waving, again at the seat of British power, again at the Palladian, neoclassical centre of the political psyche, and in the legs-spread-wide stance made famous by George Osborne and Theresa May in 2015 (see Khaleeli, 2015).

All of the recent Daniel Craig Bond films have displayed this distinctly liquid modern tenor. *Spectre*, while a far less successful film than *Skyfall* overall, still has had an immense power to shape reality as simulacrum outside of the film itself. Mexico City has just celebrated its first ever 'Day of the Dead' parade, inspired by the opening scene of the film (*Mexico City News Daily*, 2016). Landscapes and their use, as ever, are shaped by the reifications of popular representations of them as much, maybe more now, than by their actual everyday use and occupation. The resilience of the Bond franchise and its ability to reformulate itself as a liquid modern phenomenon is the result of the application and reapplication of a simple formula, shored up with uncomplicated cultural and political narratives and with common prejudices, upon new times and new spaces as they emerge. The result is that this formula serves as a sort of datum against which the fluctuations and directions of the contemporary world may be measured—and the interpretation that will remain compelling to read in the future will be written in the language of the films' landscapes and their symbolism as backgrounds for the films' action.

This chapter was first published in the collection of essays about James Bond edited by Jeremy Strong, *Bond Uncovered*, in 2018.

3

A WORD... 'BLANG'

A pewter-grey luxury sedan is parked on a pea gravel drive edged with tightly clipped shin high boxwood hedges. A pedimented entryway, door gloss black and studded with plain but highly polished stainless steel knobs and furniture, is flanked by two *Laurus nobilis* lollipop standards in square galvanized containers top-dressed with slate chips. Here we see the full suburban expression of the phenomenon known as 'blang'—bland meets bling—and we could be anywhere in the world, but the combination, neatly sidestepping any expression of taste either bad or good, is the clearest possible visual code for a particular type of wealth (Figure 3.1). This is the wealth that dare not speak its name, except in the most minutely read details— hand burnished cordovan loafers, creamy tailored beige raincoats, polished granite, an indeterminate abstract canvas in earth tones and mauve, a spray of lilies.

It's a form peculiar to a Western middle-class and upper-middle-class aversion to conspicuous display. Rarely are its symbols, which mumble instead of shouting about wealth, ironically appropriated by the subaltern classes as the trappings of wealth so often are, with the notable exception of the Burberry check (this is perhaps the ur-blang) and perhaps the Mercedes grille ornament as worn by rap artists in the 80s and 90s (though repurposed as showy jewellery, this blang actually lapsed back into bling). The totems of luxury have always been subverted and parodied by those with the least disposable income, particularly the flashiest trappings that only the most spangled celebrities would dare to sport. Wear leopard and you're either Paris Hilton, a punk, or a prostitute, though Paris is probably wearing a real skin rather than printed velour. Blang flies under the radar, avoiding any message at all except the hushed but urgent hint of money.

Our urban buildings and landscapes often used to unabashedly flaunt the wealth of our culture. Gaudy, yes, but the etymology of the word gaudy comes from an old English root meaning 'joke' or 'plaything,' and our landscapes, city or country, were festooned with ornamental swags and statuesque symbolisms of all stripes.

DOI: 10.4324/9781003164593-3

FIGURE 3.1 One recent incarnation of blang is the so-called 'grey plague,' monochromatizing affluent suburbs and erasing taste and class distinctions that might be discerned in the difference between once-aspirational Tudorbethan and ex-social housing modern façades, for example. This example is from Harpenden, a wealthy town in Hertfordshire. Credit: Charlotte Frost.

Our landscapes were playthings, fantasies, and they expressed good taste, bad taste, and wild, unprecedented taste. Just as often they expressed sensibilities that were decidedly local as well, as did Czech Cubism or Belgian Art Nouveau.

With the exception of a few token eruptions of starchitecture, though, our cities are now becoming wastelands of tepid blang as the non-tastes of bankers and developers are expressed with international money by international practices on ever-larger sites. The architectural critic Owen Hatherley, in his *A Guide to the New Ruins of Great Britain*, calls the prevailing style in architecture 'pseudomodernism.' Pseudomodernism, he says, is "Postmodernism's incorporation of a Modernist formal language" (2010: xx). It includes the usual headline-grabbing one-off architectural spectacles, but also the anodyne faceted glass towers whose sole characteristic is bulk (Shard, World Trade Center One), a whole slew of anonymous buildings with barcode façades, and sleek, Scandi-style condominium and 'luxury flat' developments. It's these last few categories that I would identify as blang, and landscape architecture in many places is doing its best to keep up with this vapid, meaningless style. The City of London's landscaping, which is decidedly suburban, tidy, and twee in its aesthetic, never fails to disappoint with its lack of true urban ambition, and all our other great cities are being shrubbed up to look like corporate campuses. We're making places with all the charm and distinction of a business hotel near the airport. So, the next time you're worried that your design might be seen as bad taste, well, you could just be onto something. Don't let that idea go! Wear a little leopard! Don't give in to the blang!

'A Word' was my column in *Landscape*, the journal of the Landscape Institute. This column appeared in the Spring issue of 2015.

4

THE FLAVOUR OF THE PLACE

Eating and drinking in Pajottenland

Belgium: Flanders and Pajottenland

The popular image of Flanders is of a flat and somewhat bland landscape. The north of Flanders does little to belie this stereotype. Driving south from Dunkirk, there is little topography, and what little exists is usually the result of human intervention rather than geology. The landscape also flattens out visually into the distance. Objects near and far are juxtaposed against one another without depth or perspective, like cut-out scenery sliding across a stage set. Flanders is famous for its towers and belfries, which gain some of their imposing nature through contrast with the low landscape. As one approaches Brussels, though, a more voluptuous landscape grows from little ripples into hills, with small towns grouped around churches, tree-lined roads, and tidy hedgerows. It is a cosy landscape with only the barest of hints that the dark forest of the Ardennes and the rusted heavy industry of Wallonia lie beyond. This area, to the west and southwest of Brussels is an area known as Pajottenland,[1] and the cosiness one sees in the approach is qualified, compromised by numerous tensions, psychological and political, that at times inscribe themselves onto the landscape.

Pajottenland is part of the province of Flemish Brabant, and it is inhabited by both Flemish and Walloons. Belgium is not one nation, but two; Flanders to the north and francophone Wallonia to the South. Pajottenland lies on the fault line between the two. This fracture is a tectonic divide of language and culture, and its

---

1 In the originally published version of this essay I used the anglicized spelling 'Payottenland' as I was concerned the reader should hear the name correctly. Subsequently I received a number of complaints about the misspelling and thus I have now opted for the correct version. I also feel comfortable to trust the reader's ear. Otherwise, though, I will stick with anglicizations, especially where place names differ in French and Flemish.

DOI: 10.4324/9781003164593-4

extreme and constant pressure inevitably results in seismic events in politics and prejudice. The big earthquakes are felt across Belgium and in the halls of its government, while the tremors are much smaller and the damage local: shattered glass, a lick of flame, a shadow disappearing into night.

Pajottenland also sits on another kind of divide, and one equally difficult to define, that of the urban fringe. It is the interface between urban and rural, a seemingly haphazard assemblage of housing, industry, and open fields. It is transected by infrastructure leading into Brussels: roads, railway tracks, power lines, canals, and the lugubrious River Senne. In this densely settled part of Europe—and Flanders has been incredibly dense since the Middle Ages—one urban fringe often blends seamlessly into the next. Despite, or perhaps because of, all this Belgians have made a virtue of the uneventful and ordinary. This is a landscape that is comfortable rather than inspirational, often pretty but rarely beautiful. Its deficits are measured mainly as pragmatic necessities, not as compromises or intrusions.

The historic village life in the area would have been much the same as in many areas of Europe; an agrarian existence, shaped by the relationship between fields, home, market, and church. Flemish villages, as so many elsewhere, were traditionally centred around a church, which usually sits, even now, just opposite a café. Roads and paths lead out radially from the church. The congregation was composed of those who lived within walking distance of the centre, and thus was the community defined. The radial routes into the church would have passed farms, which, like miniature castles, formed a sort of defended enclave with the house, barn and outbuilding ranged around a yard. Farm buildings looked inward to the courtyard rather than out to the landscape, with their backs resolutely set against winds, rains, and adversity. Belgian life is still very much an interior one, focused on the creature comforts of the home and the pleasures of the table.

It is still possible to find these patterns imprinted upon Pajottenland. On a map, village cores are a dense knot of streets clustered around an, often awkwardly, organically trapezoidal church square. Radial routes may still be traced. These routes, though, have become encrusted with structures, in the same way a string suspended in saltwater collects crystals. It is often no longer possible to tell where one town leaves off and another takes up as the intervening space is filled with car dealerships, furniture showrooms, budget supermarkets, and all other such markers of the urban fringe. Passing through the area by car along certain routes, it might never be apparent that one was in the countryside at all. And countryside is just what the people who live there wish it to be. In Pajottenland, a new generation is attempting to imprint a rural ideal upon a stretch of land that for many years served only as a hinterland—a zone hitherto beneath notice, registering only, if at all, as a mysterious realm of uncertain use and occupation beginning at the garbage cans behind the endless strip and extending to the back doors of the next strip. Perpendicular to this grain is a "gradient from urban core, to community urban fringe to urban fringe farmland to urban shadow" (Ravetz, 2000: 14). It is perhaps this lack of definition, spiced with dereliction, that makes it possible to cast this productive area as

FIGURE 4.1 The N285 road from Asse to Enghien at Ternat, just north of Eizeringen: Where urban fringe blends into urban fringe, but where very authentic lives are also led. Credit: Tim Waterman.

a mysterious landscape that is perfectly capable of accepting romanticization. This area of exurban overspill is actually a tremendously valuable stretch of cultural land-scape fertile with latent potential (Figure 4.1).

In the village of Eizeringen—just off the intersection of the busy road from Asse to Enghien (and eventually Mons) and the road from Brussels to Ninove (both so crisply straight that one can feel the bite of the cartographer's pen against the ruler)—is to be found a delightful traditional Pajot café called *In de Verzekering tegen de Grote Dorst* (Insurance against Great Thirst).[2] It is open only on Sundays "for those on their way to church, those on the way home from church, and those who say they are going to church, but don't make it" (Webb et al., 2004: 62). It is run by the brothers Yves and Kurt Panneels, who took over as proprietors from its octogenarian landlady in 1999. Since their careful restoration of the café, a window opens into the past every Sunday. It has become common for beer connoisseurs to make pilgrimages to the café, where they stock an exhaustive selection of trad-itional Pajot beers. This is historic preservation as it should be. It preserves not just a building and the surrounding spaces, but the way of life that animates them. It is an

---

2 *In de Verzekering tegen de Grote Dorst* has a website at www.dorst.be/en/ that gives directions and their opening hours. It is well worth a visit.

urbanite's ideal of country living, but one that works with the place and its people rather than imposing a ludicrous fantasy.

It is a cliché that 'everyone eats well in Belgium,' though, as with many clichés, it is well-founded. The patterns of living that make it possible for the *In de Verzekering tegen de Grote Dorst* to continue to exist are still alive and well in the Belgian kitchen. The North Sea makes possible a mouth-watering range of seafood, particularly the sweet, plump mussels that have become emblematic of Belgian cuisine. They are at their best in the autumn and winter before their spawning season begins, and a giant pail of mussels steamed with cream and white beer is just the thing to take the chill off. Succulent 'eel in the green' (*paling in 't groen* or *anguilles au vert*) is another favourite—thick slices of eel in a sauce of wine and green herbs such as sorrel, sage, and chervil. *Waterzooi* ('watery mess') is either a chicken or seafood stew made with leeks, potatoes, eggs and cream. The seafood version may contain eel, pike, or carp, and possibly also shellfish.

The influence from the south, the Ardennes, contributes a love of game. Rabbit is served grilled or cooked slowly and sauced richly with its own blood. Wild boar, partridge and venison make regular appearances at table in myriad forms from roasts to stews to patés and sausages (sausages are often served with *stoemp*—mashed potatoes and vegetables). Every menu also features beef, and always *stoofvlees* or *carbonnade Flamande*, the quintessential Belgian stew of beef and sweet brown beer. Belgium, though a fraction of the size of France, produces roughly as many different types of cheese. Few but the formidable, perhaps notorious Limburger cheese are known outside Belgium, though, as most are produced locally by small producers. It can be a challenge, even, to find Belgian cheeses in Belgian supermarkets.

While the Belgian diet is almost always anchored by meat, vegetables also receive more than their due. The princeliest of vegetables are at their best here, many raised in the dark, secret earth and plucked in tender youth—it is the illicit air of decadence that lends them their cachet. The delightfully bitter Belgian endive or chicory (*witloof* or *chicon*) features in many typical dishes. They are almost always cooked, whereas elsewhere in the world they may appear more commonly as a salad vegetable. Asparagus, either green or white, is consumed with gratitude in season. A speciality that has experienced a resurgence lately are the shoots of the hop plant (*jets d'houblon*). These are harvested like asparagus, but in February and March, and are commonly served with a *mousseline* sauce (*hollandaise* folded with whipped cream just before serving) and poached eggs.

It is no surprise that the hop plant should make an appearance in cuisine, as everyone drinks well in Belgium too. This is the cool, damp north, though and few wine grapes are found here. Belgium's extraordinary range of local cheese is matched or outmatched by a dizzying variety of exquisite, hand-crafted beers. Even the mass-produced lagers are a cut above, and the run of the mill such as Bel, Maes, or Stella Artois[3] are flavourful and stimulating. At the other end of the

---

3 Stella Artois is also brewed under licence outside of Belgium, and outside Belgium the quality is not the same.

spectrum are the six world-famous and highly alcoholic beers produced by Trappist monks: Westvleteren, Westmalle, Rochefort, Orval, Achel, and Chimay. These are usually "double" and "triple" beers; rich, sweet brown beers. There are many other styles as well, the most common being blonde or golden ales, the most famous of which is Duvel, and white beers—fruity, cloudy light beers typified by Hoegaarden. Every beer in Belgium is meant to be served in its own distinctively shaped glass, and the best cafés will ensure that they have the correct glass on hand for every beer they serve. Many of the beers I have mentioned (with the notable exception of Westvleteren, which is available only at the abbey in limited quantities or by reservation) have international brand profiles, but most of the rest are distinctly local products, produced on a small scale locally by people who brew as a labour of love on a marginal wage.

The people of Pajottenland, and Belgium as a whole, are often fiercely (though not exclusively) loyal to their local producers, and it is this characteristic that allows these producers to exist and yet limits their range and commercial viability. It also, presumably, has the effect of ensuring a continuing market despite incursions from the big supermarkets. In turn, it keeps the pressure on supermarkets to provide quality products. It helps to ensure that the average food consumed in Belgium is not merely adequate, but delicious too.

The *Terroir* of Lambic

Terroir is a French term that is most often used in relation to oenology, the study of wine.[4] In this sense it refers to the effect of soils, geology, topography, and climate upon the flavour of wine from a given region. The French *Appellation d'Origine Contrôlée* (AOC) system defines and protects agricultural products such as wines and cheeses from specific regions. Other countries, as well as the European Union as a whole, also protect the names of foods and beverages based on their origins. These products are held to possess character and qualities that can only be produced by certain methods in a certain region. While *terroir* certainly refers to this, it also refers to the patterns of inhabitation and the practices of daily life that have evolved in an area as a complex interrelationship between a landscape and its inhabitants. In this sense, the idea of *terroir* is not too terribly different from the definition of cultural landscape. The UNESCO World Heritage Commission defines cultural landscapes as those "that are representative of the different regions of the world. Combined works of nature and humankind, they express a long and intimate relationship between peoples and their natural environment" (UNESCO, n.d.: n.p.) The implication is that, while the flavours of some agricultural products are deeply dependent upon a region and upon human practice in a certain area, these products also exert a strong influence upon the personality and cultural identity of people in

---

4 Oenology also refers to the making of wine, a field separate from, but related to viticulture, which is the science, study, and growing of grapes.

that same area. You are what you eat. And what one eats, at least ideally, is an indelible connection to one's environment.[5]

The French AOC system is very specific about certain products, such as wines and cheeses. Elsewhere, though, and for other products, there is less or no emphasis on *terroir*. Beer is one such product, and possibly this is because of a long-standing association of wine with the cultured upper classes and beer as a drink of the masses. With wine prices being pushed ever downwards, the premium prices of many top-quality beers would seem to reverse that social order, especially with restaurant mark-ups. Still, the question must be asked whether the term *terroir* can apply to beer? I believe so. A few years ago, when I had first moved back to England, I was riding on one of the last 'slam-door' trains through the area around Faversham, what is now possibly the last remnant of the Kentish hop-growing landscape. I was drinking a bottle of Spitfire, a bitter beer brewed in Faversham. When fresh, the beer has a most stimulating spicy, fiery hop character, and it would be better named for this than the fighter plane to which it actually refers. As I drank, the train passed farm workers loading freshly harvested hops into a truck. The sharp perfume of the hops filled the train through the open windows. The hops being loaded were probably destined for the brewery in Faversham, and the experience of tasting the beer and smelling the fresh hops simultaneously was both electrifying and somehow chthonic. It was like being plugged into the landscape and, literally, grounded.

Many readers will be familiar with English bitter beers, but far fewer will have ever tasted, or even be aware of the existence of lambic and gueuze beers. Lambic is particular to Pajottenland and Brussels, and its production is now limited to a handful of brewers. Lembeek, which is the home of the Boon brewery, is the source of the name 'lambic.' Lambic beers are produced in what must be the original method of brewing beer around the world. "In traditional lambic fermentation, freshly brewed wort [the liquid extracted from cooked grains in the brewing process] is left in an open shallow vat to cool, usually overnight. Naturally occurring yeast land on and drop into the sweet mixture. When properly cooled the next day this wort is drained into large oak casks, where it ferments slowly for between six months and three years" (Webb et al., 2004: 6). The wild yeasts that settle into the wort are a mix specific to the Senne valley, and they include the yeast *Brettanomyces bruxellensis*, which is named for Brussels. Most if not all other brewing processes, at least in Europe, are highly controlled and sanitary. Lambic breweries, in striking contrast, exhibit exposed wooden beams draped with spiderwebs (the spiders control the fruit flies) and an overall atmosphere that can only be described as, well, *yeasty* (Figure 4.2).[6]

5 Elspeth Probyn, in her *Eating the Ocean*, writes that oysters remind us that the flavour of the seascape is often very particular, and she calls this not *terroir*, but *merroir:* "this designates the physical factors of place, techne, and tide that give each microenvironment a different flavor" (2016: 52).
6 This atmosphere may be savoured at the Cantillon Brewery in Brussels, which is not far from the Gare du Midi. It offers self-guided tours and tastings and it refers to itself as Le Musée Bruxellois de la Gueuze/Het Brussels Museum van de Geuze. It is well worth a visit and their beers are first-rate. In the years since I wrote this essay, the popularity of lambic and gueuze has increased so much that this once sleepy museum is now heaving with tourists every day.

FIGURE 4.2 Oak casks stacked in the Cantillon brewery in Brussels. Credit: Tim Waterman.

The enjoyment of lambic is definitely an acquired taste. It is a flat beer, served fresh at cellar temperature in earthenware jugs. It packs an attack of tartness at the front of a whole range of earthy, antediluvian flavours that may invoke leather, mildew, or mud. The flavour of lambic lifts and separates the tastebuds in the same way that fresh, unsweetened grapefruit juice does. It is a down-home drink that is as macho as bourbon, and there is also a slight thrill of danger from the relatively uncontrolled and antique brewing process. As Luce Giard writes, "In the time before the reign of products that are sorted, graded, carved, prepackaged, and packaged in an anonymous form where only the generic name attests their original nature, everything had flavour because everything was dangerous" (de Certeau et al., 1998: 205).

At the Woolpack pub in Chelmsford, Essex, I met with Chris Pollard, an expert on Belgian beers who co-authored the book *Lambicland*. He told me that lambic is the taste of Pajottenland and associated with country life and labour in the fields. Gueuze, on the other hand, is the taste of cosmopolitan Brussels and "the Champagne of Belgium." Gueuze (the name of which may be from the Norman word for wheat, which is a common ingredient along with barley) is a sexed-up, blended lambic that undergoes a secondary fermentation in champagne bottles and is topped with a wired-on cork. The second fermentation makes it a sparkling beverage. Gueuze is produced from the output of various lambic breweries and of various vintages, in much the same way that blended scotch is handled. The blending adds complexity and depth, and the natural carbonation satisfies more effervescent urban tastes. Fruit is also added to lambics, the most traditional being sour cherries, which produce a drink called *kriek*. Raspberries and blackcurrants often make an appearance, and occasionally sugar or caramel is added to make *faro*. A range of Belgian malt beverages flavoured with fruit syrups is currently causing confusion with the more traditional beers, but these are tailored to juvenile tastes, and have little character other than sweet/fruit pablum. The flavour of real lambic beers is stamped with the moist air of the Senne valley and it is a palpable link to a whole history of inhabitation of the area. To taste it in Pajottenland is to experience the same sort of chthonic connection to place that I felt drinking bitter in Kent.

The complex and earthy flavours of lambic and gueuze beers make them the perfect complement to much of Belgian cuisine, from the gamey flavours of boar and rabbit to the decadent spears of asparagus and jets d'houblon as well as fat, bitter little chicories. The sharp, citrusy flavours of gueuze also cleanse the palate between bites of what is often rich or creamy food. They may even help to curtail the appetite somewhat, helping to reduce the damage done by all that saturated fat, though this may be wishful thinking. To acquire a taste for lambic and gueuze is to gain entrance to a spectrum of sensation and a way of life that is peculiar, and special, to Pajottenland.

Acquired taste, discovered taste, accrued taste

Taste, though it can be defined as a single sense, is never truly autonomous. The boundaries between taste and olfaction are blurred. Those without the sense of smell find it difficult to taste anything as a result. Taste also involves touch—the way a food or drink feels in the mouth has a distinct influence on its flavour. In fact, the boundaries of the sense of taste continue to swell ever outwards to include all the human senses and numerous variables such as colour and composition in the presentation of food, positive or negative associations, and so on. Taste, ultimately, has psychosocial and cultural meaning that is not altogether inseparable from the five senses at any time.

Babies rely early on their sense of taste to explore the world around them and make meaning of it. If possible, every object is inspected, felt, and tasted. Through these encounters, the infant pieces together a composite portrait of the surrounding environment and landscape that is the basis for taste preference and has a strong influence on personality, identity, and character. In this way, even if children are not consuming the produce of their immediate landscape, which is likely the case for first-world children who may eat a largely processed diet sourced from supermarkets and franchised restaurants, they are probably still responding to taste stimuli that are rooted in their native landscape. Local preferences, even in a globalized market, may still be the result not just of local acculturation (nurture), but of a direct relationship with soil, air, climate, and vegetation of a place (nature). Many basic tastes, then, may not be completely universal, but may be tempered to one degree or another by the landscape of place.

Innate tastes for bland, salty, and/or sweet foods—'comfort foods'—have instant appeal to infantile tastes. Some tastes may well be nearly universal. There is probably only a handful of people of any age, anywhere in the world who wouldn't be seduced by a plate of perfectly golden-fried Belgian *frites*, for example (though some might object to the Belgian preference for serving them crowned with mayonnaise. I myself can't fathom the practice of eating them with ketchup). Because of the instant rewards of comfort foods, products are engineered for the market to pander to and encourage these basic tastes, which can often be quite addictive. The food industry probably has much to gain from playing to childish or 'kidult' tastes and from actively infantilizing the consumer. Unfortunately, the consumer has little to gain from this market dynamic except weight.

In a healthy environment where the development of taste is not inhibited, taste is slowly developed. The more we learn to like, the broader our range of choices and combinations becomes, and the more open we become to further taste possibilities. I will call this *accrued taste*. Accrued taste is acquired taste that is learned, constructed and additive, contextual and associative, but not necessarily intentional. It may be the discovery that a food is pleasing because it is sauced with hunger, or it may simply be that repetition has bestowed familiarity, which has grown into fondness.

Educated taste I shall define as acquired taste derived from intentional taste explorations. If a people come to believe, wish to believe, or are coerced into believing that learning to like something will enrich their lives, then they will undertake to do so, even though the process may be unpleasant. *Educated* acquired taste is active whereas *accrued* acquired taste is passive. It is the taste equivalent of 'working out' or 'reading up.' Scotch whisky is the sterling example of this. I have slowly grown to find single malt whisky quite indispensable, though at first only the gentler brands were acceptable. The first time I brought home a whisky from the Isle of Islay, I was horrified at the taste that assaulted me. It was as though I had uncorked a Molotov cocktail. The bouquet was of tarpit, and the flavour was of diesel. I don't believe I finished the glass, and the offending bottle remained at the back of the cabinet for some months. A visit from an American friend, though, prompted a tasting of the various scotches I had on hand. Tentatively, I retrieved the bottle, brushing off the dust, and warning my companion about the violence I was about to do to his palate, poured some. This time, however, I was more prepared for its flavour. I found it challenging, but not altogether unpleasant. It was only a matter of weeks before I tried it again, and by the time the bottle was finished, I was quite enjoying it and looking forward to trying more Islay whiskies. Now a couple of the Islay malts rank amongst my great favourites, profound comforts.

Educating taste is usually quite rewarding in this way. There is the satisfaction of having overcome an obstacle, the pleasure of adding a new experience to a repertoire of experiences, and the lift of knowing that one's tastes are now a marker of difference, perhaps even superiority. Further, the acquisition of tastes through intention, educated taste, leads to the possibility of more innocently accrued tastes building upon a new framework and expanded context. To complicate matters, though, educating taste is also a process of elimination. Often, in acquiring new tastes, we leave others behind as an act of casting aside the training wheels, perhaps, or as a conscious step up the class ladder, and this expression can be quite violent in its refusal. Pierre Bourdieu, in his landmark study *Distinction: A Social Critique of the Judgement of Taste*, states:

> Tastes (i.e., manifested preferences) are the practical affirmation of an inevitable difference. It is no accident that, when they have to be justified, they are asserted purely negatively, by the refusal of other tastes. In matters of taste, more than anywhere else, all determination is negation; and tastes are perhaps first and foremost distastes, disgust provoked by horror or visceral intolerance ('sick-making') of the tastes of others.
>
> *(1979: 36)*

Fitting into a social and physical environment involves both accrued and educated acquired tastes, in the process of the accumulation of Bourdieu's 'cultural capital.' We first become attuned to the landscape in which we are raised, beginning with the infant's explorations. Geophagy, the consumption of soil, is common amongst children, and is one quite vivid and literal way in which the landscape might be internalized, understood, ingested, digested. Later in life, educated acquired taste will be a way to identify with a certain group, whether this is acquiring upwardly mobile tastes for champagne and truffles, or simply a liking for lager to facilitate and lubricate conviviality at the local watering hole. Bourdieu again, this time at some length:

> Taste classifies, and it classifies the classifier. Social subjects, classified by their classifications, distinguish themselves by the distinctions they make, between the beautiful and the ugly, the distinguished and the vulgar, in which their position in the objective classifications is expressed or betrayed. And statistical analysis does indeed show that oppositions similar in structure to those found in cultural practices also appear in eating habits. The antithesis between quantity and quality, substance and form, corresponds to the opposition—linked to different distances from necessity—between the taste of necessity, which favours the most 'filling' and most economical foods, and the taste of liberty—or luxury—which shifts the emphasis to the manner (of presenting, serving, eating etc.) and tends to use stylized forms to deny function.
>
> *(Ibid.: 6)*

The larger issues of identity can be descried in these taste ambitions (or lack thereof), and the elements of personality both drive those ambitions and are informed and shaped by them. It is possible that acquired tastes have little to do with basic needs, but rather could be seen as practices or tactics to enable us to discriminate and navigate through everyday life. They may well be essential, though, to making a home in a community. Pierre Mayol, in volume two of *The Practice of Everyday Life* points out that "the practice of the neighborhood introduces gratuitousness instead of necessity; it favors a use of urban space whose end is not only functional" (de Certeau et al., 1998: 13). It also favours a deployment of taste whose end is not only functional—a fact reinforced by the tendency of the wealthy and privileged to be distinguished by being thin—a perverse reversal in which the existence of plenty is displayed through the appearance of scarcity. Less signifies more. Educating taste, in this case, becomes not only *like* working out, but the appearance of it actually *requires* working out.

The agony of taste

Agony and ecstasy dwell in close proximity to one another. Agony is a sensation not only allied with pain, but with competition, with striving and aspiration. It's not unusual for the most satisfying emotions to have both a dark and a light side. The bittersweet and the melancholy, for example, are experiences with a piquancy derived from a mixture of pleasure and pain. It is also a measure of the emotional content of taste that terms relating to taste, such as 'bittersweet' and 'piquant,' should so aptly describe a state of being.[7] In all its aspects, life is a jumble of emotions that are always queerly juxtaposed, and the ability to savour the mix is the ability to apprehend all of life and to draw nourishment from it. Chocolate, dark chocolate, perfectly contains this delightful opposition—and Belgian chocolate is without argument the best in the world. Without the sweetness (and light) of sugar, chocolate is too intense for most tastes. It is almost black, the colour of oblivion, but the mild euphoria it delivers is elevating. Cocoa grows in messy, fetid conditions necessitated by the habitat of its pollinators, but the best chocolate is sold in immaculate, light-filled boutiques like Pierre Marcolini in the Place du Grand Sablon in Brussels. Marcolini's exquisite chocolates certainly walk the razor's edge of agony and ecstasy, a taste that can only be delivered on a small and exclusive scale by producers with passion.[8]

Pajottenland has its own producer with the same sort of passion as Pierre Marcolini. Armand Debelder is the owner and brewmaster at the Drie Fonteinen brewery in Beersel, a tidy, intimate town with a small but well-formed castle and pleasant, composed views over Pajottenland. He is an elegant, confident, and well-spoken man who is a proselytizing believer in lambic beers and who produces some of the very finest. I spoke with him in the 'Lambik-o-Droom' tasting room at his brewery, and he underscored many of the themes that have been appearing increasingly, and for good reason, in the media; the importance of the small producer, the

---

7 To 'bittersweet' and 'piquant,' we might add sour, sweet, salty, spicy, etc. as emotions, moods, or descriptors of personality.
8 Marcolini has grown into an international brand over the last decade, but it is still very fine chocolate. It's now worth seeking out a range of new boutique chocolatiers in Belgium, Laurent Gerbaud being a good example. The little historic café in Brussels, La Fleur en Papier Doré, is also worth a visit to get a gueuze-filled chocolate with your coffee.

virtues of sourcing goods locally, the need to maintain patrimony and tradition for future generations, and shedding empty consumerist ambitions in favour of those things that are 'free.'

He has lived his life in Pajottenland, and he told me that there are two moments of that life that stand out as possessing singular beauty. The first was the birth of his granddaughter, and the second was the death of his mother. His mother died in winter, a season she loved. As the family gathered around in the last moments of her life, they threw open the shutters into the yard, where the light from the window picked out the flakes of falling snow. Why these two moments? Because they contain agony and joy; sorrow, pain and hope. Because they are about the continuity of life in a landscape, belonging in family, community, place. As I listened and sipped an astounding gueuze, it seemed that the flavours presented in that drink held all the richness and depth of such a story. Tart like tears and brash like laughter and with undertones of sweat and soil, longing and belonging. If a drink can be a true reflection of a place and a people, of *terroir*, then Armand Debelder's gueuze is a textbook example.

It is, of course, difficult to discern how much of the intensity of this taste experience is held within the beverage itself. Does it, in fact, intrinsically contain all this information? The question could well be metaphysical, and it is delightful to contemplate that the flavour could tap into an ancestral collective consciousness. More pragmatically, as a cultural construct, educated taste is the product of foreknowledge and context that shape the experience. The story thus influences and enhances the taste, though it would be unpoetic and unnecessary to rule out metaphysical factors. Indeed, beliefs and spirituality are integral to the formation of place through practice. Bourdieu notes: "But one cannot fully understand cultural practices unless 'culture,' in the restricted, normative sense of ordinary usage, is brought back into 'culture' in the anthropological sense, and the elaborated taste for the most refined objects is reconnected with the elementary taste for the flavours of food" (1979: 1). And the elaborated taste for the most refined places, for homeland, for landscape, are inextricably tied to culture in the anthropological sense, and thus to the flavours of food in a way that is basic to identity and is fundamentally both ideological and spiritual. *Terroir* implies that taste is much more than simply aesthetic judgement, but is (or at its best can be) part of the total framework of identity that is a construct not only of human associations, but of the full matrix of associations across home, work, and community, which are bound together by modes of occupation and daily practice in the landscape.

The Tower of Babel

The Tower of Babel has somehow haunted me the whole time I have been in the process of writing this essay, appearing in conversation and print and image, though I doubt I have heard the story mentioned in years. Armand Debelder spoke of it when he talked about the appreciation of those things that are 'free,' like bluebells in the spring rather than those that are accorded value due to supposed rarity or exclusiveness. Indeed, many things are accorded value simply because they are expensive. Debelder's brewing is an attempt to find a better way of operating in the world, a more authentic mode. He sees society as building a new Tower of Babel, one that is surely destined to collapse.

The story of the Tower of Babel is the classic tale of hubris. It ends with the fall of the tower, and the fragmentation of a great, unified society that is undone by its own arrogance. The punishment for attempting an ascent to heaven from the mortal earth is the dispersion of the people across the lands and the appearance of myriad different languages. Thus the groundwork is laid for misunderstanding and misinterpretation, the drawing and re-drawing of boundaries, fractiousness, skirmishes, battles, wars, ethnic cleansing, and all-out genocide and ecocide. Ironically, the linguistic and geographic distance between people is also the foundation of exotic difference, of the allure of the foreign. It is this other that draws us but also is thrown into relief to remind us of the comforts of home. Linguistic and cultural differences are interlinked with geography, producing *terroir*. Producing the taste *of* the place, informing the taste *for* the place.

Our most enduring images of the Tower of Babel come from the Flemish painters. That of Pieter Breugel the Elder, in particular, shows a tower possibly modelled on the Colosseum in Rome, but placed in a landscape that is ineffably Flemish; tall, pointy houses fill a lowland landscape that merges effortlessly with the sea. In the castle at Gaasbeek, which looks out over the Pajot landscape, there hangs a large rendition of the same scene by another, later Flemish painter, Marten van Valckenborch (Figure 4.3). The lesson of the Tower of Babel seems to have been taken to heart in Belgium and is taught with the same gravity in a very secular society that it once was in a rigidly Catholic Medieval Flanders. The tale, after all, has resonance for a society that is so starkly separated by language. The popularity of the story may also reflect the Belgian respect, even love, for the ordinary or quotidian. The popularity of the story in Belgium also reflects the divide in language and culture that so bedevils the country.

In the current economic collapse, we are once again being punished for heedlessness and hubris. We have become further fractured, not just nationally or regionally, but into single solitary individuals who are losing the ability to communicate and cooperate. We have become tiny islands of greed whose actions may be justified solely by invoking the rights of the sovereign individual or the privilege bestowed by the status of wealth. Yeast—even the noble *Brettanomyces bruxellensis*—will eat sugars voraciously, dividing and increasing as they sate themselves. In the process, though, they produce alcohol, which in sufficient quantity paralyses the mass of them. Capitalism works like yeast. We keep eating, consuming, producing waste until the environment is toxic, until the tower falls. In these times it is ever more crucial to seek out the cultural ties that bind, to reach out to one another to rebuild community and to begin to live in and use the landscape once more. We look at landscape through a frame, at a distance, and it is landscape that puts food on the table, that provides open spaces for meeting and greeting, that provides air and light

FIGURE 4.3 Tower of Babel (1595), Marten an Valkenborch (1535–1612), oil on panel, collection of the Castle of Gaasbeek.

and health. It is a good time to reconnect, and Pajottenland provides some compelling possibilities.

The new Pajot landscape

For much of western Europe, the legacy of the Industrial Revolution seems to have receded impossibly far into the past. The economy is now often based upon retail and services, especially financial services. The frustration and disorientation that people may have felt leaving behind meaningful trades and well-defined roles and struggling to make their way in a world without any definitions except rich and poor, labourer and master of industry, are hard to fathom today. And yet, one of the characteristics of the Industrial Revolution was the "struggle to maintain wages, material welfare and moral values against the exploitive and alienating implications of the new form of social organisation being forged in the factories and cities" (Cosgrove, 1998 [1984]: 224). This struggle seems suddenly desperately pertinent again, despite the fact that the shifting ground of social organization is utterly different. We may now be moving into an age when people will once again define themselves in terms of trades and activities rather than simply wage, class, and branded lifestyle. Characteristic of the struggle during the Industrial Revolution were the actions of the Luddites and the *saboteurs*, but their actions have come to be seen as merely anti-progress or anti-industry, rather than defensive of a *moral economy*, one "founded on custom and attributed status as the dominant conditions of human relationships." The emergence of a *political economy*, one "founded upon contract and the status provided by access to capital and the means of production" (ibid.: 224) during the Industrial Revolution, affected not only the cities, but colonized the countryside with mines and mills while it consolidated the means of agricultural production and distribution. The emergent relationship between city and countryside was less clear than it had been in the Middle Ages, where dense cities were separated from the surrounding territory by a strong demarcated boundary. Now cities displayed a dense core and a diffuse boundary where agricultural production, noxious industry, waste, and transport corridors interwove. The haphazard nature of the resulting landscape was so disorganized as to be apparently placeless. Carolyn Steel, in her book *Hungry City*, which manages to be simultaneously delightful and ominous, says, "As civilisation is city-centric, it is hardly surprising that we have inherited a lopsided view of the urban-rural relationship. Visual representations of cities have tended to ignore their rural hinterlands, somehow managing to give the impression that their subjects were autonomous, while narrative history has relegated the countryside to a neutral green backdrop, good for fighting battles in, but little else" (2008: 7). The geographer Yi-Fu Tuan had earlier noted similar trends, but emphasized the ideal of the country as pleasure ground: "In modern life physical contact with one's natural environment is increasingly indirect and limited to special occasions. Apart from the dwindling farm population, technological man's involvement with nature is recreational rather than vocational" (1990 [1974]: 95–96).

The creeping desecration of, and separation from, the rural landscape was accompanied by a conflicting set of attitudes towards the country in city dwellers: the first an Arcadian idyll, and the second of a forgotten and forlorn, muddy, dusty place inhabited by inbred and ill-educated country bumpkins. While there may be an element of truth to both, city life contains the same sorts of extremes (and stereotypes) from the cosmopolitan high life to Skid Row. Country life has now changed so drastically that there is hardly anyone left in it to whom stereotypes might be applied. Steel goes on to say,

> Meanwhile, the countryside we like to imagine just beyond our urban borders is a carefully sustained fantasy. For centuries, city-dwellers have seen nature through a one-way telescope, moulding its image to fit their urban sensibilities. The pastoral tradition, with its hedgerows and its meadows full of fluffy sheep, is part of that tendency, as is the Romantic vision of nature, all soaring peaks, noble firs and plunging gorges. Neither bears any relation to the sort of landscape capable of feeding a modern metropolis. Fields of corn and soya stretching as far as the eye can see, plastic polytunnels so vast they can be seen from space, industrial sheds and feed lots full of factory-farmed animals—these are the rural hinterlands of modernity.
>
> *(2008: 8)*

Pre-industrial cities depended heavily upon their hinterlands, often in a virtuous cycle in which fruits and vegetables were cultivated in soil enriched by human waste collected in the cities as 'night-soil.' This loop has been broken, with waste pushed ever further away and produce shipped from the four corners of the Earth. The rural hinterland that Steel speaks of is at a significant remove from most of our cities. Thus a rural hinterland is no longer synonymous with an urban hinterland. The urban hinterland has ceased to be a landscape whose importance is primarily production and is now cast in the same role as an Arcadian landscape, as a landscape of leisure, consumption, and recreation. In many European countries, as in America, the countryside is now the setting for luxury second homes, often in a rustic style or in reinhabited farm buildings (homes as well as barns and other outbuildings) as seen in the French *fermette*. What is missing is a romanticized notion of what might constitute a life in such a setting. These places are often not truly inhabited in the fullest sense. They are commuter dwellings in bedroom communities, weekend country boltholes or holiday homes that may only function seasonally. These dwellings could, though, begin to form the basis for a new style of settlement in the urban fringe and shadow, following the Jeffersonian model of the gentleman farmer and his smallholding, though the ranks of servants may need to be replaced by technology. This indeterminate exurban landscape needs only be seen again as a lived place, the kind J.B. Jackson taught us to see: "The beauty that we see in the vernacular landscape is the image of our common humanity: hard work, stubborn hope, and mutual forbearance striving to be love. I believe that a landscape which makes these qualities manifest is one that can be called beautiful" (1984: xii).

It is vital to find a way of inhabiting the urban fringe, a way that people like Armand Debelder and Yves and Kurt Panneels seem to be, that values the association between people, place, food, drink, and landscape, that is based in a moral economy and a delight in the miraculous and transcendent act of dwelling in a mundane and quotidian world. We need to come to live in a multisensual landscape once again. Dolores Hayden compellingly highlights this association between the senses and our inhabitation of the landscape:

> If place does provide an overload of possible meanings for the researcher, it is place's very assault on all ways of knowing (sight, sound, smell, touch, and taste) that makes it powerful as a source of memory, as a weave where one strand ties in another. Place needs to be at the heart of urban landscape history, not on the margins, because the aesthetic qualities of the natural and built environments, positive and negative, are just as important as the political struggles over space often dealt with by urban historians and social scientists.
> *(1997: 14)*

Key to imagining a sustainable future for the urban fringe is the reinhabitation of the landscape with people who do so out of volition or earnest vocation, in the same way that the ideal inhabitation of the city is by people who aspire to city life, rather than those who see it as drudgery. Why not envision a future in which all people do what they love? This may sound utopian, but perhaps only because it is an idea that is at odds with the present industrial and agricultural complex. It also may be queried because it is a dangerous oversimplification to romanticize the nature of life on the land. Nathaniel Hawthorne had his spirit nearly broken shovelling manure on George Ripley's transcendentalist (and later Fourierist) utopian community at Brook Farm, and countless hippies returned from 'getting back to nature' to a very earnest 'getting back to civilization.' To 'simplify' or 'get back to nature' shows a profound misunderstanding of the relationship between soil, climate, place. It's complex. It's very hard work. There is still value to romanticizing the life of the small farmer or small producer, though, especially if visionaries like Armand Debelder are around to show us what an earnest and satisfying life can be made in a newly reinvented hinterland. It is possible to learn to savour the agony and ecstasy of a textured and flavourful life in the countryside as part of a vibrant community that might show the re-emergence of a moral economy. Perhaps all that is needed is that we acquire a taste for it, an educated taste.

This chapter originally appeared (as 'The Flavor of the Place: Eating and Drinking in Payottenland) in the 2011 University of Nebraska Press collection *Educated Tastes: Food, Drink, and Connoisseur Culture.*

5

THE GLOBAL CUCUMBER

On the Milan Expo 2015

A city like Milan reflects the strivings of generations. It has a rich quality of everyday life that includes a sophisticated food culture which, as in so many Italian cities, is both distinctly local and, because of its history of trade, cosmopolitan. The evolution of the city's form has intertwined with the tastes and appetites of the Milanese. The convivial quality of many of its spaces comes from enclosures such as its ubiquitous courtyard gardens, its cool semi-private zones where neighbours come into contact, or its sidewalk cafés. Milan was once *Mediolanum* (meaning "in the midst of the plain"), the capital of the Western Roman Empire. It was enclosed by walls, but open to its countryside in the Po River Valley, where alluvial soils raised abundant grain and wine, and roads brought influence from all over Europe.

Milan's economy suffered, as did all of Italy's, from the crash in 2008, and recession and unemployment are tenaciously rooted. While its economy continues to be underpinned by industry and agriculture, notably by small, family owned farms, government policy has looked to urban and infrastructural development for solutions to the crisis. Italy's new, post-Berlusconi government is trying to show evidence of its ability to deliver, and Milan, the financial centre of Italy, has become a showcase of contemporary neoliberal development. In particular, two developments have shown great international visibility: the Milan Expo 2015 and the business district at Porta Nuova, best known for the Bosco Verticale (vertical forest), the heavily vegetated and much-published twin luxury apartment towers designed by the architect Stefano Boeri.

Boeri has courted controversy in both sites, attracting anti-gentrification protests both from the working-class neighbourhood the towers protrude from, as well as accusations of deploying expensive greenwash that would never be possible in a lower-cost development. Much the same objections have been raised against the plans for this year's Expo in Milan, which he masterplanned with Jacques Herzog, William McDonough, and Ricky Burdett. "Feeding the Planet—Energy for Life"

DOI: 10.4324/9781003164593-5

FIGURE 5.1 A vandalized shopfront in central Milan. Credit: Tim Waterman.

is the Expo's motto, meant, as it was, to embody a sustainable ethic, clashed with the presence of food giants such as McDonald's and Coca-Cola amongst the nations represented. Lavish spending on the project further incited anger, as many people questioned the concentration of municipal spending on one site instead of many, and the inevitable siphoning away of funds that such concentration engenders. On May Day in Milan, cars blazed in the streets, windows were smashed, and 'No Expo' graffiti proliferated (Figure 5.1).

In this case, radical protesters have shown a conservative attitude to public spending. Such stubbornness is also to be found in Italy's culinary and agricultural customs. Like Milan's urban fabric, these forms and practices reflect the strivings of generations: make-do-and-mend and waste-not-want-not methods ensure the sustainability of these customary practices. Frugality is a fruitful practice, and thus the delights of the Italian table are legendary. Italy's food culture as a result provides the perfect platform to present good food practice to the world. This was the starting point for the masterplanning team, who wished to create a very different type of Expo, mixing a necessary message in with all the usual flash of a multimedia, multi-nation consumerist extravaganza.

I spoke in London with Ricky Burdett, who told me the original intention was that 50 per cent of each Expo plot should be given over to green open space, which meant that the whole would have been landscape-driven rather than focused on pavilions. Drawings from the 2009 proposal show delicate fabric awnings, fields of sunflowers, and canals. This much calm sincerity was, perhaps, doomed from the beginning, and all the partners on the masterplanning team except Boeri disowned the process and left the team when the requirement for green space was abandoned by the organizers.

The parts of the masterplan that have survived are based in Classical Roman city plans or plans of military camps. The site is bounded, in like military or urban style, by fences, guards, gates, and canals, and it is organized on a grid with two primary axes: the *cardo*, or north–south axis, and the *decumanus*, the east–west axis. Tent-like canopies, other survivors from the original masterplan, float above.

The Expo involved spending on major new highway, rail, and subway infrastructure and interchanges, enough for a permanent new city quarter, which now seems unlikely to be built in the near future. No developer has yet been found for the site, which is located on Milan's western edge immediately adjacent to one of Europe's largest convention centres, Fiera Milano. The area is typical urban fringe, a loose agglomeration of industrial uses, working-class neighbourhoods, and strip development, all studded with islands of remnant agricultural land. Reports of scandals and boondoggles were rife, as all the usual problems with corruption, profiteering, and inflated land prices, along with a now-familiar story of worker exploitation and poor working conditions, unfolded. The growing cost of the event forced the organizers to search for more corporate sponsors, which included McDonald's (Figure 5.2) and Coca-Cola, as well as the confectioners Lindt and Ferrero Rocher. Their presence is "perverse and bizarre," Burdett says.

This familiar mix of corporate influence and official and private corruption angered not just those who demanded satisfaction in Milan's streets, but also workers at the Expo who have a keen sense of the politics ("In Italy, politics is everything," says Ricky Burdett). I toured the children's area, which was filled with installations for interactive play designed to teach children about plants, food, and environmental responsibility. It was the end of the day, and there was a handful of children left. Many of the workers were gathered together and winding down. Amongst them was Stefano Bisi, who is scandalized by the presence of the food giants and convinced that "the only people who will gain [from the Expo] are the big firms and those who poured the concrete." Against a backdrop of giant multicoloured fruits and vegetables, he warns me that we must "beware of the global cucumber." Naturally, I'm mystified at this, and he explains by acting it out—he presses his back flush to a wall—"we have to guard our behinds from the global cucumber."

There are some moments of real beauty, and pavilions that have kept to the original idea of 50 per cent green space. These pavilions are without a doubt the most successful. Austria and the UK are the big showstoppers. Austria provides a steadily misted and cool, wooded undercroft (Figure 5.3). As the path climbs into the pavilion through trees, a neon sign which reads "breathe" comes to read "eat." The UK Pavilion by the evocatively named Wolfgang Buttress and BDP is hardly a building at all, but rather a swarm of steel members hovering over a wildflower meadow humming with bees (Figure 5.4). Everywhere else, plants are growing on green walls at wild angles, as at Israel's pavilion, or even upside down in a number of

FIGURE 5.2 Sited between national pavilions, food giants, perhaps appropriately, take on the status of nation-states. Credit: Tim Waterman.

pavilions where any number of techno-contraptions are employed in horticulture. It's a relief to see plants growing happily, right-side-up, in soil.

The US Pavilion is presented with our usual national swagger, second only in height to the Italian pavilion, and with great techno-pomp, a massive lighted sign at its entrance announces the dawning of the new age of "American Food 2.0." This means that plants are grown both sideways and upside down, and that an enormous living wall encrusted with lettuces undulates rhythmically from stem to stern, apparently (avowedly) to evoke the vaunted national image of 'amber waves of grain.' Not even your patriotism can overcome such leaden high-concept and over-zealous technophilia, though they're certainly appropriate to the Expo format. The Belgians, punching above their weight, also bring high-tech farming that looks like the inside of a laboratory, and the Ikea-like serpentine circulation system through it spits the visitor out into a wonderland of costly chocolates, beer, and *pommes-frites*.

Some countries get the point of an Expo but not the foodie theme. Brazil has a bouncy climbing structure, while Russia's mirrored, cantilevered erection is, says Ricky Burdett, "something an oligarch would build." And, of course, a glib comparison to the global cucumber is apropos. The centrepiece of the whole exhibition, at the south end of the *cardo*, next to the vast, white Italian pavilion, is the 'Tree of Life,' designed by the event entrepreneur Marco Balich, and the focus for a fountain and multimedia light show every night of the Expo (Figure 5.5). Like the

FIGURE 5.3 A path leads to the Austria Pavilion, which was designed by a team led by Klaus K. Loenhart, who is both an architect and a landscape architect. Credit: Tim Waterman.

'Supertrees' at Singapore's Gardens by the Bay, the form is the shape of a vortex like a tornado or a whirlpool, or perhaps the bell of a horn (to describe the shape an old friend suggests it might be called "vuvuzeliform," in reference to the stadium horns made famous by the 2010 soccer World Cup in South Africa). Since the conflation

FIGURE 5.4 Wolfgang Buttress and BDP's UK Pavilion works with the trendy metaphor of "the hive." Credit: Tim Waterman.

of tree and vortex in Singapore, it's become possible to see this "vuvuzeliform" as invoking the symbology of the tree of life, though this is an uncomfortable pairing, given that the tree of life is so often depicted with roots equivalent to its canopy. Rooted in the ground, reaching to the sky, a reflection of the cycle of life. The vortex/tree form appears everywhere at the Milan Expo, but it's rootless.

This article was published in *Landscape Architecture Magazine*, July 2015.

FIGURE 5.5 "The Tree of Life" is a sound and light spectacle every evening that includes dancing waters and a techno soundtrack. Credit: Tim Waterman.

6

A WORD... 'THEATRE'

A landscape architect who found his way into the profession of landscape architecture after tiring of working as a building architect recently told me he had
started to see buildings as nothing but "boring utensils." Still, the reality of creating
buildings as tools means that good architects are highly aware of the performative
and instrumental functions of both buildings and of their profession. They see not
just the programmatic possibilities of built spaces, but also the theatrical possibilities within them, whether this be the dramatic play of light across a wall surface
or the potential for a person to appear, vaunted and elevated, at the top of a flight
of stairs.

The idea of the *theatrum mundi* is a very old one, certainly predating William
Shakespeare's verse from *As You Like It*: "All the world's a stage, / And all the men
and women merely players; / They have their exits and their entrances, / And one
man in his time plays many parts..." In Shakespeare's time the roles that people
played on the stage of life would be clearly delineated, with public dress, speech, and
mannerisms reinforcing class and other hierarchies such as those of the trades. Each
individual would be acting out a role on the public stage. Though this is less true in
an age where we value individualism and self-expression, and in which we like to
pretend that we are still not bound by hierarchies of wealth and class, there is still
great value in thinking about our public roles and how we play them.

Building architects are often great actors with a clear understanding that they
inhabit a role. Think, for example, of Le Corbusier's great stage presence as evidenced
by films of his lectures. Or perhaps Philip Johnson's chameleon-like adaptations of
both his public role and his style throughout his career. For more contemporary
examples, we might point to Richard Rodgers' pink and acid-green ensembles, or
to the great swirl of hair, cloth, and haughtiness that is Zaha Hadid. When a client
procures the services of an architect, they are also paying for a performance, and the
better an architect delivers a showstopping presence, the better they are paid, and

DOI: 10.4324/9781003164593-6

the better their services are seen to be. Though to be sure the majority architects are not quite such celebrities, many architects carry off their roles with a certain élan.

Possibly because of the vast range of our profession, landscape architects aren't nearly as good at 'owning a room.' There are few landscape architects cast in the 'starchitect' mould. Notable exceptions might be the formidable Martha Schwartz or the colourful Ken Smith, but of course it is of note that they are exceptions. If we grumble about being asked too little to lead projects, or that we receive too little media attention, then in many ways we have ourselves to blame for not mastering the performance of design and putting ourselves in the public eye. We needn't appropriate either the arrogant egos that are building architecture's stereotype or try to be starchitects. Then again, those of us who are capable should work towards creating an image in both dress and action that creates the theatre of power and of the lightly exotic that gives spice to the performance of our professional lives.

This column was published in *Landscape*, Spring 2014.

7

FEASTING IS A PROJECT

When I was in my tweens, my family made a trip from Harwich to Copenhagen on a cruise ship.[1] It is the one and only trip on a cruise ship I've ever taken. Even though it lasted only a couple of days and one night, it was dull, especially for a youngster. Every meal was a buffet, and every meal was enormous, overflowing the table. Britain in the 1980s was not exactly cornucopian in either the quality or quantity of the meals served. Still, when every meal is a feast, the excitement begins to wear off.

In the ship's cinema we were treated to a screening of the film *Quest for Fire*, which I admit I only dimly remember, as though in flickering cave-light and also queasily rocked by the sea. The film is set 80,000 years in the past and was filmed in the Scottish Highlands. The plot, narrated by the actors in a speculative prehistoric language created by Anthony Burgess (who speculated on future tongues, of course, in *A Clockwork Orange*), is necessarily thin, revolving around the possession of a carefully kindled germ of fire. Around that glowing nucleus, in the 80,000 years that would follow, would form the campfire, the hearth, the kitchen, the dining room, the feast.

The cooking of food, whether or not it started exactly 80,000 years ago or not, may be one of the most important moments in human cultural evolution. First of all, cooking food makes more nutrients available, and second of all cooking and eating together is very much at the heart of human association. Biological evolution is a series of more or less happy accidents—mutations. More than mere happenstance, cultural evolution has shape and direction. It has memory and it is concerned with the future. It is human. To understand the evolution of the feast as

---

1 Actually, it was the now-defunct Harwich to Esbjerg overnight ferry, but it seemed like a cruise ship to me at the time.

DOI: 10.4324/9781003164593-7

a form of human association coupled with a utopian drive, a little reimagining of prehistory is necessary.

A fair amount of biological evolution can happen in a few thousand years, but only cultural evolution can explain the exponential advances of the human species. Primatologist Michael Tomasello speaks about the 'ratchet effect,' in which innovations are held in place while new innovations are geared up and advanced upon them.

> The process of cumulative cultural evolution requires not only creative invention but also, and just as importantly, faithful social transmission that can work as a ratchet to prevent slippage backward—so that the newly invented artefact or practice preserves its new and improved form at least somewhat faithfully until a further modification or improvement comes along.
>
> *(1999: 5)*

That ratcheting, for humans, begins with the campfire, the spear, and various tools for digging at the earth to forage. Many parts of the Earth provide generously, copiously for such hunting and gathering lifestyles. There is little reason, rationally, to culturally evolve from this luxurious state into sedentist agriculture. Farming is hard, risky work with long hours, and it developed in many fruitful parts of the world where it might be seen to be unnecessary.

But just as the campfire projects the possibilities of the hearth and the kitchen, so the digging stick imagines the garden. And the kitchen and garden are projects that require organization. In short, cooking, gardening, and tending animals are interesting. They give people something to talk about; a reason for language, even. The campfire, the kitchen, the garden, and the herd provide a focus for human energies and a reason for human association. The quest for fire leads to a quest for conviviality, and conviviality may well be humanity's great project.

As flame-roasted meats developed into 'lunch' and 'dinner,' so too did primal nature become formed into landscape, an even more interesting project in total than mere lunch or dinner. And the cycles of time: day and night, season, hunt, and harvest—the *genius temporum* (see Chapter 18) that accompanies landscape's *genius loci*—become frames for imagining delicious pasts and tasty futures. "We are all utopians," wrote Henri Lefebvre, "so soon as we wish for something better" (2000 [1968]: 75), and the next feast necessarily has to be lovelier.

So I come to the potluck, that great dining invention: "a beautiful act of social creation," according to Kim Stanley Robinson, "a result of living with a commons, rearing the kids together, and thinking socially and creatively" (2018: n.p.). A potluck is interesting. It's a project. It requires organization. It is a frame for conviviality. Then, perhaps most importantly, it is emblematic of the form of evolution which Peter Kropotkin calls 'mutual aid.' Kropotkin clarified Darwin's 'survival of the fittest,' stressing that the fittest relationships within species and amongst species were those which ensured the greatest advantage. For humans, stories become part of the advantage; stories about pasts and futures; stories about utopia. Our future feasts (and when I say 'our,' I mean 'all humans') are often utopias; dreams of convivial living in shared landscapes.

Utopia is a drive with the same sort of shape and direction as that of cultural evolution. When Lefebvre speaks about utopia, he speaks of it as part of a work— an *oeuvre*. Though much of human life in landscapes, whether rural or urban, is composed of drudgery, routine, duty, and hardship, what is created collectively is often beautiful, even transcendent. If human history is a dull fabric, it is woven through with sparkling utopian threads, and when seen in total the drapery of its folds is an astonishment. Those sparkling threads are the emergence of the festival in the everyday, the utopian feasts in which an abundance of food and a surplus of art, music, and dance make the everyday worthwhile.

If human feasting in late capitalism has itself become drudgery, like the overflowing tables on that Danish cruise ship of my childhood, then it's likely that a return to understanding the nature and the place of the feast as a human project is important. To make the feast interesting and fulfilling, it is not enough for food to magically appear in folkloric abundance, as it does in the land of Cockaigne, but it must be part of a planned project that is undertaken collectively. A feast is meaningless, its utopian significance eviscerated, if it isn't part of a project that links the landscape (of finding and foraging, whether roots or cheese and chocolate as well as growing) with the kitchen with the table; placemaking with companionship (from *com-panis*, breaking bread together) and commensality (coming together at table). All of life must be lived with one eye on the potluck.

This short essay was part of an online collection, edited by David Sergeant at the University of Plymouth, called *Imagining Alternatives with Feasts for the Future* in 2018.

8

AT LIBERTY

The Place de la République

Over lunch at the cheap and cheerful Gai Moulin restaurant near the Pompidou in Paris, I spoke with the man at the next table about his experience of the Place de la République. He replied that it was outside of his usual haunts, but that he had always seen the space as "a sort of absence." This is precisely how I remembered the Place from previous trips to Paris. It was somehow dark, cold, and wet in every season; a vortex of angry traffic that made fugitives of pedestrians; a margin; a non-place. What a pleasure, then, to return to find a space filled with warmth and activity, even on a damp winter day.

The design, by the French architecture and urbanism practice Trevélo and Viger-Kohler (TVK) with Martha Schwartz Partners and the Belgian landscape architects Areal, has brought the city back together where it had been fractured by traffic planners and years of small streetscape adjustments unaided by strategy. TVK was responsible for much of the design, the meetings, the consultations. Two great successes of the space are owing to creative input from Martha Schwartz Partners; the partial pedestrianization of one side of the square and a very sophisticated grading strategy.

The Place de la République sits at the corner of the 3rd, 10th, and 11th arrondissements and at the centre of a spiderweb of streets with no fewer than seven roads connecting (and more diving into forks just before). There are also five Metro lines that converge just underground and eject people at five points around and within it. The square's current shape is the result of the talented megalomaniac Georges-Eugène Haussmann's interventions in the Second Empire. The construction of the square and the adjoining boulevards involved the destruction of a row of theatres on the Boulevard du Temple. One of the earliest photographic images, a daguerreotype of the Boulevard du Temple, shows the area before Haussmann's picks began to swing (Figure 8.1).

DOI: 10.4324/9781003164593-8

FIGURE 8.1 The Boulevard du Temple by Louis Daguerre, 1838. Credit: Louis Daguerre/ Wikimedia commons.

The centre of the Place de la République is the top of a gentle hill on which sits a gaudy statue of Marianne, France's national emblem, brandishing an olive branch with bombast (Figure 8.2). Before the renovations of the square she sat marooned on a traffic island, her pedestal covered with graffiti deposited during demonstrations. Now she floats over the dome of space, and the topography bends away from her and down the many radiating streets. The hilltop has been gently smoothed in every direction, which gives it a decisive tautness. It doesn't have 'hospital corners,' tucked into itself nicely as so many squares can be; rather, the tautness extends beyond the square and down each connecting street. As Schwartz says, "The project's big win was to attach the square to the rest of the city." The decisive, perhaps brutal confidence of Haussmann's avenues has met its complement. The square and the surrounding streets have all been joined in grand unity.

The redirection of the traffic, which partially pedestrianizes the northeastern side of the square, is almost a photocopy of London's Trafalgar Square, which was also a choked gyre of traffic until Peter Heath at Atkins and Norman Foster and Partners corrected it in 2003. Whereas Trafalgar Square is completely pedestrianized along one side, its Parisian counterpart allows bus and taxi traffic along its quiet side. It's hated by taxi drivers, who claim that there is now a permanent bottleneck at the Place de la République. The London version is not loved by taxi drivers either, nor by the National Gallery, which, with characteristic English reserve, claims the

FIGURE 8.2 The statue of Marianne photographed after the Charlie Hebdo shooting in 2015. Credit: Tim Waterman.

space is now so overrun with tourists that it has turned into an undignified carnival. In 2009, the gallery actually tried, as a reaction, to have the traffic returned to the square.

The Ville de Paris is willing to wait out the taxi drivers, though. The intentions are overall to make Paris a place much more friendly to alternative transportation modes, and the hope is that congestion will ease as car usage declines. Paris also gives over automotive spaces to the pedestrians, bikes, and other wheels along the Seine during the summer when a beach appears on the road, and on Sundays all year.

On my midwinter visit the tourist throngs that plague Trafalgar Square weren't in evidence at République, but the square was certainly thronged on my arrival. Thousands of Kurds and their supporters had turned out to protest the murder of three Kurdish activists in Paris the previous year. Flags of a variety of countries waved from the hands of young protesters who were climbing Marianne's pedestal. Food vendors set up at the edges of the crowd, and then, lining every street in incredible numbers, were armoured gendarmes and their vehicles, drinking coffee and waiting for trouble (which never came). From my hotel room just next door I could hear the indignation of the crowds and the speakers coming in waves.

At midnight, the square was full of piles of refuse being gathered together and trucks with pressure washers. A couple of flags still fluttered around the statue. The next morning, a Sunday, was clear and bright, and early on in the day the traffic around the square was light. With a cup of coffee and a croissant I watched the Place de la République awaken. First there were just a few of us—a couple of homeless people on a bench, the other coffee drinkers, a few people whizzing by on bicycles. Gradually, though, a wide variety of other types of wheeled vehicles began to appear, attracted by the large, clear, smooth space. First a father teaching his tiny son to ride his bike, then a mother and a young girl both with pink rollerblades, and a toddler on a scooter who let it fall to the ground in order to have a good full-throated cry. Later, two girls with unicycles carefully threaded their way through a group having a kickabout with a soccer ball.

While watching all the activity dependent upon a clear, level space (Figure 8.3), a delightful paradox became evident. It does, as I've mentioned, slope off into streetscapes in every direction. It's far from level. However, along the pedestrianized edge of the square, a series of four flights of stairs provide balconies over the space below and help to give the illusion of levelness. Thus it is possible to stand in the square and simultaneously comprehend it as both meticulously level and pronouncedly domed. What's even better is that this isn't an accident. It required some very canny and careful grading by Martha Schwartz Partners. Not one of the flights of stairs meets the slope in the same way, and there are cross-slopes to the cross-slopes.

There's a particular irony that MSP should have helped to design a space where the design work flies so low under the radar. Her practice is founded in her flair as a provocateur. She has always wished to move the landscape profession by exciting

FIGURE 8.3 Aerial view of the square. Credit: Pawel Gaul/iStockphoto.

comment and provoking debate, and always with highly visible design moves. "I am the army ant that sacrifices its body to build a bridge," she says. She utterly rejects the old dogma within landscape architecture that it is at its best when it is invisible. I couldn't help asking whether such a minimalist space was enough for her. No, of course not. If she had her way she would have swept the old Plane trees away that guard one side of the space, replacing them with a series of big fountains. But it was not to be.

She explains the Place de la République's subtlety in terms of the fabric of Paris itself. Paris, she explains, doesn't need landscape spaces that shock it back into functionality. It's already working in so many ways, and so sure of itself. Paris, she says, "… doesn't need a defibrillator." Still, one gets the sense she would have used one anyway if she could have. Maybe it doesn't need it, but it can certainly take it.

There are also difficulties trying to make a design splash in a public space where so many people have ownership. "The public landscape is the most contested of all spaces," Schwartz says. "It is where everything overlaps. It's more political territory than it is environmental or social, for example." In addition to the many stakeholders, how much can happen in a project depends upon the political will of the powers that be, whether they will take on risks, which may depend upon where they're at in the electoral cycle. "TVK took the largest part of the project—they were sitting there with the politicians."

It is the big moves that work here, and perhaps also the hard work with the politicians. Other gestures are much less assured. The square's simple austerity allows the warmth of human activity to fill the space. TVK seems to have become frightened of such minimalism and have added to the square a small wooden stage at the southeast corner, but it looks paltry and tentative. Worse, the square is dotted with wooden benches, the outsized timbers of which seek to reference overstuffed sofas. These appear jokey and compensatory. Finally, the northwestern end of the square is held in place with a small rectangular café, grandly named the Monde and Médias Pavilion. Its glazed walls allow a seamless interaction with the surrounding space, and a roof cantilevers out over seating adjacent to a water feature. It is perfect for parents wishing to watch their children. There is gently glowing lighting that adds a delicate ambience. From the water side, this is a successful ensemble, but viewed from the street side the café's lines are far less confident. The floating effect of the cantilever doesn't elevate the building here—it is decidedly grounded. The heavy beam that forms the cornice, and which counterbalances the cantilever, overpowers the building with top-heaviness, and as an otherwise unadorned box the architecture offers no other tactic with which to counteract this effect. Viewed from the major approach down the Boulevard Saint-Martin across the busy street, it is a graceless and unwelcoming presence.

I leave Paris in the mid-afternoon, with a walk to the Gare du Nord to catch the Eurostar back to London. The southern expanse of the Place de la République is now filled with youths skateboarding, and the clatter of boards is so constant it sounds like the pop and crackle of a poorly tuned radio. To all the other wheels in the square I add the two of my suitcase. TVK created a beautiful *bande dessinée*

FIGURE 8.4 Wheeled vehicles. Credit: Pawel Gaul/iStock photo.

graphic to convey the various programmes and activities that were to be contained within the new Place de la République, and they're all in there—he kids, the Kurds, the skateboards (Figure 8.4). Even the sullen taxi drivers might reluctantly find themselves in the mix.

So many of the groups that have ownership of the square have been there through the weekend. The grout is already coming away from between the stones from all the pressure washing at night—a direct result of so much activity. It's gone from being an urban margin to something that integrates the city around it, making it legible. The charming little cafés near the Square du Temple are now part of the same city that contains the tranquil Canal St Martin, which on just the other side of the Place de la République dives into a tunnel through the same hill that is crowned by Marianne. What the graphic fails to show is that the site's narratives aren't contained here. They are now part of all of Paris's trajectories again—they stretch outside, they connect, and bring the whole place into focus again.

This article was published in *Landscape Architecture Magazine*, April 2014.

9

A WORD... 'PROFESSION'

In the middle of the seventeenth century, at the dawn of modernity, the philosopher Thomas Hobbes, in his *Elementa Philosophica de Cive* (1782 [1642]: xxv), described human relations outside the constraints of civil society as *bellum omnium contra omnes*—a war of all against all—an idea which subsequently came to underpin dog-eat-dog conceptions of social Darwinism, and which characterizes the mindset that made possible the transatlantic slave trade and the enclosures and clearances in early capitalism. Contrasted to this are the premodern commons, those shared lands and practices that were the basis for communal well-being and wealth, *unus pro omnibus, omnes pro uno*—all for one and one for all. The dog-eating dogs continue to consume each other and to enclose the commons globally, and the ideology that allows it still echoes Hobbes. It is known as competitive individualism (see Curtis, 2013; Gilbert, 2014) and it is the foundation for neoliberalism, the ideology under which we have seen governments everywhere become more authoritarian and market-driven.

It is commonly assumed that the commons are historic conditions, but people still work together everywhere for mutual advantage, and we might even regard professions as types of commons. What does a profession do and how does it function? It consists in a variety of interlinked supports and guarantees: it ensures trust both internally and externally by providing the certification of the group and adherence to a robust code of ethics; it provides support for students and young professionals through education, training, and/or apprenticeships; it provides promotion, advocacy, and communications; it lobbies in government; it provides statutory protection for the work of its professionals. Last but not least, it provides for togetherness and sharing of ideas, friendship, and the common good. Professions thus have great importance both for their members and as models of what society can and should be.

DOI: 10.4324/9781003164593-9

Professions and institutions of all sorts are now increasingly under threat from competitive individualism, however. The relentless intensity of our working lives makes it ever more difficult for us to make time for togetherness and sharing. Downward pressure on professional wages in many sectors makes long periods of time and quantities of money spent on education and qualification seem wasteful instead of the vital structure of our mutual guarantee. Finally, and probably not only, our perception of society as composed of disconnected individuals means that we are putting greater trust in crowd-sourced certification (Tripadvisor springs to mind, with its five-star ratings for popular but unexciting restaurants) rather than expert or institutional judgement.

Competitive individualism complicates professions even further. We tend to see achievements as the work of disconnected and miraculously inspired individuals—this is evident in the trend towards starchitecture—rather than as the work of professions and the sharing and supporting networks engendered by them, from education to practice. We have come to see value as being created by the lone genius rather than by a great collective work over many years.

It may be that the multiple threats which professions face, as they are presently constituted, and in a winner-takes-all world, will be enough to overwhelm them completely. Or they may change and adapt to new forms that we cannot yet predict. Or finally, we may decide that we need to make a case for the continued survival of professions and stand stalwart together in defence of the idea of mutual aid. As for me, I know I'm one for all.

This column was published in *Landscape*, Spring 2016.

10

SITUATING THE DIGITAL COMMONS

A conversation with Ruth Catlow

The negotiation of the commons takes place in two distinct realms that are increasingly reaching into and shaping one another: the long history of the landscape commons both in cities and in the countryside, and across digital networks. In both realms we find the continued project of the enclosures, appropriating forms of collectively created use value and converting it, wherever possible, into exchange value. In this conversation, Ruth Catlow and Tim Waterman discuss the 'Reading the Commons' project together with Furtherfield's work on understanding the commons.

Artist, theorist, curator and recovering web-utopian Ruth Catlow is co-founder (with Marc Garrett in 1996) and co-director of Furtherfield (and furtherfield.org), London's longest running (de)centre for art and technology. Furtherfield provides labs, debates, and exhibitions around critical questions in arts, technology and society.

TW: I'll start with a little background. 'Reading the Commons' is an ongoing project[1] which we initiated that seeks to find a place of power in order to defend the continual project of the creation of the commons in all realms in the future and to augment and magnify other similar endeavours by other groups and organizations. We knew that there is already a lot of work being done in and around the idea of the commons, so we were less interested in staking out any intellectual ground than we were in making connections and finding ways of sharing research and experiences amongst ourselves and other interested parties. So far, two groups have been assembled to read and discuss. The first was convened in the summer of 2014 at Furtherfield Commons, the community lab space in the southwest corner of Finsbury Park, and was composed of a broad range of academics and practitioners

---

1 'Reading the Commons' is no longer an ongoing project, though its legacy lives on in continuing work at Furtherfield and, of course, in this book.

DOI: 10.4324/9781003164593-10

FIGURE 10.1 The Embroidered Digital Commons at Furtherfield Gallery 2012. EDC initiated by Ele Carpenter is a collectively stitched version of 'A Concise Lexicon of/for the Digital Commons' by the Raqs Media Collective (2003). In the background is the installation "London Wall" by Thomson and Craighead. Credit: Furtherfield.

from different disciplines.[2] It met once a fortnight for several months and discussion was wide-ranging. The second was in the Summer of 2015 and involved a group of Master's students in curation at Goldsmiths under the direction of Ele Carpenter[3] (Figure 10.1). Future incarnations of the group will each try for different configurations of people, disciplines, and callings.

RC: The first group was very diverse—from backgrounds in geography, sociology, law, political science, technology, landscape architecture, art, and more. We faced an immediate challenge talking across the boundaries of all these disciplines and philosophical and cultural traditions. This was illustrated immediately in the first session.

2 The original group involved the following scholars as well as the convenors: Anne Bottomley, Emeritus Reader in Law and Property at Kent Law School; Joss Hands, Director of Postgraduate Research Studies, School of Arts and Cultures at Newcastle University; Alastair McCapra, Chief Executive at the Chartered Institute of Public Relations and board member of Wikimedia UK; Nathan Moore, Senior Lecturer in Law at Birkbeck School of Law; Christian Nold, artist, designer, educator, and research fellow at the Extreme Citizen Science group at University College London; Penny Travlou, Lecturer in Cultural Geography and Theory at the Edinburgh School of Architecture and Landscape Architecture, University of Edinburgh; and Ed Wall, Associate Professor of Landscapes and Cities and Academic Portfolio Lead—Landscape Architecture and Urbanism at the University of Greenwich.
3 Ele Carpenter is now Professor of Interdisciplinary Art & Culture and Director of UmArts Research Centre at the University of Umeå.

One of our group, a scholar in Law and Property, was irked by our early introduction of two Americans, Garrett Hardin and Yochai Benkler. We had introduced these theorists along with Elinor Ostrom, Oliver Goldsmith, and Michel Bauwens. The law and property scholar was irked for a number of reasons, but particularly because they represented a bias towards a US and UK (English speaking) over other European traditions—of property and ownership over civil liberties. Another participant, with an established practice in arts and technology looked pained throughout. I think this was because we seemed to be scratching the surface of topics, works, and discussions that make up the discourse around the network, and the digital commons.

TW: We partially remedied this problem by asking the participants to provide readings for future sections and to give a brief verbal introduction.

RC: For instance, Christian Nold led a show-and-tell at the second session, based on a book, *Autopsy of an Island Currency* (2014) that he had worked on with Nathalie Aubret and Susanne Jaschko. The book problematizes a project called Suomenlinna Money Lab, a participatory art and design project that worked with money and local currencies as a social and artistic medium and that sought to involve a community of people in a critique of its own economies. This reinforced for me the contribution that situated practices have to make to theories of the commons, as the book tells a revealing story of resistance to critique in a place and community with an established interest and investment in the cultures associated with private ownership.

TW: Nevertheless, there were a lot of times when people 'looked pained,' because basically we had just jumped in and started discussing the idea of the commons without realizing that we were all speaking with different understandings of basic terms. In other words, we were all operating on different registers that sprang from our hailing from different philosophical and disciplinary roots and traditions. It might have benefited us to begin by trying to map out our terms. On the other hand, this might have prevented us from ever even starting! This mapping, perhaps, is a project that we need to figure out how to undertake.

RC: The difficulty of wrangling different registers was also exacerbated by the seemingly unbounded scope of the discussion (Figure 10.2). The relatively recent growth of the World Wide Web introduces enough material for months of readings about how the digital commons has helped to shift thinking about the commons away from merely the management of material resources to knowledge and cultural work.

Still, we felt—perhaps because Furtherfield's physical venues are located within a public park—a sense of urgency to think about the social layers of physical and digital space in relation to the commons, as a way to resist the unquestioning total commercialization of all realms.

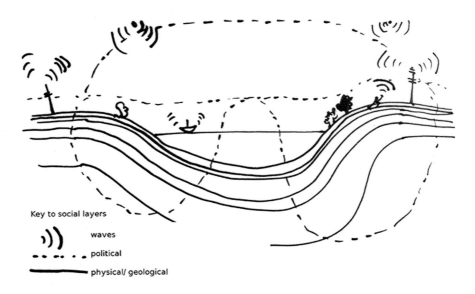

Key to social layers

))) waves

. _ . _ . . political

▬▬▬ physical/ geological

FIGURE 10.2 The social layers of physical and digital space—drawn by Ruth during this conversation. Credit: Ruth Catlow.

RC: To take a couple of steps back ... There are misconceptions about the commons that require rectification. Political economist Elinor Ostrom showed, in opposition to Garrett Hardin, that in theory and in practice, the collective co-operative management of shared socio-ecological resources was a lived reality in many localities (Ostrom, 1990). While her research drew on management of material resources, her Eight Design Principles for Common Pool Resources shares many characteristics with digital commons.

Hardin's (1968) essay "The Tragedy of the Commons" had argued that commonly owned resources were doomed to exploitation and depletion by private individuals; therefore, justifying the role of hierarchical, centralized systems of power to maintain private ownership. On the other hand, Jeremy Gilbert in his book *Common Ground* (2013), quotes radical economist Massimo de Angelis, to define the commons as social spheres which help protect us from the market. This becomes particularly useful to help us to recalibrate our definitions of 'free' and 'sharing' as we reveal so much of our private lives (so nonchalantly) via ubiquitous, proprietary digital devices and commercial social platforms.

TW: Hardin's one-dimensional projection of the commons as unworkable and disastrous was based upon an understanding of human relations that assumed that competitive individualism is 'human nature' and that all such 'experiments' were doomed to failure as a result. This is Darwin's survival of the fittest rendered as 'dog eat dog'. The voice almost contemporary with Darwin's that I think most clearly articulates how evolution (human and otherwise) is based upon cooperation is

Peter Kropotkin's, in his amazing book *Mutual Aid* (1902). Evolutionary science and theory is moving ever more towards Kropotkin's conclusions rather than Darwin's, or at least Kropotkin's work is becoming ever more relevant and complementary to Darwin's. For me, it's also impossible to imagine how cultural evolution could work at all except through the cooperation, sharing, and processes of negotiation that characterize the commons.

The landscape commons has always been about more than just material resources, and this is perhaps the most reductively oversimplified register on which we might speak of the commons. So, if the problem is to align the different and more mean-ingful registers along which we all discuss the commons so that a truly collective and collaborative project can emerge amongst many disciplines simultaneously, we should have a go at pinning in place a few core understandings of the commons. Shall we give that a go?

RC: Yes! From my work with Furtherfield, my feeling for the commons is strongly influenced by the cultures of freedom and openness in engineering and software. In 2011, we created a collection of artworks, texts, and resources about freedom and openness in the arts in the age of the Internet. "Freedom to collaborate—to use, modify and redistribute ideas, artworks, experiences, media and tools. Openness to the ideas and contributions of others, and new ways of organising and making decisions together" (Furtherfield, 2011: n.p.).

If we can agree that the commons represents those resources that are collect-ively produced and managed by, and in the interests of, the people who use them, then the digital commons, as set out by Felix Stalder (2010), are the technolo-gies, knowledge, and digital cultural resources that are communally designed, distributed, and owned: wikis, open-source software and licensing, and open cultural works and knowledge repositories. Licences such as the GNU General Public License and various Creative Commons licences ensure that the freedom to use, adapt, and distribute works produced collectively is preserved for the future.

Discussions of the commons have, in the liberal tradition, centred around how to produce, manage, and share scarce material resources in a bounded geographical locality. This is fundamentally changed in the postindustrial, information age, where cultural and knowledge goods can be easily, cheaply, and quickly copied, shared worldwide, and transformed. It has brought about a massive shift in the way eco-nomics, politics, and law are practised.

As distinct from the users of the majority of corporately owned search, sales and social media utilities (think Google, Amazon, Paypal, Facebook, Twitter) and digital entertainment platforms (think Netflix, iMusic, and Spotify) the community of people involved in developing the digital commons "can intervene in the design and governance of their interaction processes and of their shared resources" (ibid., 2010: n.p.) (think Wikipedia, Freesound, Wikihouse). This has long continued to be an area of intense critical inquiry, unfolding, and practice for artists who are cre-ating digital and networked artworks that take the form of platforms, software, tools, and interventions such as: Upstage software for online "cyberformance"; Naked on Pluto, an online game whose 'players' become unwitting agents in the invasion of their own and others' privacy; and PureDyne, the USB-bootable GNU/Linux operating system for creative multimedia.

Consumer cultures invite us constantly to outsource responsibility for knowledge, information and cultural works to the markets. Artists and technologists involved in the digital commons make these otherwise abstract (and often invisible) shifts in power and social relations "feelable" for more people. In this way they are asserting alternatives to the prevailing economic models—often privileging collaboration and free expression that disrupt outmoded models of copyright and intellectual property.

Discussions about the role of affect in the development of the commons will be the subject of the next explorations of Reading the Commons, and we will certainly come back to these.

TW: Let's look at this from another direction. In landscape terms, the idea of the commons has evolved a great deal over time, as, for example, feudal forms gave way to different hierarchical forms based in capitalism and private property, and now in late capitalism and neoliberalism's adaptation to, and co-optation of, various forms of horizontality, especially in managerial practices. The importance of the commons has also shifted from defining notions of shared ownership and management of agrarian resources to include various manifestations of urban life, most recently and compellingly, perhaps, in the dogmatically horizontal democratic organization amongst participants in the Occupy! movement.

Ultimately, the commons, for me, is about dialogue, sharing, and the relationship between people and place. The earliest expressions of the commons were all about our relationship with food; its procurement, preparation, and consumption. A beautiful historic example is the importance of the chestnut tree to the inhabitants of the Cévennes in southern France, and how it not only embodied the commons, but symbolized it as well. It's not possible to romanticize this story, as it's one of very hard-scrabble survival, but it does illustrate the point. As a staple food, the chestnut was a matter of survival for the inhabitants of the Cévennes. It would seem, metaphorically, that the idea of rootedness would follow naturally from this as a characteristic of the commons, but the reality is more nuanced. Chestnuts were introduced to the Cévennes by the Romans, and then tended centuries later by monks, who would share plants with the peasants with the expectation of future tithes. Labour-intensive chestnut orchards were farmed not just by locals, but by migrant workers as well. If we fast-forward to the 1960s, chestnuts were rediscovered by those wishing to get 'back to the land,' reviving agricultural practices that had withered away during the years that capitalism had lured (or forced) people from the countryside into towns.

This shows a very complex picture of the commons: one in which colonization and imperialism, monasticism, peasantry, migrant labour, and then finally arcadian anti-capitalist mythologies of the 1960s each play a part—and I'm skipping over a lot of historic detail and nuance. There is a tendency nowadays to see the commons as exclusively autonomous and horizontal, but historically the commons has been inextricably bound to patterns of ownership and domination. Far from discounting the commons, this shows how the commons can exist within, and exert pressure against, prevailing forms of domination and ownership. We need not wait for total revolution or the construction of utopia or arcadia. We can get to work now and make a shining example of what is possible, making use of existing networks and existing places. The anthropologist David Graeber, in his book *The Democracy Project* (2013), calls this 'prefigurative politics': the idea that by acting out the model of politics and human association and inhabitation that we wish to see, that we work to bring it about.

RC: Yes, and while sociality, rootedness, and affinity are all associated with embodied experience, they bubble up again and again in the critical and activist media art community who take digital networks for their tools, inspiration, and context. Take, for example, the Swedish artist/activist group Piratbyrån (The Bureau of Piracy), established in 2003 to promote the free sharing of information, culture, and intellectual property. Their entire exhibition (Furtherfield, 2014) of online and physical installations (Figure 10.3) at Furtherfield Gallery highlighted the centrality to their work of cultural sharing and affinity-building. In his recent conversation with Tatiana Bazzichelli about networked disruption and business, Marc Garrett (2014) discusses the importance of affinities in evolving more imaginative, less

FIGURE 10.3 Riot Chat by Palle Torsson, part of the Piratbyrån and Friends exhibition at Furtherfield Gallery, 3 May–8 June 2014. Credit: Furtherfield.

oppositional (and macho) engagement with regressive forces; and quoting Donna Haraway who says "situated knowledges are about communities, not isolated individuals" (1988: 590).

But Tim, I think you were on a roll. Why don't you keep going? Why is the commons important now?

TW: The exploitation of people and resources that marks the practices of contemporary capitalism is very much a continuation of the project of the enclosures, whether it is to skim value off creative projects, to asset-strip the public sector which is increasingly encroached upon by the private sector, or to exhaust land and oppress workers in the Third World. The commons, however, are being created continually, and they represent not just a resource to be enclosed and exploited, but a form of resistance that has particular power because it is lived and acted. It's not at all a contradiction to say that what is common is simultaneously enclosed, exploited, and liberatory. It's a matter of tipping the balance so that the creation of the commons outpaces its negation.

RC: As people negotiate systems for renewal and stewardship of the resources over time they also arrive at an expression of creative identity and shared values.

TW: A moral economy…

RC: By freely surrendering all collectively created culture, from use value for conversion to exchange value, our shared ecologies of knowledge, culture, and land are dismantled.

And with this we stand to lose the ability to attend to the nature of co-evolving, interdependent entities (human and non-human) and conditions, for the healthy evolution and survival of our species (Catlow and Garrett, 2012).

We are seeing a resurgence of collective and collaborative efforts. Our ongoing DIWO (Do-It-With-Others) campaign (Furtherfield, 2006) sets out to adopt the verve and tactics of DIY culture, but to move us on from its individualism towards imaginative and experimental artistic collaboration. We construct more varied social relations (than those set up by pure market exchange) into the proliferation of connected sensing, communication, and knowledge tools, in order to facilitate new forms of trans-global relations and cooperation. Most exciting is the Robin Hood Asset Management Cooperative (robinhoodcoop.org), an activist hedge fund (and the project of economists, critical theorists, artists, and financial experts) which distributes shares to members, and its profits are invested in pro-social and commons-focused cultural projects.

TW: The point about use value is an important one. Capitalism, in the familiar equation, seeks to convert use value into exchange value. This process abstracts and simplifies value into purely financial terms. The language and action of the commons resists this because it is so often emplaced and embodied. Commons are local, experienced, shared, and negotiated, and they exist within networks of friendship, family, and civil society, which operate as moral economies, not purely monetary ones. I should probably also make the point that the Greek root of the word 'moral' signifies custom—which suggests that morals exist in the relational realm of everyday life, rather than in abstract 'higher' realms or in abstract financialized realms such as 'the market'—and that 'economy' comes from Greek again, the *oikos* (οἶκος), or household—another firmly embodied and situated idea that is also incontrovertibly relational.

RC: The digital is becoming embodied and situated in a number of ways. Where once the boundaries between the worlds of atoms and bits were marked by screens and passwords, chips and implants are now on or in our bodies, devices, and appliances. People and things are becoming increasingly expressive as nodes in the machineweb. Again, this gives artists a vital role in making these effects more legible, feelable, and visible. Our actions are tracked, our utterances and exchanges are monitored, and our behaviours inform the design of future media, systems, and products. This is the cybernetic loop (see Furtherfield, 2015). We also see a growing awareness of the geopolitical questions surrounding the physical infrastructure of the Internet and its role in global markets. The problematization of the web through heated debates about ownership and control of infrastructure and data, privacy and surveillance, expressed in the SOPA debates—the Edward Snowden affair; Tim Berners-Lee's campaign for a Magna Carta for the web; calls for a Digital Bill of Rights; the development of decentralizing blockchain technologies that underpin Bitcoin, Etherium, and (many other projects; artistic projects with Situationist verve such as those of Piratbyrån and F.A.T. Lab—these all help us to clarify our place, the opportunities and limits for agency and action as we straddle the physical and digital layers.

So, then we come back to the question of resistance and the commons. If, as you've described above, the continued project of the enclosures sets the scene for new acts of resistance, how, Tim, do you see these acts taking place in landscape space?

TW: Democracy and the commons both take place (literally a historic act is situated by its *taking place*) by occupying space as well as by initiating dialogues and negotiation. Occupying digital space is important, as you have shown, Ruth, as is resisting the forms of surveillance and control that seek to close down the digital commons. I take hope from the fact that even if it takes generations to end capitalism, or at least to shift it from a form of global governance to a competitive economic system more appropriate to the scale of the farmers' market, that the commons will never be fully enclosed, because capitalism is dependent upon the commons to create value that it then marketizes and financializes.

Defending the digital commons also occupies physical space. It will be, from time to time, necessary to occupy the streets and squares of our cities in protest to stand up for them. In doing so we stand up for the physical commons at the same time. Governments have all sorts of tools against public demonstrations, such as the British government's recently renewed hostility to trade unionism and its desire to further limit strike powers.[4] Strikes and protests will happen whether they're legal or not, though, as history amply demonstrates. Often many instances of land occupations are seen to have failed, however they have to have succeeded, at least temporarily, to register in the historical record as symbolic moments. These moments have immense power. The Diggers, for example, followers of Gerrard Winstanley, were proto-anarchists who organized horizontally in their land occupation in Surrey, Northamptonshire, and Buckinghamshire in the mid-1600s. Their planting of vegetables on common land, though a brief experiment, lives on powerfully in the discourses of democracy.

More modern incarnations of this power include the access to land gained by the mass trespass at Kinder Scout (see Chapter 16), the long-term encampment at Greenham Common, and the incredibly powerful and highly visible symbolism of the Occupy! movement in various places from New York to London to Istanbul and beyond. A recent echo of the Diggers is the occupation of Grow Heathrow,[5] which seeks to prevent the airport's expansion by peacefully living on land proposed for a third runway and growing food there.

RC: So our next steps, both for Reading the Commons and in our acting out of the commons, are to define and map, for the purposes of resistance in the ongoing creation of commons; digital collaborocracy; and an exploration of affect, agency, embodiment, and the commons. Creative practices under capitalism have long contained elements of both creation and resistance (or defence), and now these actions, both positive and negative, take place across the digital and situated realms as well as what might now be termed the 'situated digital.'

TW: I'm pursuing ideas of what Kate Soper calls 'alternative hedonism' (see Soper, 2020; Soper et al., 2009) so that sustainability can be conceived of as joyful. I think satisfaction—the fulfilment of desire—can have radical transformative potential for prosperity as a collective pursuit and is perhaps the only way to tip the balance away from liberal and neoliberal individualist competitive models. My idea of the commons and commoning includes freedom, democracy, nice cups of tea, evenings spent drinking wine and talking, the elimination of poverty, and the flourishing of human habitat and human potential.

RC: Let's all drink to that!

This conversation was posted on the arts collective Furtherfield's website in 2015, while Tim and Ruth were working on the next chapter in this book, 'Dining at a distance.' The two have worked closely together for many years.

---

4 These limitations to protest and the right to assemble have become evermore stringent under the evermore fascistic Johnson government.
5 Half of Grow Heathrow was evicted in 2019.

11

DINING AT A DISTANCE

Performing the commons across space and time

With Ruth Catlow

Hole-in-Space, 1980

> "Yeah! Party time!" a young man cheers, dancing around in the New York City crowd. As he raises his bottle of beer to a bevy of young women whose image is projected life-size in real-time from Los Angeles he yells "*Hey! You goddit, you goddit, you goddit, yeah?! Here you go baby!*" The crowds in both places clap and whoop their approval as the flirtation continues. "*Yeah, where you goin'?*" She can't hear him, the crowds are too noisy. "*Huh?*". "*Where you goin'?*" "*Where I go?*" "*I say, where you goin'?*" "*Where am I going? I'm standing right here with you!*" "*Oh I like that baby! I like that, I like that! Oh yeah, baby!*"

This toast occurred between impromptu participants during an unannounced, live, two-way, television–satellite link between New York City, and Los Angeles (Figure 11.1). For three evenings in November 1980, people on opposite coasts of the US appeared as life-sized, television images, standing right next to each other, able to hold a conversation. And so they discovered and invented possibilities for new encounters across a geographical divide.

Landscape and digital in common

Hole-in-Space introduces possibilities for conviviality, sensuality, and feeling together, in the early creation of the digital commons. It is curious and telling that a clearly identifiable strain within art practice[1] that takes global communication infrastructures as its materials (and to some degree, its subject), virtual as it may have

---

1 See, particularly, the networked performance work of Annie Abrahams, and Make-shift, the cyberformance collaboration of Paula Crutchlow and Helen Varley Jamieson.

DOI: 10.4324/9781003164593-11

FIGURE 11.1 *Hole-in-Space* was "a public communication sculpture." The video is a documentary of an unannounced, live, two-way two-hour satellite transmission which took place between Los Angeles and New York City 11th, 13th, and 14th November 1980. *Hole-in-Space* took place at Lincoln Center for the Performing Arts in New York City, and The Broadway department store in the Shopping Center in Century City, Los Angeles. Credit: Kit Galloway and Sherrie Rabinowitz.

seemed to be, is directly concerned with intercorporeal human connectedness and specific situatedness or emplacement. There is a tendency to attempt to realize the social and political realms of the Internet as *mise-en-sens*, *mise-en-forme*, and *mise-en-scène*. In terms of the kitchen and table as sites for both connectedness and performance, we may also add the chef's *mise-en-place*.

This tendency is emblematic of a larger history of two distinct realms increasingly reaching into and shaping one another: the long history of the landscape commons both in cities and in the countryside and in the shorter history of digital networks, though, of course, these last exist within a continuum of the much more established realms of human communication and media, word and image. In both realms we find the continued project of the enclosures, appropriating forms of collectively created use value and converting it, wherever possible, into exchange value. The abstraction and transformation of use value through enclosure, so often created and negotiated through mutual processes and through the commons, is a hallmark of capitalism—perhaps *the* hallmark of capitalism (see Chapter 10). The commons, on the other hand, as we set out in the previous chapter, is local and situated, and exist and operate as moral economies. These commons, lived and acted, seek to outpace their negation by capitalist enclosure.

Creative practices under capitalism have long contained elements of creation, resistance (or defence), and *détournement*, and now these actions, both positive and negative, take place across the digital and situated realms as well as what might now be termed the 'situated digital.' A number of artists associated with the London-based activist digital arts collective Furtherfield have sought to embody, emplace, and perform ideas, people, and interactions that are at a distance or distributed across space and/or time as well as revealing the social relations that are produced by infrastructures for distribution and connection, including communication and information networks.

Do-It-With-Others

Furtherfield's Do-It-With-Others (DIWO) ethos, developed across the web with an international network of artists, technologists, and activists—thinkers and doers—has always aimed to enlarge artistic freedoms using the metaphors, tools, cultures, and processes of digital and physical networks. It is a distributed campaign for emancipatory, networked art practices led by experimental artistic processes rather than utilitarian or theoretical concerns to disrupt traditional hierarchies and concepts of ownership working with decentralized peer to peer (P2P) practices (Furtherfield, 2006).

Its expressions, though initiated across digital networks, have often spilled over into physical space. And coming together at table over food and/or drink—commensality and propinquity—have always been understood as an essential part of taking big steps forward in collective endeavour.

This was explored most closely through Furtherfield's *Rich Networking* series (Furtherfield, n.d.) in which the DIWO approach was employed to discover what digital culture might contribute in the context of ecological and economic stress. The series was a thought experiment about ways of convening artists, curators, technologists, musicians, thinkers, and researchers in geographically distant venues to share their knowledge, experience, perspectives, and approaches to sustainable international collaboration and exchange. It sought alternatives to the ecologically damaging international plane travel involved in hosting conferences (see Furtherfield, "We Won't Fly For Art: Media Art Ecologies," 2012). This essay's co-authorship exists as part of this ethic, and the process of its writing reflects the need for the sharing of physical as well as digital space in the act of its creation. We had to maintain the conversation during the creation of this essay; we had lunch and the conversation continued through lunch, then we wrote and worked on a web-based document editor, which allowed us to work on the same document together and to access it from anywhere. There is a thrill of recognition and of an oddly physical nearness when you are two authors, blinking cursors,[2] working together at the same time in a document that is precisely the sort of tantalizing almost-touching that is highlighted by *Hole-in-Space*. But then the need to speak face-to-face reasserts itself again, and dinner is made, wine is drunk, minds and bodies happily together at table and happily creating intellectual work. What this underscores, as Jeremy Gilbert observes in analysing Bernard Stiegler, is that "technicity as such is a constitutive feature of all human culture, that culture itself always takes a technical form, from the very earliest manifestations of tool making or cave art, and that a 'prosthetic' relation to technology is partly constitutive of the human relation as such" (2014: 133). Human adaptation through cultural evolution in this context, that of the relationality inherent between 'nature' and 'culture,' and their resultant indivisibility, reinforce the assertion that digital networks and communications cannot be conceived of separately from the rest of material and social existence, and, by extension, nor can the work of art.

The authors' experience in creating this essay is part of the history of Furtherfield's project to increase opportunities for international 'rich networking' by seeking ways to reach into global ideas and associations by creating, through digital means, commensality without propinquity,[3] bringing people as close as possible, allowing their bodies and minds to simulate as nearly as possible the actual experience of dining and creating together. The political and theoretical grounding of these efforts is explored below as case studies from projects of Furtherfield-associated artists involving networked food distribution and dining, including Pollie Barden's 'Telematic Dinner Parties,' Sophie Hope's '1984,' and Kate Rich's 'Feral Trade Café.'

Telematic dinner parties—Pollie Barden

In 2011, Pollie Barden devised a dinner, hosted by Furtherfield as part of the *Rich Networking* series, to support the design of a technology platform that would support remote guests in experiencing togetherness and playfulness within the setting of a conventional dinner party. She wanted to discover how visual and aural channels might be composed to reproduce a dining experience comparable to a traditional co-presence dinner.

---

2 "We two cursors together blinking," we think of this.

3 It goes without saying that, during the pandemic, many such meals were shared (through laptops and pads and smartphones) in which commensality was experienced without propinquity, and the authors had ample experience of this. We did not know how prescient this essay was to appear in the 'new normal.'

Two small groups of diners seated at tables, at Furtherfield's studios in London and Telenoika's in Barcelona, ate together via a telematic dinner-setting. The telematic dinner party is "a technology system for mediating remote guests in a shared dinner party experience. […] With the telematic dinner party (TDP) we explore the mediation of food, food practices, and the shared connections people build around food" (Comber et al., 2014: 65).

> Sharing bread in the course of ceremonies or simply at ordinary meals forges bonds which, in principle, will never be loosed [sic] or forgotten. Your companions, as we have seen, are those with whom you have shared bread; the word is derived from Latin *com-*, 'together', and *panis*, 'bread.'
>
> *(Toussaint-Samat, 2009 [1987]: 208)*

A live image of remote table-tops was projected down onto physical table-tops left empty for the purpose. The image of the remote plates—first set, then loaded up with food, and eventually (literally) licked clean—occupied an otherwise empty half of a long table next to four physical dinner settings (Figure 11.1b).

Food was served according to the rules of the Latitude Supper club, from the latitude corresponding to the day of the year. The hosts in each venue cooked a Russian meal. During the latter part of the evening participants all observed themselves becoming more 'teenagery'—flirty and playful—free from the more careful observances of appropriate attention to ones' fellow diners.

Participants speculated on why this might be. They experienced the technology as inherently rebellious—it just could not be relied upon to behave as intended. The reduction in raw sensory data necessitated risk-taking. Participants had to do more guessing than usual about what their remote guests might mean by their gestures, words, audio expressions. In addition to the disruption of the audio-visual signal, the physical set-up forced diners to relate to their remote guests via an image projected downwards on to the horizontal plane of the table. Ordinarily, guests' mutual verticality is very much a part of how they relate (perhaps until later in the evening for the more adventurous). The diners 'played hard'[4] to compensate for this. The language difference led diners to move to written word—writing messages to each other on paper plates in a form of improvised analogue instant messaging.

The technical set-up took on a "fully anthropomorphised presence as a sassy but uncontrollable host." "So began the telematic kissing, and the stroking, and the drawn lips, and the lying (uncomfortable and contorted) with our heads on the table to gaze and laugh into the camera for each other." "We also expressed our identities as differently located groups to each other by swapping revolutionary

---

4 Those who worked on the various video communications platforms that proliferated during the pandemic will recognize this sensation—the additional strain of trying to project one's earnest attention becoming part of what people came to call "Zoom fatigue."

slogans and competitive joke telling. The Telenoika guests thought we might be in need of a little political training" (Catlow, 2011: n.p.).[5]

What is important to note about the telematic dinner parties is that they sought to create interaction and connection using food and dining as the vehicle. Jaz Hee-jeong Choi argues, specifically in addressing human–computer–food relationships:

> We deliberately use 'human–food interactions' instead of, for example, 'human–food experiences' to denote the interconnection between the self and food; food fundamentally influences the self and, at the same time, a person's actions also significantly influence—beyond individual food choices—the existing food and related systems.
>
> *(2014: 4)*

Art critic J.J. Charlesworth has written accusatorily about the egocentricity of new art and performance (such as Marina Abramovic's *512 Hours*, staged at London's Serpentine Gallery), where participating in "an experience, being in the now, is the new aesthetic," but it is ultimately empty narcissism (2014: n.p.). The telematic dinner parties strove to be participatory, transformative, and interactive, building long-term relationships and associations through food-centred art practice. As Tim Cresswell writes in discussing the "phenomenology of bodily movement in space" in David Seamon's (1980) research, "The mobilities of bodies combine in space and time to produce an existential insidedness—a feeling of belonging within the rhythm of a life-in-place" (Cresswell, 2003: 277). In this case *two* places digitally enfolded into one—a life-in-place in two places.

1984—Sophie Hope

"I have been tortured by the experience of simultaneous experiences that we can't share," says Sophie Hope (Waterman and Catlow, 2015a). She refers to Jim Jarmusch's 1991 film *Night on Earth* as an example; the film's action takes place in five different cities in five different taxi cabs at exactly the same time, though, of course, the drivers and passengers are unaware of the other stories being played out simultaneously. We discuss how sometimes it is possible to have a too-real sense of violence occurring all at once in the world, and about how we all followed the events of 2013 during the Occupy! movement in Istanbul's Gezi Park as they happened on Twitter, fascinated that the reports and scraps of video seemed somehow more real and immediate than coverage on the evening news.

Hope chose the year 1984 as the focus of her interest and activity, a time when, in Britain, a powerful socialist municipal spirit still existed and community art

---

5 From a blog post written by Ruth Catlow to Pollie Barden, reflecting on the experience of the pilot Telematic Dinner Party held between Furtherfield, London and Telenoika, Barcelona (2011) as part of Furtherfield's Media Art Ecologies programme.

projects and activism intertwined, fertilized by public funding. Artists, activists, and politicians were all aligned, and political structures of the time enabled, for example, the GLC (the then Greater London Council, staunchly leftist, under the leadership of Ken Livingstone) Community Art Programmes, which ran from 1981 until 1986. This, though, at the time of neoliberalism's ascendancy, was in stark chiaroscuro against an inky Thatcherite background. Hope staged a dinner in London with British activists who had been highly active in 1984 and whose work continues today. She recorded the conversation during the meal and uploaded it to the web (Hope, n.d.).

She has since gone on to organize four further meals in Singapore, Melbourne, Australia, Johannesburg, South Africa, and recently in Montevideo, Uruguay, all with activists with powerful memories of politics in 1984.

Together, these meals and the conversations during them paint a portrait of a particular time—the sensations, the violence, the exhilaration. By asking participants to recall their experiences together around the table, the story and the memories are enriched. The conviviality aids a process of establishing greater veracity in memory, as participants jog memories and reconstruct events. Participants are also 'kept honest' by their interaction. The commensality provides a series of failsafe mechanisms that stop participants from rhapsodizing, romanticizing, or grandstanding in the process of recalling events.

In November of 2014, at the launch of Hope's 1984 website at Birkbeck, University of London, a collage of the recorded conversations was played to an audience seated around a table. Where the 1984 dinners up till that date had involved quite simple meals—in Singapore, chicken, rice, fruit, and chocolate cake (ibid.: n.p.; Figure 11.2), catered in rather than prepared by the participants, a process which might have diffused the theatricality and formality of the meal setting—the participants were simply served, in disposable containers, wine, crisps, and Twiglets (the peculiar yeast-extract-flavoured snack sticks). In this case, rather than drawing the participants closer to one another, the fact that the foodstuffs presented did not constitute a meal served to heighten the *exteriority* of the experience—that the audience was *outside* the dialogue from the meals being broadcast and was passively rather than actively engaging with the performance. The transformative interactions of the 1984 dinners had been transformed into an experience.

Feral Trade Café—Kate Rich

Also part of Furtherfield's Rich Networking series, the Feral Trade Café (Furtherfield, 2009; see also Rich, n.d.) took as its materials, distance, databases, and distribution. Kate Rich's artist-crafted database enabled international peer-to-peer distribution of food and drink products (often luxury products such as olive oil, mezcal, chocolate, and coffee) across social networks that took pleasure in subverting the capitalistic use of provenance in the construction of brand narratives. The story of production and distribution of food as told from the ground goes on to reveal also the politics of the places that it moves through. The Feral Trade Café was the

FIGURE 11.2 Johannesburg 1984 dinner, 20 March 2014 at The Bag Factory, Johannesburg, South Africa. Guests were Firdoze Bulbulia, Anton Harber, Faith Isiakpere, David Koloane, Santu Mofokeng, Pat Motlau, Aura G. Msimang, Molefe Pheto, Malcolm Purkey, Brett Pyper, Joachim Schonfeldt, and Monique Vajifdar. Co-hosts were Gabi Ngcobo, Rangoato Hlasane, and The Bag Factory (James French and Sara Hallatt). Credit: Sophie Hope.

first instance of an actual café (Figure 11.3). Placemats pulled from the database the ingredients (and stories that attached to them) that constituted the meals that people were served. As they ate, they could read about the producers, and the land through which the couriers travelled. The people who came to the café were both art audiences and lorry drivers who happened to be delivering raw materials and taking away manufactured goods from the light industrial park in which the gallery (then called HTTP Gallery) was then situated. The other people were regular café attendees, the artists and musicians newly moved into the light industrial space (indicating the early stages of this area's gentrification).

It is an artwork that is parasitical on art networks—goods are mainly carried in the spare space of international art networks. It brings the story of provenance AND of distribution and food systems together in a commensal space that encourages a conversation about all of these.

The Feral Trade network bears certain similarities to the burgeoning Genuino Clandestino movement based in Italy. Frustrated with corruption in the organic certification system in Italy, and the resultant meaninglessness of the certification,

FIGURE 11.3 Feral Trade Café by Kate Rich at HTTP Gallery, 13 June–2 August 2009. Credit: Furtherfield.

Genuino Clandestino has built a network of farmers and producers who ensure trustworthiness by certifying each other's products, thus operating entirely outside of European Union or Italian frameworks.[6] Each also contains an insistence upon communal luxury and each showcases that markets outside of capitalist market models are possible and viable.

Conclusion

As human beings, we have invented both the street and the table, each staging-grounds for conviviality and cosmopolitanism. In turn, the great isolating and alien-ating factors in life are inventions: capitalism is an invention, as is the hamburger eaten behind the wheel of a car, the gated community, the privatized digital social network, or the smartphone. Technologies and designed environments are assumed to have great agency, but it is the practices of everyday life that more urgently need our attention—those places where technicity and culture intersect. Practices of everyday life, indeed, are being constantly reinvented by a churning media engine

6 Genuino Clandestino's website is genuinoclandestino.it/ and there is an Italian language film at https://vimeo.com/34322825. Scholar of the commons Massimo de Angelis is currently studying Genuino Clandestino. Also worthwhile and related, as it shows similar problems of the DOC certification system in Italy that parallel the issues found in organic certification, is Jonathon Nossiter's film about rebel winemakers in Italy, entitled *Natural Resistance* (2014).

driving consumerism, commodity fetishism, and throwaway culture, to add gloss to an already well-burnished set of associations. If lifestyle has replaced or obscured class as the structure around which we arrange our identities, then there is a clear link between the creativity and invention that goes into selling us these lifestyles and the environments and technologies that contain and facilitate them. Thus, it is precisely at this locus that artists must situate themselves in order to effect change and to create the greatest possible use value in the commons. We must invent and sell the lifestyles that we require to save ourselves from isolation and helpless consumerism. We must find ways of performing the cosmopolitan lives that we desire, and by rehearsing them, bring them into the commons of our mutual practice.

Furtherfield's DIWO ethos directly supports this ambition by looking always to support the subversive possibilities opened up for inventive, informal, non-suited, playful, networked communication. It sets out to embrace and explore the whole array of relational wormholes thrown up by the experience of straddling physical and virtual space. Because dinners are such key sites for power-broking and decision-making, it would be good to see this developed so that we could imagine non-artists and researchers enticed to play and communicate in this way—changing what gets thought about, decided, and acted upon. The interplay of affect, agency, sociality, and conviviality at the dining table provides an ideal model for human fulfilment where profit disappears as a constituent of value, and thus it is perhaps the most critical locus of investigations that strive to be satisfyingly situated and embodied, such that we may find the best possibilities for the future of human habitation and association here, and build models of sustainability that are meaningful outside of the commodifying tendencies of market capital.

This essay was published in the innovative journal *p-e-r-f-o-r-m-a-n-c-e.org* in 2016.

12

ON ASTRONAUTS, LSD, AND LANDSCAPE ARCHITECTURE

Virgin space

On 11 July 2021, celebrity fossil capitalist[1] and founder of the Virgin Group Richard Branson flew in a rocket passenger plane to "an altitude of 86 km (53.5 mi)— just slightly below the Kármán Line (the official boundary of space)" (Williams, 2021: n.p.; see also Betancourt, 2021). He was the first of three billionaires (Elon Musk and Jeff Bezos complete this unholy trinity) to mount an ascent to the outer reaches of Earth's atmosphere, and the first to assault the public with triumphalist hyperbole and chest-thumping of the first order. "The entire flight was captured by flight cameras mounted on the mothership, the spacecraft, and the chase plane. Branson and crew also live-tweeted the event and shared photos of their ascent and the four minutes of weightlessness they experienced" (ibid.: n.p.). Journalists and social media influencers couldn't resist mention of "virgin territory" and "virgin space" with all its connotations of *terra nullius*, colonialism, and masculinist deflowerings. All of this so very imperial too: "Adventures, then home for tea," as Kathleen Jamie quips of a "lone enraptured male" (2008: n.p.).

Home for tea, during the "post flight press event" an enraptured Branson recruited another English trope, that of the jolly, benevolent (yet suspiciously nefarious) industrialist of a Roald Dahl character: "You'll be entered into the Omaze [Omaze, n.d.] sweepstakes for the chance to win not one, but two seats aboard one of the first commercial Virgin Galactic spaceflights. And with my Willy Wonka hat on, a guided tour of Spaceport America, guided by yours truly, and I promise lots of chocolate in the factory..." (Williams, 2021: n.p.). As well as chocolate, Branson

---

1 For a stunning analysis of the emergence of fossil capitalism in the steam age and the promotion of the consumption of fossil fuels as a project of capital and the Industrial Revolution, see Andreas Malm's (2016) *Fossil Capital: The Rise of Steam Power and the Roots of Global Warming.*

DOI: 10.4324/9781003164593-12

promised access to a life-changing experience—a holy grail of the tourist gaze—in this case no less than "By allowing regular citizens the chance to go to space, they hope that more people will experience the Overview Effect and be inspired to help find solutions to problems here on Earth" (ibid.: n.p.).

Writing breathlessly of the Overview Effect in the context of these new private space shots, astronomer Chris Churchill tells us what can happen to a person who views their home planet from space (Figure 12.1):

> something fundamental changes in you, forever, once you have seen the planet in its natural habitat of space. It's called the 'overview effect,' a term coined by Frank White in 1987. This a permanent cognitive shift in awareness experienced by astronauts. You don't see national boundaries from orbit. You don't see 'others' or races; you see humanity as a whole. You see 'us.' You see a living breathing and fragile orb filled with a variety of totally interdependent living creatures—and you see each as unique, fragile and precious. You can't un-know it. You can't un-feel it.
>
> *(Churchill, 2020: n.p.)*

Branson is offering this as part of his space tourism package: "live out your astronaut dreams" and "[e]xperience weightlessness and awe-inspiring views from space" (Omaze, n.d.). He enthuses of his flight, "We are at the vanguard of a new space age. As Virgin's founder, I was honored to test *the incredible customer experience* as part of

FIGURE 12.1 Self-portrait of astronaut Tracy Caldwell Dyson Earth-gazing in the Cupola module of the International Space Station. Credit: Tracy Caldwell Dyson/NASA.

this remarkable crew of mission specialists and now astronauts" (Richard Branson quoted in Williams, 2021: n.p., emphasis added).

It is possible to discern from these statements, and that Branson hadn't had enough of a life-changing moment to go off script, that he probably *didn't* experience the Overview Effect in those brief moments of weightlessness near the Kármán Line. It's likely, rather, that he experienced something more like a profound sense of ownership, finding his earthly power affirmed looking down with a god's-eye view over garden Earth, spaceship Earth, blue marble Earth. It's also likely that Bezos and Musk will find the same on their respective ascents—a feeling akin to what Louis XIV must have felt gazing from his windows at the gardens of Versailles—a symbolically limitless geometry of dominion illustrating the reach of the Sun King. Or perhaps an enlarged version of the sense of myth and moment Michel de Certeau wrote of, contemplating the view from New York's World Trade Center:

> An Icarus flying above these waters, he can ignore the devices of Daedalus in mobile and endless labyrinths far below. His elevation transfigures him into a voyeur. It puts him at a distance. It transforms the bewitching world by which one was 'possessed' into a text that lies before one's eyes. It allows one to read it, to be a solar Eye, looking down like a god. The exaltation of a scopic and gnostic drive: the fiction of knowledge is related to this lust to be a viewpoint and nothing more.
>
> *(de Certeau, 1984: 92)*

Haraway puts this differently, but it is complementary: she calls it the "god trick," "seeing everywhere from nowhere." This eye, this solar Eye, "fucks the world to make techno-monsters" (1988: 581). This is not probably, to be sure, something you 'can't un-know' and 'can't un-feel,' but very different indeed from the Overview Effect and its bestowal of humility, awe, fragility, and interconnectedness upon the viewer. That is something no one could ever describe as an 'incredible customer experience.' Further, the Overview Effect often excites in those who experience it a profound sense of the need to care for and become stewards of our unique planet. Elon Musk seems to be in quite an opposing position, happy to burn the planet up and "die," he hopes, "on Mars" (Kern, 2021: n.p.). Musk's Sun King posturing is, of course, evident in his new title, "Technoking of Tesla"[2] (*BBC News*, 2021) and in his tacit bid for space imperialism, evident in his rejection of the Outer Space Treaty and the idea of space as a commons (UNOOSA, n.d.; see also Storr, 2020; van Eijk, 2020: n.p.). Presumably Earth law will no longer hold purchase when Earth is a smoking ruin.[3] Clearly this is anti-utopian futurism and not a utopian dream

---

2 My first thought upon hearing this was "Technoking? What is that? How does one 'technoke'?"
3 The wording here in SpaceX's Terms of Service "for the beta test of its Starlink broadband megaconstellation" (van Eijk, 2020: n.p.): "Services provided to, on, or in orbit around the planet Earth or the Moon… will be governed by and construed in accordance with the laws of the State of California in the United States. For Services provided on Mars, or in transit to Mars via Starship

of a future of human and planetary flourishing. Murray Bookchin puts this well in his *The Ecology of Freedom* (and with a nod to Élisée Reclus's sense of humanity as nature becoming conscious of itself):

> Futurism, as exemplified by the works of Herman Kahn,[4] merely extrapolates the hideous present into an even more hideous future and thereby effaces the creative, imaginative dimensions of futurity. By contrast, the utopian tradition seeks to permeate necessity with freedom, work with play, even toil with artfulness and festiveness. My contrast between utopianism and futurism forms the basis for a creative, liberatory reconstruction of an ecological society, for a sense of human mission and meaning as nature rendered self-conscious.
>
> *(Bookchin, 2005: 75)*

Science fiction writer Sim Kern gives voice to some welcome *schadenfreude* and points out aptly that this futurism, these plutocrat space shots are doomed to failure: "[f]or all their wealth, billionaires do not have the power to make space a more comfortable place to be than Earth … Space tourism will inevitably suck. Our billionaires won't find anything up there but a whole lot of time to sit with the gaping void in their hearts, which space certainly won't fill, while forcibly holding their asscheeks to a suctioning toilet seat" (2021: n.p.).

From overview to acid

The god's-eye/solar-eye view is very different from what many astronauts describe of their experience of 'Earth-gazing' from outer space. Presumably neither of these positions can be 'un-known' or 'un-felt'—they both represent profound shifts in consciousness and cognition. The first is characterized by a myopic form of power-madness that colonizes the mind of the person who colonizes the world (or space), while the second is very different indeed. In the canonical work of Frank White, cited by Churchill above, he says of the Overview Effect nothing less than it "may point to humankind's purpose as a species" (1998 [1987]: 5). The view of the Earth from space, and the ability to watch its processes, forces, phenomena, and activities from afar—thunderstorms passing over; auroras around the poles, city lights coming on and the clear line of darkness across the planet as night falls—these combine in body, mind, and the sensorium (ibid.: 20–22). Kenneth Cox helpfully lists the characteristics of the Overview Effect: it is "1) an abiding concern and passion

or other colonization spacecraft, the parties recognize Mars as a free planet and that no Earth-based government has authority or sovereignty over Martian activities. Accordingly, Disputes will be settled through self-governing principles, established in good faith, at the time of Martian settlement" (SpaceX quoted in van Eijk, 2020: n.p.).

4 Herman Kahn was a futurist and military strategist who was known for articulating dark nuclear futures, and who, along with Wernher Von Braun, John von Neumann, and Edward Teiler, was one of the inspirations for Stanley Kubrick and Terry Southern's *Dr Strangelove* (1964).

for the well-being of the Earth [note here already a radical divergence from the position, say, of Elon Musk], 2) changed perceptions of space and time coupled with the experiential impact of silence and weightlessness, 3) an understanding that everything is interconnected and interrelated, 4) a higher level viewpoint, involving a new awareness and consciousness, and 5) the recognised need for a stewardship perspective and a global participatory management of the planet" (1998 [1987]: xvii–xviii).

What is useful and important is that, in the same way that the views of Earth from space captured by the Apollo missions—"The Blue Marble" and "Earthrise" (Figure 12.2)—were able to catalyse a resurgence of environmental and ecological consciousness as a popular movement worldwide, so too could the description and sharing of these experiences help to change the very structure of human consciousness towards a greater sense of interconnectedness and stewardship.

Around the same time that human consciousness was expanded through images and descriptions of outer space, so was *inner* space also being transformed by another great cultural phenomenon, the hallucinogenic drug lysergic acid diethylamide—LSD, or simply 'acid.' This was, of course, popularized through association with various rock music heroes, films, art, and the writing and cultural influence of flamboyant figures such as Timothy Leary and Ken Kesey.

FIGURE 12.2 "Earthrise" taken by Apollo 8 crewmember Bill Anders on 24 December 1968 while in orbit around the moon. The continent visible is Africa. Credit: Bill Anders/NASA.

FIGURE 12.3 A tenstrip of "Alex Grey" Albert Hofmann LSD blotters, dosed at 100–120 μg each. Credit: Lortordemur.

LSD

The standard experience—if something so purposely non-standard can be said to have an average—of an LSD trip begins with a square of blotter paper, impregnated with the drug and torn from a perforated sheet (Figure 12.3). This little square is placed on the tongue and ingested. Within 20–30 minutes the pupils of the eyes are widely dilated and the 'trip' begins.[5] A wide variety of different experiences may then follow, and everyone seems to have a different experience in some way. Some experience visual geometric patterns and/or 'tracers,' heightened sensation in any and all the senses including synaesthesia, joy and euphoria, and occasionally, on a 'bad trip,' negative sensations as well as fear or paranoia. It is also quite standard for those who have taken the drug to speak of the experience as 'consciousness-changing,' 'consciousness-expanding,' or 'mind-expanding.'

LSD was first made in 1938 by the chemist Albert Hofmann, who derived it from the grain fungus ergot. Ingestion of ergot historically was a cause of ergotism,

---

5 I have heard of faster methods to begin the trip—one notable method being dropping liquid LSD directly into the eyes, though I have never seen this myself or known anyone who professes to have ingested the drug in this way.

also known as 'St. Anthony's fire,' also characterized by hallucinations alongside other negative effects. Hofmann was a great protagonist for the drug, believing in its potential for use as a medicine, but also for its use in animal experiments and biological research, and, perhaps most importantly here, for its use to travel "in the universe of the soul," "which extends from the most sublime spiritual, religious, and mystical experiences, down to gross psychosomatic disturbances" (Hofmann, 1997 [1979]: n.p.). From the utopian to the dystopian, one might say. LSD's effects are not only personal but *interpersonal*, intercorporeal, and embodied and situated in ways that enable the user to feel a profound sense of connectedness and of the interconnectedness, interdependence, and unity of all things. It places the user as participant, as part of a creative collective rather than in a position of mastery, something Donna Haraway calls "partial vision" (1988: passim). Like the Overview Effect, the experience of LSD can be both oceanic and enlightening, sparking fresh love and concern for the world and its ecologies and social ecologies. "It gave me an inner joy, an open mindedness, a gratefulness, open eyes and an internal sensitivity for the miracles of creation," said Hofmann in an address given late in his life. "I think," he added "that in human evolution it has never been as necessary to have this substance LSD. It is just a tool to turn us into what we are supposed to be" (Albert Hofmann, quoted in Harrison, 2006: n.p.). Like the Overview Effect, it isn't necessary to have the drug directly, but one can gain the enlarged consciousness and evolutionary advance from mere exposure to accounts and representations, from the position of human understanding and empathy. As the philosopher of cognition Mark Johnson notes, "understanding is a form of simulation," and when one imagines or shares a scene or scenario, it "activates areas of the brain that would be activated if we actually perceived that scene" (2007: 161–162). Stories and narratives, scenarios and simulations, have the power to shape consciousness—both individual and collective—and reality (see Chapter 14). And scenario-making from the scale of the garden to the scale of the planet is part of the process of design in landscape architecture.

Landscape architecture

An explosion of careful thinking in landscape studies and the emergence of landscape urbanism (and its eventual absorption into landscape architecture) around the turn of the millennium reinvigorated discourses around sustainability, ecology, and democracy that had enjoyed time in the sun in the 1960s and 1970s, but also expanded the scale of ambition of landscape architecture once more—to the scale of the territory and the ecosystem as well as the city. Recent work by Elise Misao Hunchuck, Marco Ferrari, and Jingru (Cyan) Chen, "Prologue to the Sky River" (2021) is just one example of the expanded consciousness of landscape architecture, linking, as it does, ground to sky in the technological desire to control rain in China in an essay which moves from the scale of the Yellow River valley to planetary weather patterns—and which echoes the technocratic ambitions, god trick, and solar Eye of the present billionaire space race. Their collaborative approach to their research, too, reflects the privilege of partial vision. These writers, researchers, know that what is known and speculated is better in shared mental and creative space.

There are certainly alternatives to the god trick. Lorraine Code (2006) calls this "ecological thinking," Gregory Bateson (2000) "an ecology of mind," Murray Bookchin (2005) speaks of "social ecologies," and indeed all of these terms are immensely useful. Code's articulation I find particularly compelling, that thinking in ecological ways "is a revisioned mode of engagement with knowledge, subjectivity, politics, ethics, science, citizenship, and agency that pervades and reconfigures theory and practice" (2006: 5). It is also "about imagining, crafting, articulating, endeavouring to enact principles of ideal cohabitation" (ibid.: 24).

Approaching landscape with humility and generosity, as a way of nurturing and supporting rather than building, like Versailles, merely a geometric representation of Earthly power, is more and more what landscape architecture is becoming. This humility and generosity opens out into a willingness, even a need, to work collectively and collaboratively and to share knowledge and build new ontologies and epistemologies together. Not only must we create the landscapes of future inhabitation, but also the minds and bodies that will inhabit and build the future too (see Waterman, 2019). Landscape architecture—in fact all design—owns prodigious tools for visioning, communicating, and scenario-making and it is incumbent upon all designers not merely to use their talents for quotidian projects but also to project hopeful visions of a better future that can be shared by many—and which aren't just evidence of the god trick, but call for real embodied and situated shared experience. Without the need for hallucinogens or space exploration the study of landscape and the sharing of landscape experiences and relationships can be a tool for thinking, but also an ethical and relational frame for comprehension of ecologies, social ecologies, and ecologies of mind for knowing the interconnectedness, interdependence, and unity of all things and even, dare I add, 'inner joy, open-mindedness, gratefulness' and a commitment to planetary stewardship.

13

A WORD... 'VAST'

I'm a child in the back seat of my parents' car, with my bare legs sticking to the vinyl and the blast from the window parting my hair in the wrong direction; the first hint of the tang of salt in the air, and I'm sure I hear the cry of a seagull.

The ocean smell deepens and up, over a rise, the first glint of the water! Over the next hill and the full view opens out. The whole ocean glittering up to the sharp edge of the horizon: limitless, vast.

As the middle of three boys in a Navy family, this experience was a common one in my youth, but the quickening, the thrill of approaching the ocean is never diminished. The other emotion experienced at the coast, if it may so be called, is the sense of vastness. The phenomenologist Gaston Bachelard discussed this idea in a chapter of *The Poetics of Space* (1964 [1958]) called "Intimate Immensity." In it, he expresses the sense of vastness as something that is both internal and external, a precarious but exhilarating state of being in which the individual feels simultaneously humble and empowered. It is a state that dangles the ego out into a space where there is no boundary between immense knowledge and madness.

Oceans bring us hard up against not just the concept of immensity, but the allied one of eternity. Because it is so painful to contemplate the end of the ceaseless waves, perhaps when the sun expands into a red giant, we are forced to imagine eternity. A seascape is a landscape without end in both space and time.

Along with all the pleasant trips to the seaside, there were just as many reluctant trips to the waterfront to see my father off at the docks. It was a huge sense of loss to witness my father sailing off into vastness and eternity, but to later witness his return was proof that one man could do so and return unscathed, heroic, and enriched.

This sense of vastness, and the accompanying gratefulness and humility, are essential to understanding and working with landscape. Otherwise there is a risk on the one hand of playing god, and on the other of being overwhelmed by scale. Playing god manifests itself in the 'master of the universe' view of the city. This is

DOI: 10.4324/9781003164593-13

a strong sense of conquest and dominion engendered by the bird's-eye or carto-graphic view; the city as seen from the sky, perhaps a boardroom in a skyscraper. This is another order of vastness, one of power and mastery and, of course, hubris. It's a vastness that's bottled up, smug, and it can be a caged animal with real poten-tial for harm. It's also a myth—a 'dry' myth—about how our bodies engaged in the world. Astrida Neimanis speaks of "watery embodiment" and that the vastness of the world literally flows in and out of our bodies. This "thus presents a challenge to three related humanist understandings of corporeality: discrete individualism, anthropocentrism, and phallogocentrism" (2017: 3).

We need enough strength of will and confidence to act upon the landscape but also *with the landscape* and a sense of intimate immensity—both humility and empowerment as well as watery, intimate, open embodiment—to gratefully and eagerly approach the landscape like we approach the sea.

This column was published in *Landscape*, Summer 2011.

14

MAKING MEANING

Utopian method for minds, bodies, and media in architectural design

Once upon a time

'Once' names the specific, the particular. 'Upon' signifies emplacing, situating, taking place. 'A time' sets a temporal context. Before the phrase 'once upon a time' is written or spoken there is a suspension: a 'nowhen,' a nowhere, a nothing. The phrase prepares us to be temporally and spatially situated. It enacts a ritual that creates a space in the imagination for a story to unfold. What follows 'once upon a time' is an important set of variables that begin to happen, to take place in that cleared, prepared site in the mind's eye. Did I say 'mind's eye'? I meant to say the *mind's body*: the imagination is not merely visual, but multi-sensory and emotional. Stories are not just visual, they're visceral. I could just as easily have said the *body's mind*. Like lovers, they belong to each other. Belonging: being and longing.

> Once upon a time there was a princess who lived in a castle. The princess had every-thing she could ever want: jewels, fine clothing, the most delicious food in the kingdom. Still, though, she was sad.

The castle is a cold and sorrowful place, isn't it? Those jewels are joyless rocks, and the supposedly delicious food tastes like cardboard and smells of nothing. The sadness that enters in the last sentence sets the tone, the mood, the atmosphere. You can probably feel the rough surface of the castle's stone and the stout planks of the princess's dinner table. Yes, that's you I'm talking to. Hello out there. Welcome to my mind, and welcome to the place I've cleared and prepared for both of us in our imaginations. It's nice to share this scene with you. It's nice to have made a little space for meaning: what does anything mean without emotion and sensation?

> Once upon a time we built the places of our heart's desires

DOI: 10.4324/9781003164593-14

I want to imagine with you a scenario in which desire and pleasure are at the core of the design process. The processes of design have much in common with the processes of imaginative play. They both require the envisioning and rehearsal of scenarios, and they are both often utopian. Utopias are ways of analysing and evaluating situations through narratives that allow us to test possible worlds. They can be used as methods to imagine better worlds (not necessarily perfect ones). Or they can be used to picture what might happen if things go wrong: meet dystopia, utopia's evil twin. Sometimes our heart's desires don't lead to healthy choices, and working through utopian scenarios is a way to figure out which of our desires may feasibly be fulfilled (which moves them from the realm of the utopian to the attainable)—and to what extent. The limits of fulfilment under capitalism and its attendant structural inequalities can, in many ways, only be tested first as utopian scenarios. Both design and imaginative play also allow us to test potentially dangerous scenarios without endangering actual subjects in real life experiments.

The experiment I want to undertake here, though, is a daring but not a dangerous one, and it is potentially enriching. I want to dare to imagine a world where people live lives characterized by ease, pleasure, and sensuality and in which everyone has enough to satisfy both their basic needs and a generous selection of superfluous desires. This world is one that must be imagined in detail. This prefigurative work is an act of make-believe. Ruth Levitas refers to the "imaginary reconstitution of society" (2013: xi), but the act of imagining encompasses the imaginary reconstitution, not only of society as such, but of the spaces in which society exists. Make-believe is a practice that has agency. Our dreamworlds and our lifeworlds are constantly interacting to shape place and dwelling. Using utopian imagination as method, then, for enacting positive change in the built and lived landscape is the only way to ensure that our future world provides adequate pleasure to support a good life for all.

This article will examine the roles designers play in humankind's futurity—as makers, envisioners, and tastemakers—in light of contingent and relational models rather than the simplifying, teleological, and diagrammatic models of utopian method. Further, the creation of more fulfilling and sustainable places to live requires the reshaping of popular beliefs to change patterns of everyday life and consumption. The article specifically addresses the persuasive, propagandistic nature of representation for design and asks that designers concentrate on using their powers for good.

Naturally, none of this can happen without education, and education, like utopianism, is a practice of futurity. It seeks to prepare the minds and bodies that will construct and inhabit the future. The educational experience that most people receive, in the architectures or any other discipline, however, is one that is designed to prepare them for a *particular* future.[1] This involves preparing students

---

1 I refer to architectures in the plural because it assumes the equality of fields which are complementary, but not subservient to (or subsets of) architecture, including planning, landscape architecture, urban design, interior architecture, theatrical set design, and so on. 'Architectures' is a term which, like

for preconceived roles, often employing what Paulo Freire (2007 [1968]) called 'banking education,' in which students are envisioned as containers into which knowledge is deposited. The nation-state, for example, has an interest in creating patriotic citizens, while the neoliberal project seeks to create 'flexible' subjects who are 'lifelong learners.' A fully democratic model of education might resemble neither of these, seeking, rather, to put into practice *equality* and striving towards *emancipation* (see Simons and Masschelein, 2011; Ross, 1991): both emancipation (here the freedom that comes with ability and empowerment) and equality are mutually assured and maintained through everyday practices. The 'learning society,' while expressing 'principles of a universal humanity and a promise of progress that seem to transcend the nation' (Maarten and Masschelein, 2007: 9), is undermined by its risk-aversion and also by the absence of emancipation from studenthood, itself at formal education's end. As Gert Biesta warns:

> The desire to make education strong, secure, predictable, and risk-free is an attempt to forget that at the end of the day education should aim at making itself dispensable—no teacher wants their students to remain eternal students—which means that education *necessarily* needs to have an orientation toward the freedom and independence of those being educated.
>
> *(Biesta, 2014: 2, emphasis in original)*

While learning may continue through life, education as formal learning is a transitional period and thus should come to an end, otherwise the student becomes stuck in this threshold, forever a student; never released into full competency and agency. Education should build the capacity to apply the imaginal to the real and thus to transform it, and in doing so make other, better futures possible. In this, education might resemble what David Graeber, reflecting a common position in anarchist theory, refers to as "prefigurative politics," "the idea that the organizational form that an activist group takes should embody the kind of society we wish to create" (Graeber, 2013: 23). Graeber applies this to activism, particularly to the Occupy! movement. The "democracy project," to which Graeber refers in the title of his book, should be brought into education, in particular to encourage dissent. Democracy, conceived as a project, allies itself naturally to emancipation and equality as practices. There is no room for practices of dissent in an education that is "strong, secure, predictable, and risk-free," nor in the society which it might produce. A project of democracy exists as a 'social ecology' (another term from anarchist theory; see Bookchin, 2005) of interpenetrating, mutually informing ideas that exist in the world and in human associations. That social ecology must be nested into the ecology of the physical, inhabited world.

In both education and professional practice, design processes are currently being re-envisioned in ways that are analogous to natural processes and ecologies (see

---

'knowledges,' resists totalizing and hierarchical tendencies and values both diversity in the present and the possibility of the emergence of other allied yet distinctive fields in the future.

Corner, 1999; Meyer, 2000; Reed and Lister, 2014). This makes sense if we are to design, make, and build in responsively cohesive ways. Envisioning design as a conversation with sites, materials, processes, habitats and habits, and so on engenders the according of agency to places and all they are made of. The increasing interpenetration of social, cultural, and physical worlds with new media ecologies (see Chapter 10) further underscores the importance of envisioning these processes differently.

Design involves drawing, making, modelling, and simulating, which is yet another practice which can be envisioned as having an ecological structure. As an imaginative activity, simulation is aided by design iterations involving the standard modes of representation for design. Simulation can be immensely rich if we are simulating the right things. Simulation takes place in the brain (and the mind) during the design process, and the designer rehearses movements and activities in space during simulations, using the same neural pathways that they would if they were physically negotiating and interacting with an actual site. In this way, we use the *mind's body* rather than the mind's eye. These simulations necessarily mimic not just spaces, forms, objects, and buildings, but situations, sensations, emotions, and interactions. "Modes of attending to scenes and events spawn socialities, identities, dream worlds, bodily states and public feelings of all kinds," writes Kathleen Stewart (2007: 10). The possible futures to which we might be directed, and the possible worlds we might prefigure, are embedded in this rich, relational past and present.

Making a living or making a killing

I mentioned above that the possible worlds and narratives we imagine can positively or negatively shape our beliefs. We have all come to increasingly inhabit a dystopian world—a real world—that is shaped by an imaginary that is at once utopian and anti-utopian. This imaginary speaks a language of freedom and flexibility, but in practice it encloses and constrains while sowing precarity—and precarity puts people on the defensive, whereas flexibility implies enough security to explore options. This dys-topia is the product of magical thinking. It is shaped by an imaginary that exhibits the hallmarks of magical religiosity: "the naive, need-based, unquestioning hope in the face of experience, reason and refutation is a feature [...] not of Utopia but of religion" (Howells, 2015: 24). Howells assigns these attributes to all religion, but his formulation needs elaboration, as it could be seen to assign to *all* registers of religiosity the character of fundamentalism. Let us say, then, that this imaginary bears the hallmarks of *fundamentalist* religiosity, a construct reinforced by the prevalent use of the term 'market fundamentalism' to describe much capitalist ideology. In this imaginary, individuals are alone in the world, and their success, or lack thereof, is solely the product of their own efforts. There is no expectation that any individual who succeeds should have any obligation (or any wish) to share the fruits of their success. Individuals achieve their successes or failures in an economic system that is perceived to be guided by an underlying moral compass, the 'invisible hand' of the market, a concept crudely adapted from the writings of Adam Smith. Financial success is thus believed to be a mark of human goodness and worthiness—perhaps *the* mark. Lavish displays of wealth, even in the presence of pitiful displays of poverty, are therefore acceptable because they are the trappings of goodness and represent those 'goods' to which the impoverished should aspire and which their lack of striving has denied them. The 'invisible hand' will also see to it that the biological environment is safeguarded for the future so that the natural resources which support the lifestyles of the rich and famous remain abundant.[2] The individual who has succeeded in this system, some like to say, has 'made a killing.'

This construct, as I have noted above, is at once anti-utopian and utopian. Lucy Sargisson writes that "anti-utopianism is not just dystopianism or gloominess about the future. Rather, it is a phenomenon that resists the utopian impulse" (Sargisson, 2012: 22). It insists upon the appearance of bloody-minded pragmatism over foolish dreaming. This constrains the political left by painting it as obliviously utopian when it seeks to define what the future *ought* to be, just as it fuels the right's claims to the superiority of rationality over hope when it seeks to insist that injustice is a 'natural' condition. A stern mask of anti-utopianism is applied over the ghostly face of neoliberalism's magical utopianism, which, at its libertarian or 'anarchocapitalist' extremes, displays all the marks of fundamentalism. Fundamentalism's most wicked spectres—the Inquisition, possibly—are summoned as Sargisson continues:

> The utopianism that drives religious fundamentalism is perfectionist, closed, static and it has divine sanction. This combines with core elements of religious fundamentalism to create a drive towards purity and purge. In proselytizing religions this is even more dangerous because expansionism and territoriality are added to the mix.
>
> *(2012: 41)*

This perfectionist utopia allows free-market neoliberalism to make the claim, for example, that the market is not yet completely self-regulating because it is not yet completely free.

The cultural and political theorist Jeremy Gilbert has described this magical system as 'competitive individualism' (Gilbert, 2014) and Neal Curtis, also a cultural theorist, has used the term 'idiotism' (derived not from the use of the word as a slur or an archaic descriptor for mental illness, but rather from the Greek *idiotes* (ιδιοτες), which describes a person who is private, who lacks the ability to function publicly). I prefer the former, though I have sympathies with the latter. Competitive individualism is a key narrative of capitalism and the foundation stone for neoliberalism, the system in which governments everywhere are supposedly being minimized, but which instead have become more authoritarian, corporatized,

---

2 I'm less convinced now that the ruling class does in fact believe the 'invisible hand' will safeguard the environment than I am afraid of their abandonment of any future for Earth. The new imperialists like Jeff Bezos and Elon Musk have their eye on human life on other planets and the exhaustion of life here at home.

privatized, and marketized, and have remained large despite shedding many of their altruistic functions and obligations. This is in response to the progressive loss of power in the nation-state to the free-floating power in the 'space of flows' (as formulated by Manuel Castells, 1989) in what Zygmunt Bauman calls 'liquid modernity.'[3] Competitive individualism and neoliberalism have literally been 'making a killing' by fuelling war and terrorism, squandering planetary resources, and polluting and destroying wantonly in processes that are flatteringly described as 'wealth creation,' despite having actually created a preponderance of "illth" (as John Ruskin (1921 [1860]: 97–98) once termed wealth's opposite).

For Curtis, the *idios*, the realm of the private, is identified with the practice of the enclosures, which have been 'the primary means for capitalist accumulation over the centuries' (2013: 14). This enclosing tendency takes place across all realms of human endeavour anywhere a commons and a common good may be founded. This includes digital realms (for example, Microsoft's ongoing enclosures in the name of 'intellectual property'; see Stallman, 2005), cultural realms (such as the practices of corporate 'cool-hunting'; see Klein, 2001), and the landscape (from the early enclosures in England which pushed the peasantry, often violently, off the land and into the proletariat; see Williams, 2011 [1973]). In late capitalism, enclosures continue apace in all these realms, but are obscured by liquid modernity's incessant shape-shifting. This is the sort of world in which 'flexible' workers who are 'lifelong learners' can flourish. What is sorely needed is a positive counter-imaginary of prosperity and flourishing that is identified not with destruction but with careful management of resources and ecologies, with sharing, creating economies of care, and planning constructively for a future in which all will share. In contrast to 'making a killing,' this could and should be called 'making a living,' which would redefine success in terms of whole lives rather than whole paychecks.

Making sense

Those who argue for competitive individualism tend to frame their claims in terms of cold rationality, which allows the masquerade of eschewing morality. Decisions that are made on qualitative or emotional bases are suspect, and moral arguments are viewed as subservient to rational calculations. Ugly buildings, for example, are justified on the basis of their efficiency or their cost-effectiveness. Such decisions may be rational (arguably), but they are not sensible or reasonable. Calculation does not equal evaluation (or valuation, for that matter). What 'makes sense' to most people on a daily basis are those things that provide them with convenience, comfort, pleasure, and satisfaction, and these things are almost never merely selfish concerns. The value that people see in their lives is usually dependent upon and interactive with the lives and desires of others. Seeking the approval of others, as well as their

---

3 As Bauman explains: "What makes modernity 'liquid' is the compulsive and obsessive, unstoppably accelerating 'modernization,' through which—just like liquids—no forms of social life are able to retain their shapes for long" (Bauman, 2010: 330).

satisfaction, is fundamental to human behaviour. The decisions about what is reasonable are based in the evidence of the senses and the emotions. By this token an ugly building is unreasonable and makes no sense. It is also selfish, lacking any intrinsic worth of its own. Meaning and values are sensual and embodied—looking good and feeling good are moral and ethical qualities, and they are dependent upon their context.[4] As Tim Cresswell points out, "[t]he geographical setting of actions plays a central role in defining our judgment of whether actions are good or bad" (Cresswell, 1996: 9).

For the design process, the implications are fairly clear. If an architect is asked to design a building and the sole considerations are pecuniary—to maximize space and minimize cost, then it will be exceedingly difficult for the architect to make a sensible building. The logical extreme is demonstrated by the big box retail building, which is exactly as it sounds—a big box of a building which maximizes retail space but in all other regards is utterly ungenerous to and/or destructive of its environment. The emergence of the computer as the preferred design tool, often to the exclusion of all others, reduces the sensory engagement in the design process to a single sense, that of vision, which actively abets the process of reducing buildings (including landscapes) to mere (financial) instruments. As architect Santiago Pérez puts it: "The gap between computation and making today may be seen as a rapidly developing over-reliance on parametric instrumentality, at the expense of material invention and discovery" (Pérez, 2012: 382). It might be argued that at least buildings produced solely through digital means will 'look good,' but a building that looks good but doesn't *do* good or *feel* good in its material reality is a failed building. Again, it doesn't *make sense*.

An active engagement with multisensual materials and media is key to creating buildings that make sense. What is necessary is a particular engagement that architect Kyna Leski calls 'material reasoning.' Leski refers to Antoni Gaudí's methods of making and modelling, specifically his designs for Barcelona's celebrated cathedral, the Sagrada Familia. Its arches were tested with a model made of draped chains, which inverted the building's structure. His methods include exploration of "material behavior, material geometry, material tolerances, and material analogies" (Leski, 2015: 78). I would extend the analogy of material reasoning to include consideration of the sensual qualities of materials, something Pérez approaches more closely with his similar concept of material intelligence which "combines parametric workflows, traditional crafts and advanced rapid-prototyping and manufacturing" (Pérez, 2012: 383). But the concept still needs expanding, and the framing of design processes as 'workflows' smacks of the liquid modern vocabulary of

---

4 Morals are often taken to be universal and acontextual, and ethics contextual. In line with the theories of Mark Johnson and George Lakoff, I would argue that morals are situated and embodied, and thus just as contextual as ethics in their own way, if they are not, in fact, one and the same thing. I have written about this elsewhere: "I should probably also make the point that the Greek root of the word 'moral' signifies custom—which suggests that morals exist in the relational realm of everyday life, rather than in abstract 'higher' realms or in abstract financialized realms such as 'the market'—and that 'economy' comes from Greek again, the *oikos*, or household" (see Chapter 10).

neoliberalism. First, materials used in modelling in the studio may be employed to test textures, acoustics, and even the smell (using wood in models to bring to mind the odour of panelling or decking, for example). Secondly, the sensual qualities of materials used in the studio may be used to recall and make more vivid the sensual qualities of the site itself, and to make it more real in the imagination during design explorations. A riverside site might be brought to mind by pressing one's thumbs into clay—to recall the alluvial mud encountered—and, perhaps, to make drawings, choosing the paper and drawing medium to recall the texture of reeds and grasses. Recalling a site as three-dimensional, sensual, and real rather than merely a red-bordered abstraction drawn on a plan is an important step to resist treating it merely as a commodity or a surface that exists only to be filled. No, importantly, as Cresswell tells us: "We live in a world of meaning. We exist in, and are surrounded by, places—centres of meaning. Places are neither totally material nor completely mental; they are combinations of the material and mental and cannot be reduced to either" (Cresswell, 1996: 13). A further boon is that the designer also becomes more present, embodied, and thus becomes a more human presence in the design imaginary. Perhaps thinking in these terms will also help us to demand more, for example, from processes of remote sensing for geospatial analysis, which presently are composed primarily of statistical and visual data.

It is perhaps important to note, as well, that these processes are certainly available to capitalist modes of production, and that luxury products, for example, are often the result of careful, embodied design. What can redeem this process from the mere creation of sensually fulfilling commodities is a concomitant awareness of context, an embedded altruism, and an ecology of thinking: that is, it is not merely the tools and the product, but the whole mindset we bring to design. Contemporary placemaking processes rely heavily on the imaginal, "which emphasizes the centrality of images" (Bottici, 2014: 5), and the imaginary, which "primarily means what exists only in fancy and has no real existence and is opposed to *real* or *actual*" (Bottici, 2014: 7). This is reflected both in the luxurious imagery of the architectures—filled with birds, balloons, well-groomed people, and a flash of lens flare—and in the language, in which a different 'sense' is made. This is the 'sense of place,' or the 'sense of community,' which here refers not to immersive, reflexive, multisensual engagement, but to a general feeling that something might be the case. Places that are at best humdrum, common, and stultifying are presented as ecstatic and playful, but actual well-being created by fulfilling places is as far away from this as certainty is from a hunch. The relentless pursuit of empty glamour—where pursuit is merely the 'thrill of the chase'—has for decades trumped the pursuit of happiness. And here the importance of the *pursuit* as practice, pastime, and lived experience is key to overturning the chimerical, illusionary, neoliberal sense of happiness and well-being. Here the 'art of living' is one of *cultivated* goodness, and thus authentic in that it is 'authored.' The design of places that are capable of sustaining such authentic fulfilment requires more of the designer than merely pretty pictures and a 'sense' of goodness. It requires the deep and rigorous exercise of the suppositional imagination.

Moses supposes

Moses supposes his toeses are roses;
Moses supposes erroneously,
For nobody's toeses are roses or posies,
As Moses supposes his toeses to be.
                    —traditional nonsense
                    poem and tongue-twister

I have sometimes used a short studio exercise in which I ask students to come up with as many words for sounds and states of water as possible. The exercise, of course, begins with onomatopoeia such as 'splash' and 'gurgle.' Hilarity is allowed and encouraged with words like 'piss' and 'piddle.' States of water—waves, ripples, limpid pools, froth, are all explored. I then give them an assignment to design a garden room that provides/contains these experiences. They are encouraged to think about the sensual experience of water, for example, sliding their hand into cool, calm water on a hot summer day. I then ask the students, as part of their process, to play with water, and they are sent outside with cups and buckets. I also encourage them to draw a bath full of water at home, and play with the water as if they were children, taking delight in its qualities and listening to the amusing noises it makes. Ploop, slosh, tinkle, plash. The delight of this exercise is immediately apparent to the students, and they all comment on how different and refreshing it feels to begin with a proposition that involves senses other than vision, in this case primarily touch and sound.

Design in the architectures is a work of supposition: 'Suppose it's like this.' The designer is supposing a scenario. The designer, like Moses (who supposes his toeses are roses), knows(es) this is only a scenario, but introducing a realm of (in this case comic) possibility is at the very heart of the act. Writing about the important work of Shaun Nichols and Stephen Stich (2000) on the cognitive theory of pretence, Peter Carruthers sums up that they:

> argue that we need to recognize the existence of a distinct type of attitude, alongside belief and desire—namely, the attitude of *supposing*. When children pretend, they are *supposing* that something is the case (e.g. that the banana is a telephone, that they have an invisible friend called 'Wendy', etc.), and they act out their pretence within the scope of that supposition. Moreover, *supposing* can't be reduced to believing, or to desiring, or to any combination thereof (nor can it be reduced to any sort of planning or intending). It therefore needs to be assigned its own 'box' within a functional boxology of the human mind.
>
> *(Carruthers, 2006: 90; emphases in original)*

Carruthers points out that Nichols and Stich refer to the attitude of supposing in pretence and imaginative play, but the construct is directly applicable to design.

Further, the act of supposition is accompanied by simulation. The designer who works at the scale of architecture and landscape cannot prototype their design in the studio: they cannot work at full scale to test a design. The designer must therefore undertake to simulate the experience of the site or building as faithfully as possible, and then to work through imaginative scenarios to assess whether a design iteration is more successful or less successful.

Gaston Bachelard remarked that "it is impossible to think the vowel sound *ah* without a tautening of the vocal chords. In other words, we read *ah* and the voice is ready to sing" (Bachelard, 1964: 197). This prescient observation is now confirmed by studies in cognitive neuroscience of mirror-neuron phenomena. These, Mark Johnson says:

> suggest that *understanding is a form of simulation*. To see another person perform an action activates some of the same sensorimotor areas, *as if* the observer herself were performing the action. This deep and pre-reflective level of engagement with others reveals our most profound bodily understanding of other people, and it shows our intercorporeal social connectedness. Moreover, mirror-neuron research supports the hypothesis that imagination is a form of simulation. Research by Marc Jeannerod shows that imagining certain motor actions activates some of the same parts of the brain that are involved in actually performing that action. Imagining a visual scene also activates areas of the brain that would be activated if we actually perceived that scene.
>
> *(Johnson, 2007: 161–162; emphases in original)*

Simulation has incredible power in the human mind, and designers can think of themselves as 'flight simulators' who test flying the site's design in a simulated world before real lives are at stake in real situations. When I want to envision the power of simulation, I need only think back to certain childhood experiences. I can remember opening *National Geographic* to see photos of swarms of insects on the pages, and not wishing to touch the images directly. I can also remember feeling cold on behalf of scantily clad models depicted on billboards in winter. When asking students to run their own 'flight simulations for design,' I ask them to imagine the experience of users of the space, perhaps holding their site model up to eye level to envision that person in the space. A mother carrying a child, a person in an electric wheelchair, a tipsy woman in stiletto heels at a garden party carrying a glass of champagne and a small plate of hors d'oeuvres. What will happen when the tipsy woman laughs and steps backward into the soft lawn? In simulating, the designer's imagining mind is living the experience on behalf of the proposed site's speculative inhabitants. The imaginal provides a facsimile of real experience. Is there a correlation between the facsimile and the use of media as surrogates for experience? In representation, the medium is used to stand in for—literally, to represent—so it stands to reason that this is true.

Sherry Turkle, in her book *Alone Together*, which addresses the problem of people retreating into virtual worlds that are surrogates for real life ('RL,' she calls it, in contrast to VR, virtual reality[5]) shows that the phenomenon has a dystopian aspect as well. One of her students, she recounts, says he sees RL as "just one more window [and] it's not usually my best one" (Turkle, 2011: xii). The problems of creating an immersive virtual world that allows people to live parallel and isolated lives outside of and away from RL are not, I wager, problems to be encountered in methods for imaginal design that seek to employ a vast range of materials and methods to represent the world and the experience of living and dwelling. In design process, the imaginal always acts upon the lived, so it is vitally important that RL does not become conflated with VR for the designer. The answer here is found in clay, pencils, wood, cardboard. Scenario-making has real agency in the world, and the utopian imagination is deeply important in combination with it, tying together human experience and human striving in place. Supposition in design takes on a prefigurative function, undertaking the awesome task of translating prophecy into corporeal existence. The more the corporeal and the sensual have agency in the design process, therefore, the more effectively will we design places that feel good and the more special we can make the lives and experiences of those for whom designs are undertaken.

Making special

So far, I have not distinguished between the quotidian function of design and the art function. While they are interdependent and simultaneous, they still represent separate aspects. Landscape architecture and architecture are both fields of endeavour that must answer to practical and scientific concerns. Will what we build stand up? Will it stay standing? Will it shed water? Collect water? How can one make a big box better? The architectures must answer these concerns, and the last question points to the fact that, in the work of design for built environments, practical concerns and the demands of art are inseparable. Art is an essential component of designing and building places—in particular, if there is a wish to make places distinctive—and the goal of 'making special' is fundamental to both.

Ellen Dissanayake shows that 'making special' is definitive of art practice: "art," she says, "can be plausibly considered a biological need that we are predisposed to want to satisfy, whose fulfilment gives satisfaction and pleasure, and whose denial may be considered a vital deprivation" (Dissanayake, 1992: 38). She toys with a number of terms to describe the necessity of the superfluous, such as 'elaboration' or 'the extra-ordinary.' She ends up defending the 'special' and highlights the way elements of both play and ritual define the experience of the special. Here, when she speaks of imaginative play, try substituting the term 'design':

> In play, novelty and unpredictability are actively sought, whereas in real life we do not usually like uncertainty. Wondering whether an untried shortcut

---

5 This became more poignant again in the midst of the pandemic, and the abbreviation IRL (In Real Life) came into common usage as people were surprised and pleased when it was possible to see one another in the flesh instead of online.

will take us to the bank before it closes on the day before a holiday is different from choosing an unknown path just to see where it will lead while on holiday. Play can be said to be "extra", something outside normal life.

(Dissanayake, 1992: 43)

Design allows us to venture down those untried pathways. Design helps us to find the special and the superfluous to introduce it into quotidian spaces. Indeed, I would argue—given the need to build distinctive places—that the superfluous, the special, are just as necessary to everyday life and everyday spaces as art practices are to the practicalities of building. This superfluity is not just necessary, but utopian. What Lucy Sargisson says of literary utopias is equally applicable to design:

> Excess and play are core conventions of literary utopias [...] They perform several different functions. Excess permits radical creativity. Utopians imagine and desire radically different worlds but they often work with a light touch. They fool around with reality and tweak the nose of convention: transgressing norms, breaking rules and crossing boundaries. Utopians play with reality like a dog with a rag, twisting and shaking it until it breaks. And they poke fun; evoking satire and using jokes and wit as strategic weapons to show 'it doesn't have to be like this!'

(Sargisson, 2012: 16)

Richard Howells, in his *A Critical Theory of Creativity*, brings Ernst Bloch's utopian concept of 'educated hope' to the 'making special' narrative of art: "[v]isions of a better world are encoded—often unconsciously—in art and literature, including popular culture. [...] Bloch's vision is not teleological in nature. Rather, it is a *process* rooted in the principles of creative imagination and educated hope" (Howells, 2015: 2; emphasis in original). It is precisely the notion of educated hope in the creation of utopian scenarios that allows for new and better structures of popular belief to emerge, allowing us a ready answer to the question, 'why art?' Howells prefers the term 'making better' to Dissanayake's 'making special.' This narrows the range of the discussion, however, by asserting that utopias, utopian scenarios, should primarily be employed as devices for imagining positive possible futures. We can't merely employ unidirectionally positive utopias—we must imagine critical *dystopias* too. Lyman Tower Sargent calls this utopian/dystopian action 'social dreaming':"the dreams and nightmares that concern the ways in which groups of people arrange their lives" (Sargent, 1994: 3). We need both dreams and nightmares to imagine both what to strive for, and what to strive to prevent.

Making a scene

The imaginative 'play' that we call design has a special space—the studio. It is a physical space that is particular to the act of design. Like the theatre, the stadium, or the pitch, it has a particular construction that marks the space out for a particular role. Like 'once upon a time' and the set-ups it elaborates, the studio is a physical space that corresponds to a specific space of the imagination. While, as with other species, play can take place anywhere, there is still a particular role for this special place, which is the setting for a ritual that triggers the flow of creativity. When entering the studio this frame of mind takes over, and any interruption to the atmosphere can be catastrophic—or at least it feels catastrophic. It is certainly detrimental to the creative design process.

As I write this, I am sitting in the British Library in London, as I often do, and I'm reminded that here is a special place for imaginative play as well—and I'm also reminded how much I resent any intrusion upon my space of seemingly solitary play here. As if to prove my point, a woman has just walked in and is assertively unpacking and rustling around just opposite me, and a young man has followed right behind and sat to my right, and is wearing too much perfume. I note, looking up at the continuing noise, that the woman is plugging in and setting up three (!) laptops in her space. The space of creativity and play is mental, physical, multi-sensual (as the scene above shows), affective, and particular, and is also marked by prohibitions and restraints—'rules'—that are often internally imposed:

> One generally finds, even in animals, 'rules' of play: special signals (such as wagging the tail or not using claws), postures, facial expressions, and sounds that mean 'This is make-believe'. Often special places are set aside for playing: a stadium, a gymnasium, a park, a recreation room, a ring or circle. There are special times, special clothes, a special mood for play—think of holidays, festivals, vacations, weekends.
>
> *(Dissanayake, 1992: 43)*

The studio is the particular place where make-believe is enabled in design, and Kyna Leski addresses the role of the studio as a space of experimentation (just as the space of the library allows critical experimentation), and brilliantly and poetically speaks of the individual experience of material reasoning within it. Her narrative is a modernist one, with roots in the methods of the Bauhaus, in which learning to trust the senses, to trust the materials, involves an initial un-learning (though not a total un-learning: the student does not become a *tabula rasa*). All the prejudices and preconceptions of the future designer are stripped away, and a newly built *Homo faber* steps forth. This is a useful narrative with which to encourage the student to trust in the process: *We are taking a portion of yourself away, but replacing it with something much better.* The importance of that trust cannot be underestimated.

Leski's methods and interpretation, however, are often too focused on the personal. The studio is not merely a space of trust and a space for the interaction of the teacher, the student, and the media they will employ. It is also an intensely social space. The imaginative work that takes place in the studio is part of a larger process of co-making, co-working, co-imagining, and the studio is part of the larger world of associations, professions, families, etc., all of which inform and support the individual. The musician Brian Eno calls this larger process the 'scenius,' a portmanteau of 'scene' and 'genius.' This concept helpfully reminds us that even for the seemingly solitary 'genius' painting or writing poetry in a garret, that invention emerges from a shared background of teaching, conversation, making, exploring, and feeling together: an 'ecology of talent' (Eno, n.d.). It posits a play-space/design space of situated, mediated, and intercorporeal social connectedness—a space of what Elaine Scarry calls "aesthetic fairness"—that "creates in all participants a state of delight in their own lateralness" (Scarry, 2000: 114). When I sit and create a space of intellectual experimentation and play for myself, alone in the library, I bring along all that has contributed to my current self, and I am reaching out laterally into other intellectual worlds with every book I open and every connection I make. Then I carry that back out into the world with me, in my own text, my teaching, my engagement with my profession, and so on.

For the architectures, particularly landscape architecture, the awareness of a 'scene' must include not only those people involved in co-invention, but they must enter into a constructive dialogue with all the processes and forces that comprise a landscape: biological, geological, climatic, cultural, social. The landscape architect needs to employ a mode of thinking and acting that Lorraine Code calls "ecological thinking" (2006). I prefer a term I've borrowed from ethnology: 'toposophy' (see Kockel, 2014), thinking that is about place, grounded in place, not just about objects, but about vast arrays of intersecting and interdependent processes and forces. Unlike philosophy—'beautiful thinking'—toposophy is thinking that is always *about somewhere*. The term 'ecological thinking,' useful as it is, seems to direct us too much towards preconceptions of the natural world, while toposophy engages both nature and artifice. Toposophy is a perspective, allied to what Tim Ingold calls the *dwelling perspective*, which treats people as organisms immersed in their lifeworlds, as opposed to what he calls the *building perspective*, which supposes that "people inhabit a world—of culture or society—to which form and meaning have already been attached" (Ingold, 2000: 153). This posits that the individual must 'construct' their world in order to act on it, rather than being—as in the dwelling perspective—from birth an actor in concert with the landscape in which he or she dwells. These simultaneous and interdependent actions and interactions are described well in theories of practice, which hold that practices "should be treated as involving thought and action together, and in so far as this is the case, embodied theory, as it were, is a part of practice itself" (Barnes, 2001: 20). 'Making a scene' is connecting with and learning from others as practice and as intercorporeal, embodied, emplaced sociality. This 'scene' contains conversations immersed in their lifeworlds. This scene makes connections with past realities, past dreams and ambitions, past constructions, and incorporates them as parts of possible futures. Thus it resists tendencies within modernity to clean the slate—where past forms and meanings may be expunged and new ones written upon a *tabula rasa*.

Here an un-learning of the past is necessary for total invention. In a scene, though, "[t]hinking means venturing beyond. But in such a way that what already exists is not kept under or skated over" (Bloch, 1986: 4). What already exists probably contains fragments and relics of past utopias, ready to be called into the future as part of the next scene. To those fragments are pinned satisfaction, fulfilment, beauty, and love; qualities deserving of continuity.

Making belief

It is through imaginative renderings of possible future worlds that designers have the ability to influence structures of both belief and desire to positive and ethical ends. Worlds that we know to be physically and morally possible, but which have been suppressed by ideologies of selfish cynicism, fatalism, and nihilism, or hidden behind a smokescreen of agnotology (culturally induced or purposely sown ignorance or doubt; see Proctor and Schiebinger, 2008), can be forced to re-emerge. The 'future as a cultural fact' remains true, but its alethic valence has shifted from the negative to the positive, from the dystopian to the utopian. Truth has become the province of hope, not the grounds for the abandonment of desire and fulfilment. Another face of neoliberalism is the alluring glamour of the consumer object, which distracts us from more authentic modes of fulfilment. Here Nigel Thrift identifies this tendency, and how it is amplified by media and social media: "Each of these technologies demonstrates the singular quality of allure through the establishment of human-nonhuman fields of captivation, for what seems certain is that many of the objects and environments that capitalism produces have to demonstrate the calculated sincerity of allure if people are to be attracted to them: they need to manifest a particular style that generates enchantment without supernaturalism" (Thrift, 2010: 290). The enchantment worked by capitalism's processes militates against the sociality, the *scenius* that is needed to create true forms of common good and it distracts from education's primary goal of emancipation, which "has a tradition that is not made of spectacular acts, but is shaped by a search to create new forms of the common, which are not those of the state or of consensus" (Simons and Masschelein, 2011: 6). This emancipation, and all forms of utopian creativity, are co-opted by neoliberalism and are commodified and depoliticized by it. In the process, the project of transforming the present by reimagining the future is crushed under the weight of an endless, enchanted, commodified, consumerist present. A sense of lateralness, of interconnection, and of hope are required to displace the weight of such a present. Elaine Scarry locates this lateral position as a site of beauty, "not now the suspended state of beholding but the active state of creating—the site of stewardship in which one acts to protect or perpetuate a fragment of beauty already in the world or instead to supplement it by bringing into being a new object" (Scarry, 2000: 114). And it is not merely objects which are created, but new places and new dwellings where this beauty and connectedness can be made special, and may grow.

Hope involves desire, imagination, and belief—all three—and design insists on the addition of supposing as another attribute. First, we must simultaneously suppose and believe that hope is possible at all, and once that possibility is admitted, then the belief in a better future undergirds and impels the processes of aspiration and envisioning that are germane to design, but which can be led astray by cynical or fatalist attitudes, and/or by greed and hubris. As Pierre Bourdieu argued, hope also requires a collective effort—a scene—rather than a reliance on the emergence of a new and charismatic leader:

> The whole edifice of critical thought is in need of reconstruction. This work of reconstruction cannot be done, as some have thought in the past, by a single great intellectual, a master thinker endowed only with the resources of his singular thought, or by the authorized spokesperson for a group or an institution presumed to speak in the name of those without voice, union, party, and so on. This is where the collective intellectual can play its irreplaceable role, by helping to create the social conditions for the collective production of *realist utopias*.
>
> *(Bourdieu, 2000: 42–43; emphasis in original)*

The 'realist utopia' is here one which is mutually created as a form of social dreaming. Jeremy Gilbert similarly argues that "this is a very important issue for any attempt to think about the nature of democracy, because the assumption that agency, creativity and rationality are qualities which pertain to individuals but not to groups poses severe problems for any attempt to base a politics on the possibility of collective decision making" (Gilbert, 2014: 33).

Belief in the possibility of positive change is fundamental to what is constructed and imagined mutually, and it is precisely this collectivity that is essential to making the future, whether through design or through the education, which prepares the future makers of the future. The intellectual qualities and faculties of both individuals and collectives must be developed together. It almost goes without saying that contemporary education everywhere is subject to ideological forces which are pulling precisely in the opposite way from what I am arguing is necessary. Universities "cannot compel or otherwise bring about the production of the thing that matters most—intellectual quality, whether in teaching or scholarship or research" (Collini, 2017: 44). The prevailing ideologies of our time, if not countered with other possible futures, will lock us into a loop of increasing authoritarianism (or *dirigisme*, as identified in Collini) and enclosure on the one hand, and ever greater precarity and liquid modern placelessness on the other. I would hope, though, that far from seeming like pie in the sky, my approach shows just how disconnected from problems of education, sustainability, and civic responsibility that government everywhere and, thus, how education is managed, have become. As a result of the marketization of educational institutions, education now mirrors the construction of society outside it and reinforces it. Education is reinforcing the nihilistic loops in which our larger political economy is currently mired, ones in which, as Henry Giroux has put it, "freedom is reduced to a market strategy and citizenship is narrowed to the demands of consumerism. The upshot is that it has become easier to imagine the end of the world than the end of capitalism" (Giroux, 2007: 25).

When designers work with communities to remodel their buildings and landscapes to provide for better futures, they should work with those communities, through processes of supposing and scenario-making, to find out how they can make more and better—more special—what they already are. Design in the architectures is a process of becoming that addresses being and longing—belonging—to clear and prepare a space for play, for a shared imagining of the future and a striving towards it, that builds upon *scenius* and *toposophy* for creation that, by *making special* through make-believe and social dreaming, *makes belief* in a better and more mutual world possible.

This essay was published in the web book *Imaginaries of the Future 01: Bodies and Media*, co-edited by Nathaniel Coleman, David M. Bell, and Adam Stock in 2018.

15

OTHER STRANGER'S PATHS

In homage to John Brinckerhoff Jackson

Nearly sixty years ago, J.B. Jackson wrote one of the most insightful essays about landscape ever written, "The Stranger's Path." Jackson's warm, gentle, and wise voice and keen observation have been constants in my career as a landscape architect and writer, and I offer the following piece as a kind of fugue, a flowing together of Jackson's voice into mine, in the way that so many stories flow together in the city along the Stranger's Path. Our dearest hopes for the future will always evolve from the places and the voices of our past. The city is a cosmopolitan story we write together, and so many of us have come there to write it as strangers.

Spokane, Washington, 1986

In what was, I think, the spring of 1986, my good friend Lisa and I ran away from the small town of Moscow, Idaho where we lived and went to high school together, and spent the day in Spokane, Washington. Spokane in the 1980s was a city only in shape, hollowed out by suburban expansion as well as an economy depressed over most of the twentieth century, though it had briefly stuttered into faltering recovery in the late 60s and 70s. For youngsters like us, with sarcastic anti-establishment attitudes, vertical hair-sprayed hair, and cassettes of obscure German industrial music in our Walkmans, it was precisely Spokane's grittiness that gave us something to sneer at and to revel in. In Moscow, my friends and I would spend hours mooching around by the railway tracks, and exploring abandoned grain elevators and empty farmhouses, participating in the birth of an aesthetic based in the blasted remnants of rust-belt style decline and the demise of the small farm and farmer's co-operative.

In Spokane, these same forces were writ slightly larger, and the modern and post-modern buildings and landscapes produced in its short recovery were also empty and decaying. Spokane possesses one of the most extensive 'skywalk' systems in the

DOI: 10.4324/9781003164593-15

FIGURE 15.1 There is at least one pedestrian bridge left in Spokane, Washington. Credit: Kirk Fisher/Shutterstock.

USA (Figure 15.1), built around the time it hosted the environmentally themed World Expo of 1974. Presumably grown from the Corbusian ideal of the 'death of the street,' but also in defence against the area's frigid winters, this shopping-mall-in-the-sky had first killed the streets below, then slowly killed itself. Lisa and I wandered its empty corridors eating chocolate-covered espresso beans and contemplating a seemingly post-apocalyptic cityscape from which all the citizens had simply disappeared.

A few streets away, at the Greyhound bus station, which was full, not of travellers, but of people trapped by permanent transience and precarity, and the smell of urine and fear, we wondered together whether bus stations, once planted, would spread their black tendrils of decay into the neighbouring soil; bad seeds that would ensure a continuously poisonous urban harvest for an area. Lisa and I sat on the pavement and sang a comic jingle together from the Sex Pistols movie *Sid and Nancy* (1986), "I want a job, I want a job / I want a good job, I want a job / one that satisfies / my artistic needs." We laughed together at the irony of the postmodern condition, savvy, world-weary punks.

> We are welcomed to the city by a smiling landscape of parking lots, warehouses, pot-holed and weed-grown streets, where isolated filling stations and quick-lunch counters are scattered among cinders like survivals of a bombing raid.
>
> (Jackson, 1997 [1957]: 21)

No matter how blasé we pretended to each other to be, though, this was one of our first, rare moments of escape from home without our families. Rather than being swept solicitously past the iniquitous and ubiquitous head shops and adult bookstores of the Stranger's Path, we were now free to stand and stare at them, even enter them. Though we pretended we'd seen it all, we hadn't really seen anything yet, certainly not in Moscow, Idaho. We were both making a time-honoured exchange with the city of Spokane; its secrets and lures for our inquisitiveness and invention. But poor Spokane—where Jackson's ideal Stranger's Path would lead us from potholes to a clean, bright city centre, Spokane's Path at the time only led to a gaping absence where that centre should have been.

> [I]s it not one of the chief functions of the city to exchange as well as to receive? [...]
> These characteristics are worth bearing in mind, for they make the Path in the average
> small city what it now is: loud, tawdry, down-at-the-heel, full of dives and small catch-
> penny businesses, and (in the eyes of the uptown residential white-collar element) more
> than a little shady and dangerous.
>
> (Ibid.: 22)

London, England, 2015

It's Saturday the 14th of November 2015, and there is a steady rain. I'm starting a short walk from the base of Christopher Wren's monument to the great fire of London, just at the intersection of London's two most venerable Stranger's Paths: London Bridge, for 700 years the only dry crossing of this reach of the Thames, and, of course, the River Thames itself. London has many Stranger's Paths, which now include some routes oddly distended by public transport. Heathrow Airport, for example, sits amidst a vast terrain of potholes and parking, but travellers smear quickly across the suburbs via the Piccadilly Line or the Heathrow Express to eventually rejoin the Stranger's Path in Earl's Court or Paddington, each place raffish and lightly sleazy. The Borough High Street and London Bridge are still part of continuous Stranger's Paths that, from Borough, fan out into Kent, Surrey, and East and West Sussex. I'm walking the stranger's path out of the city, because now I'm a long-time resident here, a Londoner as much as any other, it doesn't make sense to me to walk the Stranger's Path from the view of one entering. I will walk from the civic centre, that which absorbs, towards the periphery and beyond, from which the Path flows.

> The simile was further that of a stream which empties into no basin or lake, merely
> evaporating into the city or perhaps rising to the surface once more outside of town along
> some highway strip; and it is this lack of a final, well-defined objective that prevents
> the Path from serving an even more important role in the community and that tends
> to make it a poor-man's district.
>
> (Ibid.: 26)

Vistas in the City of London, with its tangled, medieval streets, are tightly enclosed. As one approaches London Bridge from the City of London along King William Street, the view expands dramatically. It is possible, here, to quickly comprehend the topography; the high north bank and the once-marshy south bank. The surface of London Bridge, a very clean plane, emphasizes the horizontal and draws the eye out over the river. The water is shining as the sun breaks through the day's dark, moist clouds. To the east, the Tower of London with flags waving. When London Bridge was crowned with its twin walls of houses, shops, and chapels this experience would have been very different. Before 1760–1761, when the bridge was cleared of these habitable encrustations, and at the height of British naval power and transatlantic shipping, it must have been possible to catch glimpses from the crowded bridge, between the buildings, out to countless masts and ship's decks forming an unbroken but uneven ground where now there is open water. Out the gate to the south, one would have passed under the cautionary severed heads of the executed, held aloft on pikes, signifying, perhaps, that the rule of order was rather weaker outside the gate than it was inside. Outside we would find the petty criminals, hucksters and whores, bishop-pimps, betting, drinking, and theatrical acts of all scales. On the south bank I reach the Borough High Street, its narrow footpaths jostling with people and its streets full of cars splashing through puddles gurgling up onto the curbs.

> *The sidewalks are lined with small shops, bars, stalls, dance halls, movies, booths lighted by acetylene lamps; and everywhere are strange faces, strange costumes, strange and delightful impressions. To walk up such a street into the quieter, more formal part of town is to be part of a procession, part of a ceaseless ceremony of being initiated into the city and of rededicating the city itself.*

> *(Ibid.: 28)*

The Borough High Street and the myriad alleyways feeding into it are a writing and rewriting of the dialogue between congestion and commerce. A succession of narrow courts and alleys open up with only a building's width between them. On a map, they appear like the teeth of combs, and they echo the parallel streets that once thronged perpendicular to the Thames, pulsing with a constant flow of people and goods from across the heaving seas. This whole place Jackson might have described as 'honky-tonk,' and despite recent attempts to Manhattanize the area, I have hopes that it will retain its rough-and-tumble demeanour. The incredibly fine urban grain here reminds us that not only would these streets have been congested, but so would the commerce itself, with many businesses not wider than a person's girth— and the prostitutes, of course, themselves commodities—'commodity' even being a name for their most private parts. The prostitute's business fits precisely the space of her body. The carts drawing goods into the city to discharge in its markets would have been constantly clutched at and called to from these many stalls, perhaps most when the carts were returning empty and the purses were full; bellies filling, balls emptying—the city's carnal and pecuniary tides are one.

The George, down one of these narrow side streets, is a rare survivor from the seventeenth century, and its history is longer—its original building was burnt. It is a galleried coaching inn, decked with balustrades on all levels from which to watch the comings and goings of horses and carriages below. Its interior is as intricately wrought as the streets outside. There are grand rooms and snug corners and stairways that allow glimpses of action above and below and which carry snatches of laughter from floor to floor. It's full, loud, and friendly today with big groups crowding around tables filled with food and ale. It's a dry spot to wet the innards, and my glass of Southwark Porter goes down a treat as I write, perched on the edge of a high bench with my notebook on a sticky table. The men next to me are talking about women, then about smoked meats.

> *For my part, I cannot conceive of any large community surviving without this ceaseless influx of new wants, new ideas, new manners, new strength, and so I cannot conceive of a city without some section corresponding to the Path.*
>
> (Ibid.: 26)

When I leave The George, the beer has gone cold in my belly and rainy-day melancholy has begun to take hold of me. Just to the south a hoarding has gone up around a large building site. Signs show images of the excavations that preceded the construction; foundations and walls closely stacked parallel and perpendicular, layer after layer, generation after generation. Somewhere they begin in the silty ooze this part of the city is mired in. They are a reminder that the trajectories we inscribe have been written over centuries. As a species we don't simply leave trails on the surface, but also below and above. When I look through the windows cut in the hoarding, I see all that is now gone, and sheet pilings line the edge of a vast, clean pit with freshly poured concrete curing at its bottom.

At last I arrive at the Marshalsea Prison wall (Figure 15.2), a place I have brought numerous visitors and guests because it is a place where you can feel the full weight of London's terrible past. This blackened and dreadful high wall, studded with occasional spikes and rings, was the outer wall of the prison in which Charles Dickens' father was incarcerated, amongst many others of London's wretched. A site redolent of woe. Today, as the rain falls, I arrive to find the wall 'restored' and almost completely rebuilt, still solid and massive, but clean and crisp and regular. I knew I would find it this way, as I had caught a glimpse of this atrocity of cleansing while it was underway, again behind hoardings, but I'm still unprepared for the magnitude of the loss now that the hoardings have been removed. All its presence, its meaning, has been washed away, scrubbed away, normalized. That cruel history that called out to every visitor, "Never again!" has been whitewashed. What once was chillingly, silently eloquent is now merely mute. I stand in front of the wall and I can't stop the tears welling up in my eyes.

Afterwards I wander aimlessly through the Borough Market, pushing through the crowds, and then cross the river at the Southwark Bridge, where the tide is high and the river is brimming with water that looks like cold, milky tea. Behind a glass

FIGURE 15.2 Marshalsea Prison wall. Credit: Glen Berlin/Shutterstock.

curtain wall in a new restaurant in a new building near St Paul's, a woman with shining hair and perfect teeth is laughing in a way that shows practised charm, but that is clearly forced. I find my way back to the narrow streets with brick buildings shouldering in and panes of glass emitting warm, yellow light.

> *The Stranger's Path exists in one form or another in every large community …* *preserved and cherished. Everywhere it is the direct product of our economic and social* *evolution. If we seek to dam or bury this ancient river, we will live to regret it.*
>
> *(Ibid.: 28–29)*

This essay first appeared in the University of Greenwich journal *Testing Ground* in 2016 and was subsequently reprinted in 2019 in the *Journal of Critical Architecture*.

16

DEMOCRACY AND TRESPASS

Political dimensions of landscape access

Democracy and trespass

This chapter is about bodies out of place on purpose, and about when being in the wrong place is the right thing to do. Forbidding access or ejecting people is often a sign of the breakdown or denial of democracy in the public sphere and the public realm. Publicity—the ability to be public, to operate in public—requires a knowledge of one's own place, even if that place is transgressive, or perhaps *especially* if that place is transgressive.

The European Landscape Convention defines landscape as perceived: "'Landscape' means an area, as perceived by people, whose character is the result of the action and interaction of natural and/or human factors" (Council of Europe, 2000: 9). It must be stressed that in this it is the lived landscape, that which is shaped by its inhabitants and which, in turn, shapes them, that is the most crucial definition. This physical and cognitive connection, though, is being eroded in many ways. It is eroded in the countryside (as it has been since the Industrial Revolution), as people's direct engagement with land, tools, and materials has been mostly replaced with technology and machines that distance us from the physical matter of place. It is eroded as the countryside becomes lonelier and emptier and is reduced to mere scenery: a backdrop, not a background for existence. In the worst case, the rural landscape is virtually completely shielded from public interaction, leaving stewardship in the hands of a very few, with the result that the possibilities for exploitation are rife. In the city this connection is eroded by ever more remote processes of planning, finance, development, and design that militate against the ability of communities to have agency in the construction of their environment.

> When the *land* in *land*scape is perceived to have the qualities of a property defined in space, discourse will tend to revolve around individual property

DOI: 10.4324/9781003164593-16

rights, territorial rights, ownership rights, and economic value. If, on the other hand, the *land* in *land*scape, is perceived to be a place, shaped as an area for use by individuals and communities, then discourse can be directed towards customary use rights, which are fundamental to common law.

(Olwig, 2011: 39, emphases in the original)

As instruments of control and compliance—from policing and surveillance to obfuscating bureaucracy—become ever more entrenched and limiting, the necessity for trespass as an assertion of democratic principles becomes more and more the only option to effect change at any scale. Many of these acts of trespass will be illegal and will result in acts of state violence against the trespassers. In the words of Costas Douzinas: "Resistance is always situated. Resistances are local and multiple: they emerge concretely in specific conditions, responding to a situation, state of affairs or event" (2014: n.p.). He also makes the point that resistance is a bodily reaction to felt injustices (ibid.: n.p.). It goes without saying that this situated resistance is enacted by human bodies in physical places. The willingness of people to make their bodies vulnerable is part of the great power of resistance, and this vulnerability dictates that the resistance must be enacted in the most meaningful and visible places possible. Turkey's President Erdoğan, for example, has designated peripheral spaces (such as Maltepe and Kadiköy) in Istanbul for protest, but protesters only have one body each; and therefore they will take those resisting bodies to Taksim Square where any violence done to those bodies will be most visible. Protest is enactment; it is performative, and therefore it requires an audience. Power understands this, which is one reason why contemporary governments seek to control, censor, or manipulate media coverage, to deny the media access to events, or to undermine public trust in the media.

Access and landscape imaginaries

Physical landscape access is necessary for nearly all people, and even if one is confined through illness or incarceration, for example, knowledge of the possibility of landscape access might still offer an important form of mental escape. The landscape is where public lives take place, whether this is in city streets or rural fields.

An extreme and particular sort of landscape access is one of 'splendid isolation,' where a society's most wealthy and powerful citizens (monarchs and oligarchs, perhaps) might move through the landscape without needing to touch the ground or rub elbows with the great unwashed. The landscape imaginaries that are commonly encountered in aspirational advertising, particularly for the Western middle class, are just such images: the private island, the secluded estate. This is a landscape imaginary of privilege and exclusivity. There is a cost to participate, whether this is one of fees for entry or membership, or the expense of paraphernalia (grouse hunting or golf, for example, require costly equipment and conspicuous, unusual, and expensive costumes). Many aspirations globally strive for just such detachment, though it would be difficult to say whether this is a universal human tendency or whether it is the result of the manipulation of desire by advertisers. It is an imaginary that posits freedom for the few, and it of course comes up against the limits of its own enclosure: it is the proverbial 'gilded cage.' It is a perennial paradox that, while interaction with others seems to be essential for happiness, it is also a source of friction and conflict that requires negotiation and accommodation. The richer and more sustainable imaginary is that of freedom for all, which requires a civil society and significant amounts of mutual aid, all of which require human interaction in social settings. The key difference between the two is that the isolationism of the first only requires protecting a compound, whereas a democratic conception of freedom of the landscape requires protecting it all. This is a fundamental point of friction, perhaps, between the differing notions of property in economic conservatism and environmentalism. Furthermore, isolating tendencies are only feasible when resources are available to protect that isolation. For most without wealth and power it is not what doesn't kill them that makes them strong(er), but rather what doesn't *isolate* them. And the consolidation of collective power requires space in the landscape.

Another form or mode of power rooted in the manipulation of landscape imaginaries is that of nationalism. Nationalist identification with landscapes has a reciprocal effect on national identity and character—in much the same way as lived landscape does—and perhaps it is no longer possible to separate the two constructions. In the United States, for example, 'purple mountain majesty' and 'amber waves of grain' are landscape images that conjure a bountiful and limitless frontier as a cornerstone of a national ideology that has come to embrace not just acquisitiveness and growth, but wastefulness. In England, the identification with garden and hedgerow—England's 'green and pleasant land'—have contributed to an obsession with privacy and a concomitant lack of agency in public affairs beyond the reinforcement of boundaries. The English are (often justifiably) accused of merely moaning about things rather than fixing them when faced with adversity from external forces or processes. Americans are, conversely—and also often justifiably—accused of possessing a strident sense of entitlement that they take with them wherever they go. Both of these markers of identity could be either underpinned or bolstered by national myths that are constructed with the use of heroic landscape imagery.

Bounding and framing

The express link between history and geography is made clear when we say that history 'takes place'—that movements of people and great conflicts often occur due to disputes over land and resources and conditions of scarcity. The link between history and geography is as reciprocal and relational as the link between humans and their environment is in the concept of landscape. Places are produced and framed by the historical events that occur within them. These determine the scale and tenor of events in such spaces into the future. This is not necessarily always an 'organic' progression, however, as the making of landscape has increasingly, in modernity, been tied to the wielding of power, as with the enclosures in England (see Thompson, 2013; Williams, 2011 [1973]).

It is easy to naïvely assume that, before the enclosures and the planting of miles of hedgerows that demarcated its definitions, the British landscape was a largely boundless common land defined instead around centres of feudal power: the lord, the castle, the monarch. Firm definitions of territorial boundaries in Britain, however, predate the enclosures quite considerably. The ancient pagan practice of 'beating the bounds,' which continues to this day in many places in England and Wales, involves elders of a community accompanying youths on a circuit of the boundaries of the parish, and beating the children with sticks at landmarks along the way (Olwig, 2019: 27, 55). Nowadays the beating is light and ceremonial, but the seriousness of understanding precisely where borders lay in case of dispute would have justified painful beatings historically. Where surveying is now the final arbiter of boundary disputes, this more abstract practice was preceded by one in which the body and its situation—its siting, its emplacement in context—were key to maintaining order. The bodily memory and experience of bounding are explicit in ways that reinforce the body's profound part of human cognition. The senses, in this case excited to the point of pain, are fundamental to human meaning, identity, and place.

This very visceral 'knowing one's place' is both literal and figurative, and reflecting on this gives one a sense of what an outrage it was to the peasantry—physical, moral, and spatial—that boundaries could be blithely rearranged by the wealthy, 'landed' classes in the enclosures.

The peasantry, forced, often violently, off the land, became the urban proletariat in modernity, and now the underclass is defined by the desperately marginalized and often de-skilled poor or the precariat. The precariat is composed of those who are living at or below the subsistence level, lack job security, and are often in debt. For the peasantry, the proletariat and the precariat, the forces of oppression are tied directly to the practices of capitalism, and the project of the enclosures must be seen to be one that is ongoing and unfinished, perhaps (though hopefully not) interminable.

Cultural historians Peter Linebaugh and Marcus Rediker identify the oppression that has accompanied capitalist accumulation throughout modernity as 'the three disabilities of terror,' which are at root three different problems with embodiment, emplacement, and identity. These are: (i) the inability to name the oppressor (evident in forms of resistance and misplacement of anger in various forms of racism and xenophobia, for example); (ii) the desire for death (this is quite specifically engendered from the hopelessness of violence and enables people to give up their lives or those of others, such as in gang warfare); and (iii) to become deracinated—specifically to be removed from place, culture, and identity (Linebaugh and Rediker, 2000: 53–54, 60). What is disabled by terror, wherever it is deployed—which is virtually wherever it is conceivable—is the practice of alternative ways of living, often collective, and "popular attachments to liberty and the fullness of sensuality" (ibid.: 14) Curiously, the terror finds itself directed back upwards at the oppressor, as the fears of rebellion, crime, or other transgressions born of the isolation germane to wealth and power is also a form of the terror of deracination.

Acts of trespass

To know one's place in a democracy is to know that one's place is often on the other side of someone else's fence. Trespass is necessary to the defence of democracy, as is the idea of utopia: the dream of a better world beyond those boundaries. Trespass is also movement towards a future goal or a utopian horizon: the sense of such an act "lies in its direction and orientation: the future which it is travelling towards, blindly or lucidly, in other words, what is possible" (Lefebvre, 2002 [1961]: 293). Democracy is a constant pressure against the solidification of forms of authoritarian power, a solidification that is more often than not spatial and enclosing in its expression. Both hope and transgression—"a form of politics"—are the primary forms this resistance takes (Cresswell, 1996: 9). In politics, hope for the masses is tied to place and setting (and Michael Walzer (1992: 98) describes civil society as a "setting of settings"). Thus it is situated; *topos* drives change, and civil society functions in places as social and historical agent. It *takes place*. Peter Hallward (2012: 61) writes, "Democracy means rule of the people, the assertion of the people's will. Democracy applies in so far as the collective will of the people overpowers those who exploit, oppress, or deceive them. Abstracted from such relations of power and over-power, democracy is an empty word." It is also an empty word when democracy is abstracted from the places people inhabit, and in which power and over-power are physically expressed.

Trespass, as it so often has been historically, is an embodied, emplaced rejection of global capital and its processes of abstraction and extraction—and disembodied dis-emplaced corporations and people—from the land-grabbing gentry of the early days of the enclosures to the tax-dodging corporations who hide their money and existences in non-places, to the 'people' who own urban luxury flats or villas but who are never home. How can any of this be democratic?

Isolation (and splendid isolation) and its accompanying tendencies of bounding and defence breed fear, particularly the fear of trespass. On the other hand, isolation and fortification necessitate trespass in a democracy. Thus, the fear of trespass is fully justified, as is the necessity of trespass. Democracy is the project of resisting certain forms of conservatism—in particular, the form that seeks to preserve or to entrench structures of power, class (which nowadays may be read as 'lifestyle') and wealth, and their expression in landscapes.

In 1932, young members of the urban proletariat of Manchester and Sheffield, frustrated by a lack of access to the beautiful Peak District landscape around the summit of Kinder Scout (a point roughly equidistant from each city), demonstrated the power of trespass as part of the Right to Roam movement. Benny Rothman, one of the leaders of the group that undertook to trespass on the private land, guarded by keepers and used by a wealthy minority to shoot grouse, says of the group:

We were very young, almost entirely under 21. The established rambling clubs were of a far older age group, and had spent a lifetime in the rambling movement. We were impatient at the seemingly futile efforts so far made to achieve access to mountains. Conditions in towns were becoming more intolerable and unemployment, which stood at about four million, greatly added to our frustration.

(Rothman, 2012 [1982]: 21)

The Manchester Ramblers' Federation, the more "established rambling club," was hostile to the idea, afraid that it would antagonize the landowners and set the movement back (ibid.: 20). Kinder Scout, once common land, but enclosed in 1830, was a highly visible but emphatically denied attractor to those ramblers seeking to escape the smoke and crowding of the industrial cities. The ramblers must have felt the constriction of the industrial city in a very real, bodily way. The 24th of April 1932 was a clear, bright day, and the young crowd of working-class men and women took to the hills, ready to defy the keepers, who were armed with stout sticks. Rothman and his friend Woolfie Winnick led the group mounting Kinder Scout from the Manchester side, while another group made the ascent from Sheffield. Rothman and Winnick evaded a heavy police presence stationed to prevent them taking to the paths, and addressed the crowd at Bowden Bridge quarry. During the ascent the group grappled with the gamekeepers, but overcame them and walked much of the way to the peak. The ramblers enacted the freedom of access and the freedom to roam and thus won the right of both at Kinder Scout.

The Kinder Scout Mass Trespass was as much addressing problems of urban conditions and proletariat lives as it was addressing conditions in the countryside. The ongoing Occupy! movement also embodies manifold meanings, reaching from physical urban places to structural conditions in geopolitics. In particular, its actions at Zuccotti Park in New York from 17 September until 15 November 2011, at St Paul's in London from 15 October 2011 until 14 June 2012, and at Gezi Park in Istanbul from 28 May until 15 June 2013 expressed the right for resistant bodies to occupy public places at the same time as they expressed a desire for a new global political order that excluded the practices of neoliberal capitalism. Crucial to Occupy! is the performance of democracy (Chomsky, 2012). Horizontally and non-hierarchically organized, Occupy! insists not on making specific demands, but rather demonstrating "its refusal to recognize the legitimacy of the existing political institutions," and "to challenge the fundamental premises of our economic system" (Graeber, 2013: 99). Its goal is to show, by example, by acting it out, that a better alternative to the current system of government manipulated by corporations, at best ignoring and at worst victimizing the poor and serving the wealthy, is possible. David Graeber, one of the key figures of Occupy!, calls this 'prefigurative politics': it is a politics of futurity in a utopian mode, and all the stronger for it. "Direct action," he says, "is, ultimately, the defiant insistence on acting as if one is already free" (ibid.: 233).

What both the Kinder Scout Mass Trespass and the actions of the Occupy! movement demonstrate is an embodied and emplaced resistance to force, violence, and enclosures through the assertion of equality—in place, through the use of the body, and through the projection of political imaginaries. This assertion is concrete in a way that that which it resists is not. State and corporate power are increasingly abstract—abstracted away from sources of real value to simple arithmetic measures as well as the physical abstraction of people and human processes from land. Urbanization has effectively emptied the countryside of people in many places, making the rural landscape little more than a picturesque abstraction for a large segment of the population in the West. Of Henri Lefebvre's famous statement about the 'right to the city,' David Harvey (2013: 3–4) writes:

> [T]he question of what kind of city we want cannot be divorced from the kind of people we want to be, what kinds of social relations we seek, what relations to nature we cherish, what style of life we desire, what aesthetic values we hold. The right to the city is, therefore, far more than a right of individual or group access to the resources that the city embodies: it is a right to change and reinvent the city more after our hearts' desire. It is moreover, a collective rather than an individual right, since reinventing the city inevitably depends upon the exercise of a collective power over the processes of urbanization. The freedom to make and remake ourselves and our cities is, I want to argue, one of the most precious yet most neglected of our human rights.

I would argue further that the right to the city must be extended to a right to the country; that all people should have a right to the landscape, to make it and remake it 'more after our hearts' desire.'

Passage, narrative, inhabitation

Resistance in the case of Occupy! or mass trespass operates in between the space of strategies and tactics, as elucidated by de Certeau. A tactic is "an art of the weak"; "the space of the other. Thus it must play on and with a terrain imposed on it and organized by the law of a foreign power." A strategy, on the other hand, is "capable of articulating an ensemble of physical places in which forces are distributed." It establishes a "proper" space, a "triumph of place over time," a "mastery of time through the foundation of an autonomous place" (1984: 36–38). What these resistances accomplish is to use the wedge of the tactic to establish a space for strategy, and through enacting the strategy, even if established in a contingent and temporary space, they open the space of the other into the space of the proper, making possible an alternative, democratic order that had hitherto only been an art of the criminal or the subaltern.

Landscape access is a story not just of occupation of land, but of the journeys undertaken as part of the act of dwelling. Journeys can fold into modes of inhabitation across a vast landscape or even multiple landscapes, aided now by high-speed transportation. Everyday life is also composed of smaller journeys on smaller timescales: journeys between home, work, shops, cafés, parks, hairdressers, that become intricate rituals of dwelling, of connection to place and community. Everyday life unfolds in journeys and narratives, including many varieties of the interpenetration of strategies and tactics. Everyday life 'takes place' exactly as does history.

Everyday life is what Henri Lefebvre calls a meshwork, which Tim Ingold references in his remarkable book, *Lines: A Brief History* (2007). Lefebvre "speaks of 'the reticular patterns left by animals, both wild and domestic, and by people (in and around the houses of village or small town, as in the town's immediate environs),' (Lefebvre, 1991: 117–118) whose movements weave an environment that is more 'archi-textural' than architectural" (Ingold, 2007: 80) The abstraction of people, places, and processes in modernity works to directly negate or deny the existence of this very ecological and contingent overlapping.

Ingold draws a distinction between the trajectories of modernity, which tend to draw straight lines as connectors between nodes, and the 'line of wayfaring,' which is the line of a passage that is traced through place, a journey that is not disembodied, but rather textured and experiential.

> They are ceaselessly eroded by the tactical manoeuvring of inhabitants whose 'wandering lines' (*lignes d'erre*) or 'efficacious meanderings'—in de Certeau's words—undercut the strategic designs of society's master-builders causing them gradually to wear out and disintegrate. Quite apart from human beings who may or may not respect the rules of play, these inhabitants include countless non-humans that have no heed for them at all. Flying, crawling, wriggling and burrowing all over and under the regular, linearized infrastructure of the occupied world, creatures of every sort continually reincorporate and rearrange its crumbling fragments into their own ways of life.
>
> *(Ibid.: 102–103)*

These are the lines, the narratives, that compose a landscape of dwelling, a place. The conflict between the lived landscape and the abstract landscape of the surveyor and the developer is precisely in this difference. Once enclosed and inscribed by geometry, it is possible to conceive of landscape as not being a lived realm, but rather as a collection of discrete sites, nodes, joined with connectors. Performing the alternative is as much a sign act of resistance as it is a declaration of the intention to dwell, and to do so not in dominion over, but in concert with, people and place.

Democratic politics in real landscape space

The democratic idea is based in the idea of equality and that leadership should be founded in the consent of the led—at its behest, not on its behalf. David Graeber writes that democracy "is just the belief that humans are fundamentally equal and ought to be able to manage their collective affairs in an egalitarian fashion, using whatever means appear most conducive" (2013: 186). It follows, then, that if some members of a society are able to completely close themselves off to interaction with others in that society by dint of force (which can take the form of everything from high walls to patrolling to outright violence), then that enclosure is undemocratic and the citizenry has a duty to resist it.

The actions of both the mass trespasses of the 1930s and the recent Occupy! movement are both examples of prefigurative politics: "the idea that the form of our action should itself offer a model, or at the very least a glimpse of how free people might organise themselves, and therefore what a free society could be like." The organisational form that an activist group takes should embody the kind of society we wish to create—in a sense imagining a better world and then living as though it already existed—that by creating and living in a more perfect society publicly, it should be brought to pass.

Through the trespasses and through Occupy!, the enactment of utopia becomes performative, perhaps also improvisatory. It is also an act of memory and a very situated, very present act. It is to value what *is* and from that to imagine what *should be*. To say, 'I want to carry *this* into the future with me. *We* want to carry this into the future.' Improvisation helps us to riff around, find the sweet notes, the snatches of melody, and to play them again and again until they form a new song. Thus, if utopias are performative, if the right to the landscape is performative, then they are all alive.

This chapter was originally published in the 2018 collection *Defining Landscape Democracy: A Path to Spatial Justice*. I am indebted to Karsten Jørgensen's keen editorial eye and this chapter is dedicated in his memory.

17
A WORD... 'HABITAT'

In the current epoch, the Holocene,[1] beginning some ten to twelve thousand years ago, a significant leap in the cultural evolution of humankind, occurred. The Neolithic revolution brought us both agriculture and cities. Jane Jacobs (1970), famously, argued that the rise of cities may well have been what necessitated agriculture, which was directly counter to the orthodoxy of the time. The received view was that agriculture made settlement necessary, which then enabled cities and their "certain energized crowding of people" to come into being (Kostof, 1991: 37). Scholars now, however, are largely of the opinion that seeking to establish primacy, as is so often the case, is a futile goal.[2] Agriculture and urbanism simply enabled each other, and ever since then humans, cities, and the countryside have evolved together. This view also dispatches the old rural/urban dichotomy rather handily. Country mice and city mice are still all just mice, it seems.

A view of human history and geography so sweeping allows us to consider all landscape occupied by humans as our habitat; and we are a very widely distributed species. From the igloo to the little grass shack, vernacular building is everywhere uniquely adapted to local conditions, and the designed landscape and city has long been shaped by them too. So, indeed, are our ways of life and our daily rounds called, aptly, by the sociologist and anthropologist Pierre Bourdieu, our *habitus*

---

1 I'm very aware that many have pronounced our entry into a new epoch called the 'anthropocene,' 'plantationocene,' 'capitalocene,' but the whole of the holocene shows abundant evidence of anthropogenic effects on climate and environment, and thus it is more useful to see current developments with global heating, ocean acidification and siltation, etc. as merely an acceleration of processes visible throughout the holocene, and often tied to the simple act of igniting combustion.
2 For example, did the French or the English invent tinned food? The answer is that human cultural evolution and the availability of technology and knowledge made the invention of tinned food possible simultaneously in England and France.

DOI: 10.4324/9781003164593-17

(1977). The term also includes notions of class and lifestyle; the circles we move in both physically and socially. It is remarkable how well the human habitat has, throughout history, served the human animal in all these regards. Human activity and interaction, in fact, embellishes and ornaments our dwellings.

Yi-Fu Tuan (1990 [1974]) built a powerful sense of cultural identity and the love of place as *topophilia* which has helped to inform our contemporary understanding of landscape as a dialogue between people and their environment. A decade later E.O. Wilson (1990 [1984]) termed our affinity for other living things *biophilia*, and argued that this innate sense of interconnection is an aid to both our own evolution and that of many other species with whom we share the planet (although from a relatively traditional masculinist and anthropocentric standpoint). Contemporary theorists with intersectional and new materialist perspectives such as Donna Haraway (1988, 2016) and Anna Tsing (2015) have opened new avenues of thought that insist that humans should not just *love* nature but understand that they *are* nature as part of multi-species assemblages. These ideas, amongst others on parallel tracks, have allowed us to open out our understanding of civilization as a construction not just of the interdependence of humans in civil society in urban settings, but encompassing all life and all things. It could be surmised, in this case, that progress and improvement are inevitable.

A key problem that plagues us, however, is that of the 'shifting baseline syndrome,'[3] which militates against progress. This posits that each generation seeks to return to a golden age that is within memory. Thus the 'golden' age becomes ever brassier with each generation. My generation, for example, now romanticizes postindustrial landscapes. Humans now have incredible power to shape the face of the planet, our habitat, but it is possible that our vision of sustainability is progressively eroded. Perhaps this is just a new way of seeing the perennial balance between progress and entropy.

The place of the landscape professions now and in the future must be one in which we reinforce a positive and progressively more flourishing vision for our human habitat: one which strengthens our bonds to place, which brings city and country together in balance, and which benefits all species to the benefit of our own. Further, as the destructive processes of global heating and biodiversity loss continue to accelerate, so too will our human need to actively assist in the survival, and the design and maintenance, of whole ecosystems. The need for the landscape professions to be activist will only grow with each generation, indeed as organisms involved in the construction and maintenance of our habitat, every human animal is an activist.

This column was published in *Landscape*, Winter 2013.

---

3 This tendency was described but not yet named as such in Ian L. McHarg's *Design with Nature* (1992 [1969]: 67–70).

18

IT'S ABOUT TIME

The *genius temporum* of Martí Franch's Girona landscapes

"I really want to make the whole city like this," says Martí Franch of Estudi Martí Franch (EMF). His vision is for designing the green infrastructure of Girona, Spain, through a process of enlightened and engaged landscape management. We are sitting in his office, amongst shelves full of models and a table full of drawings. With us are Marc Rosdevall, landscape architect with the city of Girona and the project's director, and Marta Costa-Pau, a reporter from the local newspaper who is eager to report on the most recent transformations EMF's work has wrought on Girona, and, in an amusing bit of journalistic circularity, to interview me to find out why this work is of interest and important to an American journalist and his landscape architecture audience.

Girona is a small city in Catalonia with a population of roughly 100,000, situated in the rocky green foothills of the Catalonian Coastal Ranges and at the confluence of four small rivers. The landscape is typical scrubby Mediterranean maquis, studded with Stone Pines (*Pinus pinea*), Holm Oaks (*Quercus ilex*), and the inevitable and omnipresent formal Italian Cypresses (*Cupressus sempervirens*), which have an air of nervous, attendant stiffness in the loosely informal Catalonian landscape, like butlers at a barn dance. When I visit in late spring, there is a festival of flowers in the central city called the *Temps de Flors*. It's a mix of floral installations which range from the highly professional and artistic to the desperately tacky. However, in the spirit of spring, with the soft air at skin temperature, the rivers full of water, and the maquis replete with shades of fresh and fleshy greens on the hills above the honey-coloured stone of the old town, the exuberant bad taste is forgivable and welcome, even charming.

The town's generous web of green spaces reflects its topography, with concentrations of agricultural terraces on the hillsides, and the valleys between full of lush and wild plants all pushing into the densely built fabric of the town. It gently pushes back, curving into the green. All this gentle beauty belies a much less

DOI: 10.4324/9781003164593-18

idyllic history of the landscape's continual mistreatment. Girona's citizenry has not recently had a virtuous relationship with the land: "the forest is for violation and for dropping fridges," says Franch, referring to the long-standing problem of the regular dumping of building and household waste and appliances willy-nilly on the city's fringe. His goal is to reveal the beauty of the whole of Girona's landscape, opening up strategic views, providing access to the rivers, providing pathways and resting places, and, in doing so, encouraging the populace to value their surroundings more and creating a new relationship between the city and its surroundings. Even in the early stages of his project, he notes, there has been a visible reduction in the amount of dumping.

Beginning in September 2014, Franch embedded himself in processes of management across Girona, working closely with the city's landscape maintenance teams, known locally as "brigades," in particular with Jordi Batallé, the charismatic and energetic lead (*comisari*) for the brigades. Marc Rosdevall describes the early stages, in which his superiors decided they would humour Franch in what they assumed was a Quixotic journey. "My boss didn't expect much from Martí. 'Leave him alone and don't spend any money,' he said." Franch, inspired by the approaches exemplified by the work of Gilles Clément in France, wanted to generate design from a direct engagement with site. He doesn't see himself as a lone practitioner or a 'master'; rather, he works in an informed conversation with the ecology of his practice, the ecology of the site, and the ecology of ideas in the world of landscape architecture.

Gilles Clément, when describing his approach in his new book, *The Planetary Garden and Other Writings*, could be speaking for Martí Franch too:

> For a long time I gardened without clarifying my ideas. Nevertheless, there were plenty of standpoints: to conserve the diversity already present, to increase it, to utilize the energy inherent in the species, not to use opposing energies unnecessarily, and to end up with a pledge that I repeat as often as necessary: to do as much as possible with, and as little as possible against.
>
> *(2015: 144)*

Franch's work in Girona is healing, connective, and narrative (Figures 18.1, 18.2). The project can only loosely be called a masterplan. What he has created is a series of walking loops, itineraries, that knit Girona's neighbourhoods together, but these come together on the ground more than on the plan. "The final drawing is almost the as-built," says Franch. The work begins on site, to understand the topography, hydrography, viewsheds. With the maintenance brigades he begins an active process of clearing, mowing, pruning, and cleaning. "The main thing we do is subtraction," he says. Bearing in mind a framework of green infrastructure coaxed into presence by following the existing topography and river corridors, sites are cleared, trees are limbed up, and connections are made apparent. Only then, for the future management practice, is the work transferred to plan and section. In essence what is created is an action plan, not a masterplan.

FIGURE 18.1 The Can Colomer meadow before EMF's interventions made it a destination. Credit: Estudi Martí Franch.

A striking example of the approach is the "shore edge" project, on the bank of the River Ter opposite the historic centre of Girona (Figure 18.3). The district has had shady associations, appropriate to its formerly overgrown character, but it is now part of a legible riverside itinerary. Limbing up and clearing trees and shrubbery pulls the eye and the walker along the path with cool and luscious glimpses of the burbling river glinting in the sunlight. Where the path follows a ruler-straight maintenance road, glaringly paved in white gravel, there is now a parallel route that brings people into the space of the river. It is palpably cooler, shaded. The river becomes audible, a balm to the senses.

This path leads to a newly created beach. Since the river was dammed, the natural scouring action of the river ceased to expose it, but through a process of clearing and rototilling, a gentle forest beach, softly shaded, allows ample room for play and relaxation. For the festival of flowers, the *Temps de Flors*, a lifeguard's chair has been installed, a gleeful marker of the new mood introduced here, and a sprinkling of beach chairs adds colour and life. Many are occupied, even on our weekday visit. They're examples of what Franch calls "confetti," small, irregular site interventions that give visitors occasional reminders of the fact of design. These can be sculptures, furniture, stumps left for climbing, almost anything. Visitors themselves become confetti in this setting. We approach a man in a motorized wheelchair, which has negotiated the sand successfully. He greets us with pleasure, and speaks of his pride in how the space has been transformed and how his daily excursions here have

FIGURE 18.2 The Can Colomer meadow during its periodic mowing and maintenance. Credit: Estudi Martí Franch.

been improved. Equally important is his influence on the site, in which his regular presence serves as a daily marker of safety and comfort for others.

As we leave the shore edge, we pass a nightclub ('Pandora') advertising exotic dancers, indicative of the uses to which this neighbourhood had previously lent itself. The nightclub had opposed the improvements to the site, which included some loss of unsightly parking spaces along the river, but this year for the first time they have decked their balcony with flowers for the festival.

Franch's understated approach is not geared towards big wins—spending concentrated on visible central sites with sculptural and photogenic results, which are so often what politicians prefer to support, but it has captured the imagination of the area's politicians. We have lunch with Narcís Sastre, the Girona city councillor responsible for landscape and urban habitat, on the terrace at the Cul de Mon restaurant ('The Ass of the World'—just outside town), and he tells us his reaction to Franch's quiet, covert work. "When I first saw the meadows, I wondered what was happening. Once I knew, I wanted to spread it around the city." Since then, the city's mayor, Marta Madrenas i Mir, has also become a supporter. The 'big win' with Franch's designs is across the whole city and on every constituent's doorstep, or at least it will be once all the looping landscape itineraries are created. What politician could resist such immediate, inexpensive, and widespread impact? When I talk about how many small projects can add up to big things, Franch grins

FIGURE 18.3 Chairs provide a place to watch the drift of cottonwood fluff and the River Ter's flow. Credit: Estudi Martí Franch.

and corrects me, "This is not a series of small projects. It is the biggest project in Girona ever."

After lunch we climb from the valley to a hilltop overlooking Girona to see further interventions of the biggest project ever. Past a well-established and comfortably eclectic former favela, we come to signage indicating we are at the head of a 'water mine.' Franch has created an itinerary which includes its edge. The water mine is a curiosity—it is a horizontal well which follows the contour of an agricultural terrace. Along our route, the edge of the terrace is marked by the barrel-arched roof of the tunnel, punctuated with chimneys which I speculate may work in the manner of a qanat, using air pressure to push water along to augment the sluggish movement caused by the infinitesimally slight gradient.

Impressive views—postcard-worthy views—open to the city and cathedral below as we move from an olive orchard abutting the water mine up to higher terraces (Figure 18.4). A steely blue-black thunderhead has filled the sky on the other side of the valley below, so we enjoy the view only for a moment, and hurry back through a tunnel of Holm Oaks formed by yet more judicious pruning. Thunder and lightning and the crepuscular light of the tunnel draw attention to how the nature of the itinerary is shaped not merely by place, space, and movement, but also by shifts of time and weather that animate the space. Fat, cold raindrops begin to slap down on us.

FIGURE 18.4 View from a terrace on the Torre Gironella itinerary. In the foreground is the barrel arch of the water mine roof. Credit: Estudi Martí Franch.

Franch's management-based and hands-on methods have led him to try to find a new term analogous to *genius loci* that speaks of a deep understanding of diurnal and nocturnal cycles, weather, the seasons, and cycles of work and play framed by such markers as harvests and festivals. He suggests *genius tempi*, and I venture that *zeitgeist* fulfils at least part of that sense. We both like that each term contains time, presence of mind, spirits, and ghosts in their etymological derivations. Later, to find the right term, I ask the help of a friend, C.A.E. Luschnig, a classicist and etymologist. "Well," she tells me, "*tempi* is not correct. The genitive of *tempus* is *temporis*, *tempus* being a neuter noun of the third declension. Maybe *temporum* (the genitive plural) would work better. *Tempus* has a full range of meanings including season, lifetime, the times." This seems to crack the problem and to improve on it beyond our expectations—the term we were looking for was "the genius of time" but conceiving of time as plural and nested is even better. Thus to add to *genius loci*, we now have *genius temporum*, the genius of *times* (Figure 18.5).

There is genius, too, in Franch's propensity for action first and reflection alongside and after. He knows action is necessary, and his project is to learn by doing. There is no possibility of "analysis paralysis" because analysis, evaluation, design, and action are all part of the same impetus and bound up in the same nexus of energy. There is generative genius (or perhaps what Brian Eno calls 'scenius' (n.d.: n.p.)) in the collaboration, in the fact that the project's ownership, design, and management

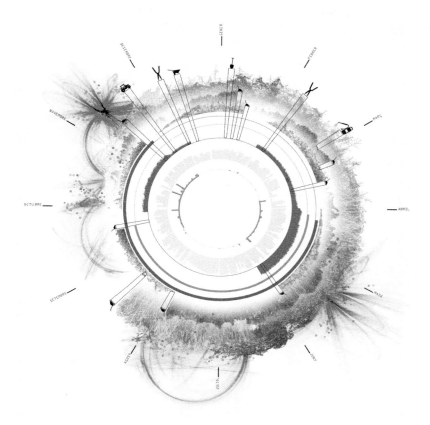

FIGURE 18.5 An annual diagram of maintenance including mowing and planting, growth of vegetation, sunlight hours, and other variables. Festivals, when maintenance brigades are busy, are shown as red sunspots. Credit: Estudi Martí Franch.

are distributed and shared. The collaboration and co-creation mean that the design is not a totalizing one, but that it is a set of ways of acting and shaping in accord with changing uses and ecologies over time, perhaps beyond the lifetimes of all concerned. There is genius, finally, in the project's tacit insistence that we must rethink the timescales, budgets, and commissioning of projects to embrace much more embedded and long-term practices of landscape management and design. Beyond the 'big win' there is something at once softer and sweeter, richer and grander, that can develop in the sets of relationships through which we build great cities. In Girona, the genius of the place and of times—*genius loci* and *genius temporum*—are conspiring to create the city as a work of landscape art for the ages.

This article was published in *Landscape Architecture Magazine* in January 2017.

19

DESPOT, MARTYR, AND FOOL

An obituary for the Garden Bridge

Sadiq Khan, the mayor of London, has switched off the life support (Walker, 2017) to London's embattled Garden Bridge (Figure 19.1), a tempestuous, contested, and deeply symbolic idea that will die tightly clutching a sheaf of contemporary perversions of the civic good, a cautionary portfolio of design's worst addictions.

Its life charts a course through the sordid world of politics and displays how the ambitions of the nation-state and the re-emerging city-state have uncoupled from democracy and attached to unplaceable global flows of power and money. The people are left helpless in a muddle of endless doubt, misinformation, threat, and the magical thrall of consumer glamour and celebrity pull. All this is held within the fading body of the Garden Bridge.

City skylines have become trophy cabinets of branded building concepts,[1] increasingly greenwashed to pull at the heartstrings of a populace that still largely wishes to see good done in the world. Although the Garden Bridge design lacked the space of the sky as isolating backdrop, which a branded skyscraper might have, it made up for it with the clean plane of the River Thames in a site chosen not for its dearth of transportation opportunities but for its eminently Instagrammable setting.

Its protagonist was the former mayor Boris Johnson, for whom it was another high-profile vanity project, like his cable car to nowhere (the "Dangleway," as it is known), and the awful red loopy thing (Figure 19.2) at the London Olympics (see Douglas Murphy, *Nincompoopopolis*, 2017). Johnson's habit is to say truly horrible things that represent his sinister ambitions (or prejudices), and then to chortle at them as if they were jokes, in a chummy, conspiratorial way that makes his audience feel like insiders (though they're clearly mugs). Thomas Heatherwick uses the same trick when speaking to the *Guardian* critic Oliver Wainwright in the early

---

1 Witold Rybczynski has written compellingly of this in his "The Franchising of Architecture" (2014).

DOI: 10.4324/9781003164593-19

FIGURE 19.1 Still from the Garden Bridge commercial showing the visualization of the bridge. Credit: Garden Bridge Trust.

FIGURE 19.2 The awful red loopy thing, a.k.a. the ArcelorMittal Orbit at the site of the London 2012 Olympic and Paralympic Games. Credit: Tim Waterman.

days of the design. Wainwright quotes him saying, "with a twinkle in his eye," "It feels like we're trying to pull off a big crime" (2014: n.p.). He has compared his design to guerrilla gardening, dubiously recruiting an edgy, idealist grassroots urban practice into his globalized brand. Heatherwick has been called the "Leonardo da Vinci of our times" by Terence Conran (Wroe, 2012), which is tragic not just for what it says about Conran's judgement, but for what it indicates about our times. High-concept gimmickry, branding, and spin are the new hallmarks of genius, as is whom you know, of course, but that, at least, has probably always been the case with so-called genius.

Heatherwick and the English actor and bridge booster Joanna Lumley have both hastened to the Garden Bridge's deathbed to declare the injustice of its consignment to the Tomb of the Unbuilt Project and to register their shock at its passing (Heatherwick, 2017). It did not die a natural death of public disapproval! No! It was killed by naysayers and philistines! And it was loved by what Lumley calls a "silent majority" (Morrison, 2017)!

In reality, it was a show of exuberant wastefulness against the black cloth of a cruel, calculated national policy of austerity. It also helped to bolster suspicions outside London that the city draws in wealth like a drain and spews it out again in showy geysers to the delight of a sweetly wettened metropolitan elite (Harris, 2014).

How will the Garden Bridge die? It will die a despot—unaccountable to opinion and the needs of the people. It will die a martyr—a symbol to the wealthy and powerful of how ungrateful the little people are for their benevolence and thus how, perhaps, they ought to disregard their feeble desires. It will die a fool, a folly—a leering Punch and Judy show to the sweeping drama of genuine and necessary civic endeavour.

But what can we learn from all this foolishness—so that this is not a tragic life lived in vain? That the whole debacle came this far shows that we might have a human predilection for showy waste, and that channelling it fruitfully and beautifully rather than damagingly is an important job for designers. That greenwash might be losing its power to persuade people of the environmental worthiness of projects, which means designers had better get serious quickly about building deep ecological value into their projects. That there is a growing public distaste for signature projects as urban baubles, and that civic and public value must be considered as a priority. That the architectures must work together to identify, create, and promote worthwhile projects, even to become their local developers. And, finally, that design education and practice must strive immensely to work with building projects that are not just viewed as objects and concepts, and to embrace, understand, and value context while striving for spatial justice.

The costly scandal of the Garden Bridge was brought to an end in April of 2017, when tens of millions of pounds had already been squandered. None of the perpetrators of this crime have ever been brought to justice. This 'obituary' was published online in *Landscape Architecture Magazine* in May of 2017.

20

NOTES FROM THE FIRST DAYS OF LONDON'S LOCKDOWN

The most noticeable thing before the lockdown was that a sense of threat had crept into every public encounter, and suspicion of contagion was pervasive. Three days in a row, out for a walk, I saw someone fall. First, an old man in a pork pie hat who fell against a bollard on Gerrard Street in Chinatown (Figure 20.1), still festooned with red lanterns for the Year of the Rat. Then outside the hoardings for the as-yet-unopened new entrance to Tottenham Court Road Underground station on Oxford Street, a young man was collapsed and unresponsive, being attended to by paramedics. In Covent Garden (Figure 20.2) an older woman fell, carrying a bag of medical supplies—a knee brace, possibly—and when my partner and I instinctively went to help, she held up both hands to keep us at bay. Now the government has shut down, for almost a week and indefinitely, pubs, restaurants, and shops, and has ordered people to stay at home except to shop for groceries or to exercise. People are still wary, but are much better at keeping to the rule of maintaining a two-metre distance from all others at all times. This is relatively easy to observe outdoors, but indoors it turns shopping into an odd, halting dance. But in London, where it is unheard of for people to speak to strangers in public, or even to make eye contact, both of these things are seen to happen daily.

My partner (who works in public health) and I live a stone's throw from Oxford Circus in central London, within easy walking distance of many of London's tourist sights: London Bridge and Borough Market are less than an hour's walk, Buckingham Palace is a half hour at a stroll, and it is ten minutes to either Regent's Park or Piccadilly Circus (Figure 20.3). The quarantine has changed our neighbourhood drastically. Living here, we never go to the places the tourists visit, and we have numerous strategic walking routes that allow us to skirt around the busiest areas. Now we can sashay through Carnaby Street or right past M&M's World in Leicester Square without seeing a soul—though we still avoid M&M's World

DOI: 10.4324/9781003164593-20

FIGURE 20.1 Lanterns in Chinatown. Credit: Tim Waterman.

FIGURE 20.2 Inigo Jones's St Paul's Church, Covent Garden. Credit: Tim Waterman.

FIGURE 20.3 Piccadilly Circus on a Friday night. Credit: Tim Waterman.

because even though it's closed it still smells of sugar and sick-up, like a birthday party at a nursery school, which of course is now also closed.

What this holiday from other people's holidays has shown us, though, is how hollowed out the city centre has become. There has been much talk and worry for years about the large number of empty apartments, bought as financial instruments (sometimes for money laundering) rather than as homes, and also about the proliferation of Airbnb listings turning whole apartment blocks into hotels, driving out residents, and driving up rents (see Minton, 2017). Soho, usually the epicentre of evening entertainment, licit and illicit, was empty of all but the occasional delivery bike or homeless person at 7:30 p.m. this Friday, and all the upstairs windows were dark. I want to say it was eerie, but it was somehow more than that: The sense of absence was transcendent, oceanic, existential.

Further evidence of this preternatural emptiness was on Thursday, when applause for the heroism of the National Health Service (NHS) workers was scheduled. While social media began to flood with live smartphone videos from the suburbs documenting the uproar as everyone leaned out their windows to clap, our neighbourhood was silent except for the occasional empty bus passing by, as lonely on these city streets as a long-distance truck on a desert highway on a winter night.

Only five minutes from us, on Broadwick Street, is another sort of epicentre, in this case the water pump to which John Snow mapped and traced the origin of a cholera outbreak in 1854: a reminder that epidemiology is a spatiotemporal science,

FIGURE 20.4 Just across from Pesthouse Close/Dufour's Place stands the John Snow pub—named for the physician and epidemiologist—and a replica of the pump from which he was able to trace a cholera epidemic in Soho. Credit: Tim Waterman.

and that testing, tracking, and mapping disease is the best way to control disease. Sadly, our government in Britain displays the same ideology of belief over knowledge and influence over expertise that is so much in evidence in bad government everywhere. It has opted instead for a course of action that will probably prolong the pandemic and further the damage to livelihoods.

Just off Broadwick Street, the Marshall Street Baths back onto an unprepossessing court, once the site of a quarantine for those stricken by the plague, and one of London's many plague pits where the bodies of the victims were unceremoniously dumped. Before the name was changed to Dufour's Place, the site was known as Pesthouse Close (Figure 20.4). Scratch London just a little, and what you'll find is sordid or insalubrious. It's worth reading Daniel Defoe's *A Journal of the Plague Year* (1995 [1722]) just to be reminded that bad government has always been bad government, and people have always reacted to a pandemic both with selflessness and abject criminal opportunism. Just as today, there were closures too, of "tippling" houses: "That disorderly tippling in taverns, ale-houses, coffee-houses, and cellars be severely looked unto, as the common sin of this time and greatest occasion of dispersing the plague" (ibid.: n.p.).

The other reminder we get from Defoe, just as spring weather and daffodils nodding in the park (Figure 20.5) beckon to us from our fusty interiors, is that the

FIGURE 20.5 Pelicans in St James's Park. Credit: Tim Waterman.

plague of 1665 was at its peak in July of that year, which means that there must have been many beautiful sunny days full of birdsong when humans were very busy with dying wretchedly.

This article was published online in *Landscape Architecture Magazine* as part of a series of pandemic lockdown dispatches from around the world in March 2020.

21

DURING AND AFTER THE PANDEMIC OUR STREETS NEED MORE DEMOCRACY

Where does democracy take place? Ask this question of many, and they will answer variously 'congress,' or 'parliament,' or, perhaps, 'the voting booth.' If, however, we take democracy in its truest sense, as the ability of people—all people in a given place—to govern themselves, then it is possible to view all given places in which people have a need to manage their affairs collectively as places in which democracy is practised. Practices are key: democracy, like equality, to paraphrase Jacques Rancière (1991: 137), is not a pre-existing quality to be drawn down from on high as a Platonic ideal, something given or claimed, but rather it exists only in our mutual conduct towards, and regard for, one another in the spaces in which life is lived.

Democracy is explicitly an orientation against forms of hierarchy or domination: against unaccountable forms of control such as absolute monarchies or oligarchies. Centralized forms of government (congress, parliament, etc.), though they may *call themselves* democracies, are always a tug-of-war between democracy and its opposites. Traditional battle lines between left and right on the political spectrum are often defined along the lines of 'public' and 'private,' but democracy may be practised anywhere, and forms of both public and private life can be seen to be undemocratic.

Let's look at the space of the street, and think of the street as a landscape—as a relation between people and place—a relation which is, in Kenneth R. Olwig's terms, a land*ship*, which holds the idea of mutualism and reciprocity as fully as does a term like 'friendship' or 'fellowship' (see Waterman et al., 2021). In the landship of the street, which may be legally either public or private, democracy is practised through mutual regard and civility, by responsibility of all *in place* and *for place*. The forms of behaviour in the street which are undemocratic are the ones which undermine the equality of citizens, who, for our purposes here, might be thought

DOI: 10.4324/9781003164593-21

of simply and reductively as citizens of the street, owing their allegiance only to the other citizens of the street.

For a citizen of the street, equality is something that is practised and mutually assured. I, as a tall, white man from a roughly middle-class background, could easily dress in a way that indicated status, and adjust my bearing to claim 'ownership' of the space of the street, 'taking my half out of the middle,' which is neither fair nor democratic. It is much more difficult for a person who is visibly part of a minority to do so, and it only takes a short time watching interactions on an ethnically or gender-mixed sidewalk to see this in action.

There are also inequalities between modes of transportation. In a giant sport utility vehicle, I am effectively an oligarch or monarch of the road, which is precisely why people buy them. On a bicycle I have the power to intimidate pedestrians, but I am seriously vulnerable to the prodigious Range Rover. It may well be that the only way to minimize the overwhelming impact of motorized transport on the landship of the street is to limit it to forms which are shared and low-speed, and which are confined to trackways, but this is a separate discussion.

What the COVID-19 pandemic has thrown into high relief, due to social distancing and the suddenly magnified need for pedestrian and bicycle space, is the vast amount of space given over to the kings of the road compared to the tiny slivers accorded to plebeian pedestrians, but also the need for rules of thumb for civility—and remember, a rule of thumb is a loose guide for behaviour which has the flexibility of custom rather than the rigidity of tradition.

When most cars have gone from the roads, all of the mechanisms for compliance and control in the street lose their significance: all those billions of litres of paint poured on the ground; one-way systems; pedestrian crossings; bike lanes; 'refuge islands'; traffic lights.[1] All meaningless, but what is evident, especially in Britain where I write, is the lack of rules of thumb for public behaviour.

I have asked many different kinds of audience in Britain the same simple question, the answer to which would clearly and simply be the first best answer to democratically managing social distancing in the street: 'What side of the pavement should you walk on?' I ask. Almost every audience is split in three, with one-third answering 'to the right,' one-third answering 'to the left,' and one-third answering 'there is no rule.' In fact, all of these answers are wrong. Britain's Highway Code asks pedestrians to walk on the outside of the footway if they are facing oncoming traffic (Department for Transport, 2007: 5).[2]

This would, in a world without one-way systems, mean everyone should keep left (Figure 21.1) to ensure the safety and comfort of others, thus practising reciprocity and equality, but effectively this advice is impossible to follow, and is further

1 For a superb history of how the car came to dominate the street, see Peter D. Norton's *Fighting Traffic* (2011).
2 For a far more detailed essay on this topic, see my essay "Publicity and Propriety: Democracy and Manner's in Britain's Public Landscape" (2017), and for another short but sweet piece, see "Pedestrian Etiquette, Gormless Phone Users, and the Rise of the Meanderthal" (2014).

FIGURE 21.1 London Bridge on the last day of May 2020 shows multiple messy layers of design for compliance and control, from construction fencing and other temporary barriers to 'temporary' anti-terrorist barriers, and painted lines to manage pandemic distancing for virus control.

confused by the Highway Code's direction for pedestrians to keep right on roads with no marked footway: this, in fact, is in many cases wrong, as in practice it is best to walk where one is most visible, which might mean multiple road-crossings on a curvy byway.

Even more confusingly, some towpaths, for example, have rules all their own, or the London Underground will direct people to walk either right or left in their tunnels.

Thus, for more democratic post-pandemic streets, the following recommendations may be made:

- Provide *substantially* more space for pedestrians and bicycles and many more streets dedicated only for pedestrian and bicycle use (this does not mean providing bike lanes, which requires pouring more paint on the ground and more compliance and control, but simply providing plenty of space for bike riders and pedestrians to negotiate the space).
- Eliminate one-way systems for motorized vehicles (see Gayah, 2012).
- Eliminate, wherever possible, motorized personal transportation—cars and trucks/4X4s—in favour of shared forms of motorized transportation.

- Seek a rule of thumb, to keep to one side of a footway generally, following the customary flow of traffic (in Britain, to the left, in the rest of Europe, to the right, for example).
- Work to make all aware that all have a just and equal place in the landship of the street, where mutual regard should also be a rule of thumb.

This article was published in a series of pandemic dispatches from 2020 called 'Covid Thoughts' on the Landscape Research Group's *Landscape Exchange*.

22

A WORD... 'INEVITABLE'

There are so many things in the world that we have come to believe are inevitable and upon which, because of their apparent certainty, we can comfortably base our arguments. These inevitabilities can be quasi-mystical, such as the 'invisible hand' of the market, homely but ominous aphorisms like the one about 'death and taxes,' or political expedients with hidden profit motives for the elites, such as the 'need' for austerity politics. One of Margaret Thatcher's slogans that still rules us today was TINA—'There Is No Alternative'—which tried to present the resurgence of cynical winner-takes-all monopoly capitalism, championed by her government, as inevitable. Austerity politics is just the most recent incarnation of this particular agenda. This also set up the now-familiar equation of hope and idealism with immaturity.

I have seen countless presentations in recent years that have based their arguments about landscape and urbanism on a couple of assumptions presented as inevitable which are certainly not, and which bear examination. The first is that human population will continue to grow, and the second is that the forces of urbanization are everywhere relentless and permanent. These 'inevitabilities' are then presented as the bases for planning and policy from all scales, local to global.

The one thing that's actually certain about both of these factors, though, is their very uncertainty. The four horsemen of the apocalypse are always saddled up and ready to ride roughshod over population growth, and we might witness a 're-ruralization' of populations for any number of reasons, from high property prices driving people out of world cities like London and New York, for example, or perhaps a scenario in which people have to return to working the land because of a need for more labour-intensive methods resulting from such true inevitabilities as the exhaustion of finite resources in agriculture.

The other thing we forget to bear in mind is that human populations and their geographic distribution are not just the basis for planning and policy, but are also

DOI: 10.4324/9781003164593-22

rightfully the *subject* of planning and policy in and of themselves—and planning the most destructive, wasteful, carbon-intensive populations of the world into decline should be a top priority.

I believe now that, in Britain as elsewhere, we need to begin to push back against these 'inevitabilities.' If urbanization continues to empty our countryside, decisions there about how land is used will increasingly come to be made by the landed gentry and/or huge agribusiness concerns with no stake in places other than for productivity, efficiency, and as financial instruments (or, in the case of the gentry, as a scenic backdrop for shooting). And rural areas need to be populated by people with a stake in, and stewardship of, the land so that those areas are ecologically healthy, fulfilling, convivial, and supportive places to live.

We also need to reverse the process of Britain's North emptying out into the Southeast, and that will take prolonged efforts to ensure there are strong local economies, pleasant places, and meaningful work everywhere. This will take local planning, design, and funding everywhere—and small local landscape practices of all sorts, from ecological to architectural, everywhere too. We must replace the inevitability of austerity politics with the emergence of a hopeful and positive *prosperity politics* for city and country, north and south. Hope and idealism, far from being immature, are hallmarks of a sane and mature society. What we should make inevitable are prosperity, well-being, and the creation of great places everywhere and for everyone.

This column was published in *Landscape*, Summer 2015.

23

TWO LONDON SQUARES AND A THEORY OF THE BEIGE HOLE

Two new squares (POPS—privately owned public spaces) have appeared in a very fine-grained part of London's historic West End. They reflect the processes, and are products of, development and real estate speculation in a wildly distorted market; of place and non-place, and taste and non-taste. The first project, completed in 2016, is GROSS.MAX.'s design for Fitzroy Place, and the second is Gustafson Porter + Bowman's Rathbone Square, completed in September 2017. These two squares are only a block apart, though "block" is a term that doesn't quite apply to the irregular knot of streets that is characteristic of the area. A further complicating factor is me. I live a block away from Fitzroy Place and two blocks from Rathbone Square, and as a landscape architect, urbanist, and resident of the area, I have some fairly strong opinions.

Rathbone Square and Fitzroy Place (so named because there is already a Rathbone Place and a Fitzroy Square) are both developments that are responding directly to market forces. They are, as Carol Willis (1995) suggests, results of the fact that "form follows finance." Each plays games with elevations and massing to hide its excessive bulk and deep, dark floor plates. Fitzroy Place even went through the acrobatics of hiring two architects (Sheppard Robson and Lifschutz Davidson Sandilands) to provide differentiation between the blocks. In both cases the distribution of the buildings on the site and their massing were determined by the architects, with the landscape architects brought in later in the process.

In each, no expense is spared on the landscape, as these landscapes are what will drive the sales of the apartments on overseas speculative markets, along with images of the interiors. All aspects of the design are geared towards their imageability on real estate websites and in glossy brochures. Wainwright doesn't pull any punches when I talk to him about the developments: They are "the kind of generic could-be-anywhere development that sucks the life out of Fitzrovia," he said. "The developer claims to be giving back to the public, by opening up a space in the centre of

DOI: 10.4324/9781003164593-23

the site that has long been off-limits, but the residual canyons have clearly only been designed as a 'visual amenity' for the well-heeled residents above—it is not the kind of space where anyone would want to dwell." Of the development at Fitzroy Place, he says it feels like "a bleak promotional computer-generated image."

I also spoke with Anna Minton, a journalist and the author of the recent *Big Capital: Who is London For?* (2017) and *Ground Control: Fear and Happiness in the Twenty-first-century City* (2009). She agrees. "Fitzroy Place and Rathbone Square are the sort of developments that are ripping the heart and soul out of London. There is nothing about this sterile, privately owned, high-security enclave that connects it to the wider area—it could be a high spec development anywhere in the world." Indirectly, Eelco Hooftman of GROSS.MAX. acknowledges as much. "The market has changed," he says. "All the public work in London now is with private clients." And further, "Landscape is a commodity."

Of course, it can be argued that landscape has always been a commodity—certainly when it is employed as the scenography of power and private wealth, as it has so often been. It is an irony, though, at a time when our profession is more focused than ever on themes of sustainability and ecology and social benefit, that the most lucrative work for Britain's best landscape practices is rooted elsewhere—and nowhere. The scenography of contemporary capital demands a virgin space, a "friction free space" (Spencer, 2016: 1) so that its business logic is not disrupted by the ethical obligations that the real city demands. Zygmunt Bauman puts it well in his essay "City of Fears, City of Hopes": that the goal of such development is "to raze to the ground the old quarters of the city; to dig up a black hole in which old meanings sink and disappear, first from view and soon after from memory, and to fill the void with brand new logic, unbound by the worries of continuity and relieved from its burdens" (2003: 10).

Fitzrovia

The neighbourhood of Fitzrovia fails to appear, for the most part, on most people's mental maps of London, which might seem surprising once one finds out just how central it is. It is bounded on the west by genteel Marylebone, on the east by leafy Bloomsbury, on the north by the thundering Euston Road, and to the south by all the hubbub of Oxford Street and Soho. It has, in the past, been known as North Soho,[1] and briefly in the 1930s, as the Old Latin Quarter (see Chancellor, 1930), but since the 1940s it has taken its name from the Fitzroy Tavern on Charlotte Street. Fitzrovia is a fancy sounding name, but the Fitzroy Tavern (still standing) is a good emblem for the neighbourhood and its history.

---

1 Real estate agents and developers have also tried to re-brand the area as 'Noho,' which residents find galling, and which makes little etymological sense—New York's Noho derives from the contraction 'North of Houston (street)' and Soho from 'South of Houston.' London's Soho is said to derive from a hunting cry, 'so—hooooo'!

The Fitzroy Tavern sits on a corner of Charlotte Street, which has long been home to exotic restaurants, and which has even longer been home to artists, artisans, actors, writers, socialists and anarchists, gays and lesbians, immigrants, and, as the town planner Nick Bailey notes in his book *Fitzrovia*, "the eccentric and impecunious" (1981: 8). Bailey goes on to comment that the area has always been marginal though at the heart of the West End. "The explanation for this must lie in the way the area was developed—mainly by piecemeal speculation over many years—and the resulting medley of different ownerships, tenancies, and leaseholders" (ibid.: 8).

The philosopher Walter Benjamin could have been speaking of Soho and Fitzrovia when he writes, with Asja Lacis, of the dense, fine-grained urban landscape of the city in the title of his famous essay "Naples" that "Building and action interpenetrate in the courtyards, arcades, and stairways. In everything, they preserve the scope to become a theatre of new, unforeseen constellations. The stamp of the definitive is avoided. No situation appears intended forever, no figure asserts it 'thus and not otherwise.' This is how architecture, the most binding part of the communal rhythm, comes into being here." Like Soho and Fitzrovia, Naples is "anarchic, embroiled, village-like in the center," (Benjamin and Lacis, 1996 [1925]: 416) and all its nooks and crannies were haunts for a who's who of nineteenth- and twentieth-century luminaries: Karl Marx, Peter Kropotkin, Oscar Wilde, Arthur Rimbaud, Aleister Crowley, Dylan Thomas, Virginia Woolf, Quentin Crisp, Roger Waters, Siouxsie Sioux.

Fitzrovia's urbanism is both the result of, and the reason for, its particular sociality. Everywhere different floors of the same building yield space for different uses: a tailor or a lampshade maker below street level under a mansion block; a studio over an embroiderer over a café. Tiny mews streets filled with workspaces are capped at their ends with cosy pubs that become raucous as Friday approaches. The scale and grain of the area is changing fast, though, as it 'modernizes' (Figures 23.1, 23.2).

The beige holes of modernization

Robert Fitch, in his *The Assassination of New York*, wrote of the postindustrial city that it "is a mutation masquerading as a modernization" (1993: 235). The industrial city in the *extensive phase* of capitalism, in which labour, resources, and thus 'surplus' wealth were extracted from far-flung empires and agricultural hinterlands, could afford the illusion of 'inevitable' progress. Earlier a more agrarian extensive capitalism had declared vast stretches of land "empty"—as *terra nullius*—to justify colonialism, simply erasing lives and cultures in the process. The Jeffersonian grid is an emblem of that ideology of emptiness. Now the postindustrial city is driven by *intensive* capitalism, which is forced to transform itself from within, shaping itself around markets and services that cannibalize the city.

Asset stripping in colonialism gridded vast territories, mapping them for exploitation. Now cities are turned inward, and the new *terra nullius* must be found within. All the nooks and crannies necessary to everyday life in urbanism are ironed out, and the Jeffersonian grid manifests itself as vast floor plates: office space and lateral

FIGURE 23.1 Fitzrovia's nooks and crannies: Glorious Arts and Crafts in polychrome brick; Colville Place, one of many soulful narrow streets; once the haunt of George Orwell and Dylan Thomas, the Wheatsheaf caps a working mews street. Credit: Tim Waterman.

FIGURE 23.2 More views of Fitzrovia: Newman Passage, just north of the new Rathbone Square; an old lampshade maker's sign on Whitfield Street; the BT Tower is visible along Charlotte Place. Credit: Tim Waterman.

apartments. The ideology rationalizing these tyrannical spaces visualizes them as 'open,' 'democratic,' and 'free' 'spaces of engagement' just as the colonial grid was spuriously theorized as a guarantor of spatial equity. As the grid of extensive capitalism worked a mutation upon rural land, so the grid of intensive capitalism now skews the space of the city. As Darwin saw, however, mutation rarely actually leads to evolution.

The urban spaces within which these vast grids are being realized are a phenomenon I have come to think of as 'beige holes.' Like black holes in the universe, they have the power to attract, compress, and trap money in the financial system as black holes consume all matter in their supergravity. Beige, though, because driven by real estate imageability they must be styled to be sleek, tidy, and generic; currency which, like the Euro, must be all things to all people and therefore nothing. Beige because they reflect the non-tastes of the elites in the FIRE (finance, insurance, real estate) sector. Beige because they must place the power of the transaction over local distinctiveness. Realtors and developers themselves call these places 'safe-deposit boxes in the sky' or 'concrete gold,' which clarifies their function as financial instruments rather than as places for living, working, or playing, or for dwelling.

A whole generation of architects and landscape architects has, as students, read Marc Augé's book-length essay *Non-Places*,[2] and yet they find themselves trapped in a system that endlessly replicates the model. The non-place is defined as a place of transit, a space that defies acts of dwelling, and is exemplified by the modern airport. "The space of non-place creates neither singular identity nor relations; only solitude, and similitude" (1995: 103). "Since non-places are there to be passed through, they are measured in units of time" (ibid.: 104).

The beige hole is a type of non-place—a place of transit. In this case the beige hole is a place of transient wealth and of money in transit—the units of time with which these spaces are measured are amortized in mortgages, counted in leasehold years, in annual contracts, in fluctuations of boom and bust. They are the relics of a financial system in which transience itself is the operative factor. If money in the current system ever stopped for long enough, it would only take a moment's examination to discover its value is baseless and placeless, a fiction in motion, of motion. As Augé says, "the user of a non-place is in contractual relations with it (or with the powers that govern it)," and these contracts are temporal (ibid.: 101). Beige holes are non-places that exist as records of transactions and contracts, as intangible and impermanent as flickering numbers on a stock market screen.

Fitzroy Place

"Certain projects should not shout," says Eelco Hooftman of GROSS. MAX. landscape architects as he and his partner Nigel Sampey show me the small site at the centre of the large new development at Fitzroy Place in London's Fitzrovia. "This is not a statement project." Indeed, it is luxurious understatement as a cipher for a certain moneyed sophistication and the financialized non-taste that characterizes the project. I have written scathingly about the architectural style of these developments in the past, which the architecture critic Owen Hatherley has described as "pseudomodernism," (2010: xix–xx) and which I have derided as blang—a mix of bland and bling (see Chapter 3). Hatherley is careful but broad with his definition. Pseudomodernism is:

2 Augé seems to have fallen from favour amongst architects in recent years, probably due to the fatigue caused by over-citation. Much in the essay is superfluous to architects to be sure, as it engages heavily with squabbles internal to anthropology. The short section, though, in which Augé gets to the meat of the argument, still remains an important tool for thinking and was once a bellwether of postmodern structures of feeling.

postmodernism's incorporation of a Modernist formal language. Pseudomodernism has several elements. The cramped speculative blocks marketed as 'luxury flats' or 'stunning developments', with their attenuated, vaguely Scandinavian aesthetic; the glass towers whose irregular panels, attempting to alleviate the standardized nature of such buildings, have been dubbed 'barcode façades'; and most of all, the architecture spectacles generated by 'signature' designers.

(Ibid.: xx)

Fitzroy Place, launched in 2016, is a major full-city-block development in the style damned by Hatherley as pseudomodernism, exemplifying his first two categories. It sits on the 3.2-acre site of the former Middlesex Hospital, where many Fitzrovians both came into the world and left it (those leaving it including Rudyard Kipling and Peter Sellers). It is now home to Estée Lauder's London office and some of London's most expensive apartments, starting at about £1 million for a one-bed-room flat (in Britain, price is calculated more by number of bedrooms than by square footage).

All that is left of the hospital is an exquisite chapel by the architect John Loughborough Pearson (designed 1891, completed 1929), and a street-length façade along the west side of the site, both exhibiting on their exteriors the very high-quality bricks, brickwork, and stone and stonework lavished on early twentieth-century public projects in London. The chapel juts into the new square, but because it is so dwarfed by the scale of the surrounding buildings, it was clearly not possible to use it as the square's focal point. A Cor-Ten steel colonnade and pergola, developed by GROSS.MAX. with the architects Lifschutz Davidson Sandilands, helps

FIGURE 23.3 The landscape design at Fitzroy Place faced a huge challenge to step down the scale from the massive buildings to the precious chapel. Credit: Tim Waterman.

to step down the scale of the surrounding buildings to the chapel. Then the chapel is shrouded behind a screen of evergreen *Magnolia grandiflora* trees. A stone sculpture (*The One and the Many* by Peter Randall-Page), suggesting a Neolithic standing stone, and etched with polyglot lettering, echoing the Rosetta stone housed at the nearby British Museum, serves to refocus the square, while further stepping the scale down to the human. These are deft tricks, exercising the designers to new levels of virtuosity, but to ends that could have been avoided earlier in the design process (Figure 23.3).

The plantings in the square have suffered since they were installed, and this may be the result of further tricks by the architects to appease the planners or the clients. It is my hunch that renderings of sun and shade might have been overly optimistic, and that the physic-garden plants chosen to reflect the site's medical history simply aren't getting enough sun. The plants that have flourished most are graceful multi-trunk *Amelanchier lamarckii*, which have been placed in giant gunmetal-grey containers on the pedestrian lanes that serve the square (Figure 23.4). These receive angular shafts of light longer into the afternoon. Elegant as they are, their body language is aggressive. They are placed as obstacles, as effective deterrents, as beefy bouncers to physical and visual access into the site from the surrounding neighbourhood. This is a clear statement that the pretensions to publicness expressed in the planning applications were the usual whitewash.

FIGURE 23.4 Planters crowd the entrances at the north of the square at Fitzroy Place. Credit: Tim Waterman.

Rathbone Square

Rathbone Square (Figure 23.5), just completed in 2017, has become the new London headquarters for Facebook as part of a mixed commercial/residential complex. Its central gated square was designed by Gustafson Porter + Bowman, and the surrounding buildings by Make Architects. The square, like Fitzroy Place, opens up important east–west pedestrian access in an area with a pronounced north–south grain. Here no beloved community building was cleared to create the site; rather, a grim postal sorting office and a barbed-wire-frilled parking lot were the pre-existing condition. It was a palpable relief when they were demolished.

Here the gravest planning error was committed early on, with a failure to provide a direct east–west pedestrian connection at the very north of the site that would have created ease of passage for locals as well as new small retail possibilities. Instead, the route jogs south, frustrating access in the same way the *Amelanchier* planters do at Fitzroy Place, and the passage is constricted through verdigris-green ceramic-clad gated tunnels. These do have the effect of squeezing the visitor just a bit so that the square appears to open out generously after they issue forth into the space. Inside the space, the building massing is more successful than at Fitzroy Place. The buildings step down to allow generous light in from the south, so the prognosis for both the success of the plantings and the square's actual and emotional warmth is better.

Donncha O Shea, who along with Mary Bowman designed the square, spoke proudly of the oblong rectangular fountains that organize two of the entrances to the square. "They celebrate the entrances and pull people in with the reflections and the sound of water." Gustafson Porter + Bowman may well be the finest designers

FIGURE 23.5 Lawn and bench curve into one another to provide informal space for lounging and interaction below the new Facebook headquarters at Rathbone Square. Touching the fountain is nearly irresistible. Credit: Tim Waterman.

with water in Britain, and these fountains are no exception. Each was tested extensively. "You have to test water—you can't wait for day one," says O Shea. Testing began with foam and moved to stone, "each time becoming more real." Visitors to the square reflexively dabble their fingers in the placid water as they pass, and it sheets elegantly down the fountains' convoluted stone sides.

Seating is similarly refined, stepping up and down at right angles to provide a maximum of sittable space and defining a dark grid against the light grid of the Canadian granite paving that establishes a rhythm with the building's façades. Here, though, the richness of the square's materials is at odds with the building cladding, which, as does the cladding at Fitzroy Place, appears to be stretched as thinly as cling film across the surface of the buildings. Windows are set into metallic panels at Rathbone Square that possess the dull lustre of a disposable aluminium turkey pan.

At the centre of Rathbone Square, curving into the edge of Facebook's offices, a crescent of lawn has been provided. Lawn is *de rigueur* in London squares, and in heritage squares is often a statutory requirement. Here it is intended as a catalyst for activity. "Private squares in London don't support actual activity," says O Shea, and time will tell whether Rathbone Square, with its alluring water features, actually comes to serve as a community space or whether it merely serves as a place for the building's workers to perch at lunch.

A world less beige

I hope I have not portrayed GROSS.MAX. and Gustafson Porter + Bowman as villains or failures. They are neither. Indeed, they are two of Britain's most illustrious landscape architecture practices, stuffed to bursting with talent, ambition, and verve. If there is villainy or failure, it is systemic, and bred in the bone of development processes that are conceived of first and foremost as extractive and profit-driven. These forces also militate against artistry and urbanism, catering to generic international non-tastes and imageable outputs. William Morris, whose famous furnishing company was located near Fitzrovia on several sites, diagnosed the same problems in his time in *Hopes and Fears for Art*, and the words are still true: "Only we must not lay the fault upon the builders, as some people seem inclined to do: they are our very humble servants, and will build what we ask for; remember, that rich men are not obliged to live in ugly houses, and yet you see they do; which the builders may be well excused for taking as a sign of what is wanted" (1882: n.p.).

If we want a world less peppered with beige holes, then we will have to work with other professions and political and economic processes to transform development. There is hope here, with cooperation and communication improving year-on-year between architects, planners, and landscape architects, and with new models for development emerging in forms such as community land trusts. Then, perhaps, we can begin to make our cities more in ways that are genuinely wanted by those who authentically live in them.

This article was published in *Landscape Architecture Magazine* in July 2018.

24
A WORD… 'STORYTELLING'

This year's Serpentine Pavilion (Figure 24.1), by Bjarke Ingels Group, was welcomed with descriptions in the architectural press of Ingels as 'the king of one-liners.' A good one-liner (in comedy, that is) involves a pithy statement, usually that skews a simple situation or idea with a pun, a *non sequitur*, or perhaps that exotic-sounding bit of wordplay, the paraprosdokian: "I've had a perfectly wonderful evening, but this wasn't it," or comedian Mitch Hedberg's famous quip, "I used to do drugs. I still do, but I used to too." A good one-liner in architecture, presumably, would remix spatial tropes surprisingly, perhaps, to comic effect. There is good reason to believe that the architectural one-liner is most suitable to an ephemeral building such as the Serpentine Pavilion. Once uttered, a one-liner doesn't stand up very long. One-liners are hardly ever appropriate to landscape, with the exception of very ephemeral landscapes such as those of the major flower shows such as Chelsea, Chaumont, or Métis. True landscapes—the ones that people live in—offer layered, nuanced, complex narratives with plots, subplots, and sub-subplots. Apologies for the pun on 'plots.' That's clearly enough with the one-liners.

A one-liner goes down well these days, though, especially in social media, where a single arresting image and 140 characters of text[1] are absolutely key to communicating and promoting a project. But what works for buildings is simply too reductive for any landscape project worth its salt. We need to find a 'narrative hook' to jar the reader and engage them with a complex act of storytelling that will follow. "Septimus, what is carnal embrace?" is the opening line of Tom Stoppard's play *Arcadia* (1993: 1). We want to know more—and any Stoppard fan will know that what follows is layered, nuanced, complex, probably carnal, and will require their full attention.

---

1 When this article was written, the maximum length for a 'tweet' on the social media platform Twitter was 140 characters.

DOI: 10.4324/9781003164593-24

FIGURE 24.1 BIG's Serpentine Pavilion in Hyde Park in London, 2016. An architectural one-liner. Credit: MartineDF/Shutterstock.

If there is one characteristic that award-winning landscape projects, unlike many architecture projects, usually display, it is the quality of storytelling, and probably also the employment of a narrative hook. Awards judges need to understand the story of a project, and why it is worthy, as quickly and efficiently as possible. The practices that consistently win also happen to be consistently good storytellers who use words and images together most effectively. Now, some of them (though not as many as one might suspect) also have PR people to help with this, but this should not deter those without such resources from giving it their best try.

Awards are not just about communicating the best work of a profession to the world; they also serve as a moment when designers can all communicate with each other. Further, they offer an opportunity for designers to sit down and figure out what important messages from their work need to get out to the rest of the profession and the world at large. This is really crucial for everyone to sit down and do at least annually—what is the year's story? That time to take stock and communicate what we do is particularly important when justifying our work from day to day. Everyone, particularly in the beleaguered public sector, who needs good storytelling more than any other, needs to figure out how to find the time to enter for the awards. The reward will be greatest in everyday work, and in everyone's understanding that it is part of a necessary story.

And finally, another thing about communicating—I spoke to a friend at a major practice who had finished what I think was a superb project, and very simple. By thinking (beautifully) through some problems of parking and pedestrian access, they had utterly transformed a whole small town. Their award entry didn't manage to get that simple message across, though, and the judges were frankly a bit dismissive. I think a lot of public sector work probably falls into this category—nothing whizzy and sparkling, but a lot of earnestly good stuff that is hugely transformative for people's (and other species') everyday lives. These projects all have a narrative hook somewhere that can be exploited to good effect.

This column was published in *Landscape*, Winter 2016.

25

NATIONAL PROGRESS

Who are we? Where are we from? Where are we going? How will we get there? These are all questions lurking within the idea of national progress, and progress always implies a forward direction towards a goal, a *telos*, and technology is usually the tool to get us there. William Morris, in his utopian novel *News from Nowhere or, An Epoch of Rest* (1993 [1890]), imagined this goal to be a withering away of the state (he was a socialist, but not necessarily always a *state* socialist), and a mutual and pleasurable management of all affairs without the domination of government. Famously, he envisioned that the Palace of Westminster in the future would be used for storing dung: clearly a punitive downcycling form of adaptive reuse, and, of course, a symbolic home for what he saw was the primary product of governments, bullshit.

If we see technology in its broadest terms, as the application of a system to a task or set of tasks, then it is possible to see both nations and buildings (including those at Westminster) as technologies or means. Systems and technologies are mesmerizing, and mastery of them deeply satisfying and engrossing. Thus, it is easy for them to become worlds unto themselves, bounded and complete, ends rather than means. Questions of government become questions of procedure and policy rather than equality and emancipation, and questions of architecture are framed in terms of procurement, practice, and construction rather than the classic Vitruvian ideals of firmness, commodity, and delight.

The ideals Morris and others of his time were cooking up (including Ebenezer Howard, Peter Kropotkin, Edward Carpenter, Emma Goldman, Patrick Geddes—not all of them architects or landscape planners (see Ryley, 2013))—were dreams of whole life economies; how whole community and individual lives could be wholly lived in whole, flourishing places. The task was to bring together head, heart, hand, and land: Geddes sought the encouragement of 'insurgent life' (1885: 27). Before the hard political boundaries of the twentieth century had formed as ideological

DOI: 10.4324/9781003164593-25

schisms and concrete walls, the anarchists, socialists, and a broad range of other radicals were discussing an insurgency in which they all had a stake. The Paris Commune, author of its own unique form of socialism and victim of massacre in 1871, had not died without releasing the ideal of communal luxury into the world, and this was the egalitarian, emancipatory framework for shared human and planetary flourishing in which the forms of garden cities and green belts as planning tools (or technologies) would emerge.

The green belt is an example of how these grand dreams have progressively been stripped down. From the view of a planner's, politician's, or developer's map, it is merely empty space. From both a radical perspective and a landscape perspective, with a goal of insurgent life and life economies, it is empty not of buildings and development, but of all the rich layers of use, belonging, and conviviality it might contain. And what is humanity's great project if not conviviality? Green belts are not just technologies, tools, or mapping strategies. They are also landscapes that demand convivial practices of dwelling and meaningful, productive, interesting use. They need life to surge up within them.

All technologies, from smartphones to planning frameworks to buildings, need to be detached from the worlds they create unto themselves and reconnected with larger practices of dwelling. Our lives have become arenas of permanent destructive revolution ('disruption,' restructuring, 'flexibility' meaning precarity, gig economies), and instead we need insurgencies that rise up from within, holding together those things that are truly of value while transforming all that is malign. Technologies must be bent upon the convivial, upon belonging, upon connecting to landscape. And national progress? The technology of the nation should always be working to minimize its own self-absorption and to prepare us all for finding conviviality in the substantive landscapes in which we dwell: the real towns, cities, countrysides, watersheds, bioregions, and continents to which we belong. The technology of nations should drive progress towards landscape citizenships and towards their own obsolescence.

This short piece was written at the request of a student for the Bartlett School of Architecture's 2018 Unit 11 studio publication, *National Reserve*.

26

THE TASTY CITY

Democratic life and the education of desire

> *People ask me: Why do you write about food, and eating and drinking? Why don't you write about the struggle for power and security, and about love, the way others do?*
>
> *They ask it accusingly, as if I were somehow gross, unfaithful to the honor of my craft.*
>
> *The easiest answer is to say that, like most other humans, I am hungry. But there is more than that. It seems to me that our three basic needs, for food and security and love, are so mixed and mingled and entwined that we cannot straightly think of one without the others. So it happens that when I write of hunger, I am really writing about love and the hunger for it, and warmth and the love of it and the hunger for it [...] and then the warmth and richness and fine reality of hunger satisfied [...] and it is all one.*
>
> (Fisher, 2004 [1943]: 353)

This essay is about food and landscape, both of which, as M.F.K. Fisher shows in her intermingling of food and care and place, are ways of talking about almost everything. It is also about utopias, which are tools for thinking about whole worlds, and the all-at-onceness of everything—processes of worlding. The concept of landscape, as it has been enlarged and enriched in the last few decades (see, amongst many others, Cosgrove (1998 [1984]); Council of Europe (2000); Cronon (1996); Olwig (2019, 2005, 2002); Watt (2016)), now allows a mode of thinking far beyond its once-scenographic connotations to embrace the simultaneous and interdependent existence of cities, suburbia, countryside, and wilderness: landscape speaks of relations between processes and forces involving the human, the more-than-human, the climatic, the inorganic, and more. Landscape thinking, as a tool for worlding, has become an ally of utopian thinking. Food, also ubiquitous and embroiled in every aspect of organic life, figures large in the (human) landscape, from its production in the countryside, its processing, its purchase in streets and markets, and its

DOI: 10.4324/9781003164593-26

preparation and consumption in homes and restaurants. People's associations with one another and with the spaces they occupy are conducted in landscapes and over tables, and many of the metaphors and metonyms with which meaning and our human experiences are described are drawn from these interactions: companion-ship, for example, as I mention in Chapter 7, is to break bread together. Food tells the story of humanity and how people build and dwell in and with landscapes. It is in these relationships that we humans everywhere must look to find our dearest hopes; our ambitions for ourselves, our families, our communities, our societies; ultimately the inevitable striving for paradise in the forms of utopias or arcadias or both. It is not possible to talk about food without talking about hunger, taste, and appetite, nor indeed to talk about cities and landscapes without also addressing these drives. I will argue that they must also be taken into account when we discuss utopias, or perhaps that utopias are precisely the focuses and drives of desires aimed at transforming the future.

Liveable cities are shaped by appetite and desire, not by hunger. Gaston Bachelard's assessment of the human condition applies as much to the city as it does to individ-uals and their communities: "The conquest of the superfluous gives us greater spir-itual excitement than the conquest of the necessary. Man is a creation of desire, not a creation of need" (1964: 16). Pierre Mayol applies the same observation directly to the city, in particular the "practice of the neighbourhood" which "introduces gratuitousness instead of necessity; it favours a use of urban space whose end is not only functional" (de Certeau et al., 1998: 13). The city that only answers hunger is the most spartan and desultory machine for living. Hunger is dearth, an aching lack which springs from the poison well of poverty. Hunger drives the need to fill the gap with whatever is handy, and it need not even be nutritious. Tales of famine are filled with descriptions of eating shoe leather and cannibalism (Morell-Hart, 2012). The urban analogue—space filled by the immediate and urgent need for shelter— is the shantytown. The belly of the city is full, but it continues to starve. Appetite may at times be indistinguishable from hunger as a sensation, but one need not be hungry in order to have an appetite (see Chapter 5). The Linden Flower tea I am presently drinking is presumably providing little nutritional benefit, but it is cer-tainly satisfying my appetite for flavour, aroma, warmth, and even novelty (Linden flowers being out of the ordinary as herbal teas go) and it is giving me greater pleasure than did the peanut butter sandwich I absent-mindedly nibbled for lunch. To have an appetite is to strive for something, to have a desire. Our greatest feats of building are the product of great appetites and their dimensions are always far greater than their functions. The Hoover Dam, for example, is far more than just a generator for electricity.

Joseph Rykwert, in his influential *The Idea of a Town* (1976), opens his narrative with the observation that the city as an artefact is "more like a dream than any-thing else" (ibid.: 24), and that, although the study of dreams has gained currency in many fields, in the study of the urban it is regarded as offensive. When so much money and so many practical considerations are at hand, it is seen as rash to consider the forms born of hopes and dreams. "Here again we are up against the poverty of much urbanistic discourse," he writes, the "psychological space, the cultural, the juridical, the religious, are not treated as aspects of the ecological space with whose economy the urbanist is concerned" (ibid.: 24). In many respects, little has changed in professional attitudes to urbanism in the decades since he wrote this. Henri Lefebvre, in a recently discovered and translated manuscript also written in the mid-1970s, writes about the importance of considering enjoyment (*jouissance*)[1] as a foundation for architecture and urbanism. Lefebvre brackets the focus on purely physical or technical problems in urbanism with cynicism: "Only an economy of enjoyment that replaces an exchange economy can end that which kills reality in the name of realism (in truth, cynicism)" (Lefebvre, 2014: 131). For Lefebvre, 'reality' includes the "space of enjoyment" which is "a genuine space, one of moments, encounters, friendships, festivals, rest, quiet, joy, exaltation, love, sensuality, as well as understanding, enigma, the unknown, and the known, struggle, play" (ibid.: 152). For Lefebvre this enjoyment is expressly, explicitly utopian: "nothing is closer than this utopia. It is as close as can possibly be to the living body, for it experiences it without interference. Otherwise, it dies, and this death in no way resembles spiritual or material (physical) death" (ibid.: 132). This death is zombiehood by starvation; starvation from pleasure, conviviality, and transcendence.

The city as built by cynical processes of contemporary neoliberal development suffers from this same starvation or impoverishment: a focus on the new and on the spectacle as a driver for real estate sales, coupled with a financialization—'form follows finance,' as Carol Willis (1995) says—that value-engineers out all that is genuinely of lasting and sustaining savour and which calls up a history of together-ness and mutual striving and both the tools and methods and the hope, and, indeed, the obligation for the continuance of this history. Zygmunt Bauman, in his essay 'City of Fears, City of Hopes,' writes of contemporary development that its goal is "to raze to the ground the old quarters of the city; to dig up a black hole in which old meanings sink and disappear, first from view and soon after from memory, and to fill the void with brand new logic, unbound by the worries of continuity and relieved from its burdens" (2003: 10). If one of utopianism's goals is the fulfilment of as-yet unfulfilled desires, the 'not-yet' or the 'ought,' then this erasure is not dystopian, but anti-utopian, a charge that has justifiably been levelled against the contemporary politics of neoliberalism by writers such as Lucy Sargisson: "Anti-utopianism is not just dystopianism or gloominess about the future. Rather, it is a phenomenon that *resists* the utopian impulse" (2012: 22; emphasis added). What Bauman calls a 'black hole' I have called rather the phenomenon of the proliferation of 'beige holes' (see Chapter 23).

---

1 Lefebvre's original title was *Vers une architecture de la jouissance*, translated in the 2014 edition as *Toward an Architecture of Enjoyment*. The translation to 'enjoyment' doesn't quite do justice to the term *jouissance*, but it does avoid the inevitable associations with the Lacanian sense of the word, which is more narrowly (sexually and orgasmically) defined than was Lefebvre's intention. Jouissance, for Lefebvre, included ideas of playfulness and enjoyment, and also of the Gallic notions of *bonheur*, *plaisir*, *volupté*, and *joie* (see Stanek, 2014: ix–x).

Beige holes are anything but accidental. When queer theorist Eve Kosofsky Sedgwick speaks of the repression of subversiveness by hegemony or of the status quo, she talks of a process of "strategic banalization" (2003: 13) which complicates that simple binary repression/liberation (assuming for my purposes that utopian Lefebvrean enjoyment is liberatory) by pointing to what is happening not at the poles, but in the lived space of the middle ground. Another problem with reifying the status quo is what it does to the middle ranges of agency. One's relation to *what is* risks becoming reactive and bifurcated, that of a consumer: one's choices narrow to accepting or refusing (buying, not buying) this or that manifestation of it, dramatizing only the extremes of compulsion and voluntarity. Yet it is only the middle ranges of agency that offer space for effectual creativity and change (ibid.: 13).

In the same way that queer life is simultaneously glamourized and banalized by homonormativity and commodification, so too is urban life banalized and reduced to mere surfaces by contemporary pseudomodernist development and commodification. Real estate advertising applies a sheen of glamour, allure, "mechanisms of fascination" (Thrift, 2010: 290), to what is to be accepted or refused by buying or not buying, and glamour can go a long way to obscuring the need for space for effectual creativity and change, or, indeed, lying outright that these new developments are actually *providing for* creativity and change (often by using the language of the 'creative city' movement, popularized amongst hegemons by Richard Florida). Watch the lurching march of glamour's zombification in this passage from Nigel Thrift, in which he describes how "life becomes a cavalcade of aesthetically charged moments that can be used for profit":

> [T]he allure in allure is largely produced by the creation of worlds in which the boundaries between alive and not alive and material and immaterial have become increasingly blurred, so that what was considered as alive can become thing-like and what was considered as dead is able to show signs of life.
>
> *(2010: 296)*

Appetites here become zombified: as with an artificial sweetener, the satisfaction is apparent, but is not nutritious. In the case of the developer, a simplified and focused appetite for cold hard cash has raged out of control. In the case of the consumer, there is only an illusion of control and a false choice (buying or not buying). Appetite in the human body (and also in the social body) requires control, as it can be a greater force than mere hunger. Both hunger and appetite for food are regulated by a system known as the 'appestat,' which involves the nervous system, the gut, various hormones, and, of course, the brain. When the appestat is broken—in normal circumstances let alone in conditions of zombie consumerism—extremes of behaviour result in disastrous bodily consequences from anorexia to obesity. What is it that controls our wider appetites for earthly pleasures and grand things—our psychosocial appestat, if you will? If it is appetite that impels us, what is it that steers us or stops us from going too far? This force is taste. "Taste," I have written, "though it can be defined as a single sense, is never truly autonomous" (Chapter 4). First, taste and olfaction are interdependent, but also the sense of touch is involved. Indeed, gustatory taste is inseparable from all the other human senses. Consider, though, how these senses are engaged. Colour and composition are also important for the appreciation of food, which directly connects the aesthetic in its largest sense—that of the sensorium—with aesthetics as the appreciation of art and beauty. Further, too, *where and in what circumstance* taste is experienced has a bearing, bringing in positive and negative associations that are wholly situational. A fried egg, for example, will taste different (or better or worse) if it is eaten with close friends while camping in the mountains, alone at an anonymous breakfast in a business hotel, or with family at home. This points not just to taste in both its aesthetic senses, but also to taste as ethical, relational, situational, circumstantial, aspirational, psychosocial, cultural.

The fact that it is impossible to separate gustatory taste from taste in its socio-cultural sense is also true of appetite in both senses. Taste and appetite are also both quite specific. If one has an appetite it is generally *for* something—cakes, jewels, blondes—and if one has taste it generally shows that one's aesthetic boundaries are delimited according to a particular social position. Educated taste is that which is constructed knowingly in order to fit into a particular social position and its attendant environment—whether this environment is perceived to be highbrow or lowbrow. In utopian terms, this also relates to the 'education of desire,' which I will address below.

The food philosopher Carolyn Korsmeyer speaks of taste as good judgement, however it must be assumed that if taste as a sensation can be unpleasant, then taste as a judgement can also be perceived as negative as well as positive. In other words, 'bad' taste is still taste. But here is Korsmeyer: "Taste is construed as the ability to perceive beautiful qualities and to discriminate fine differences among the objects of perception, differences that might escape notice by someone without Taste[2]" (1999: 42). She goes on, though, later in the book, to admit a different standard (and compare the 'taste of necessity' to the idea of hunger as dearth, which I have critiqued above):

> Bourdieu characterizes the eating habits of the leisured bourgeoisie as 'the taste of liberty or luxury' and those of the working class as the 'taste of neces-sity.' [...] Bourdieu emphatically rejects the qualitative distinction between literal and aesthetic Taste. There is no universality of Taste untainted by class privilege, no pure judgment of aesthetic pleasure. And therefore there is no need to stipulate a particular sort of Taste to ground universal aesthetic standards. Both kinds of taste are part and parcel of the same social forces.
>
> *(Ibid.: 65)*

Similarly the notion of 'good' or 'correct' judgement appears in the architectures. Nathaniel Coleman describes how taste is conceived in the work of theorist-archi-tect Claude Perrault (1613–1688). Perrault "argued that taste, which lends itself to

---

2 Korsmeyer distinguishes between gustatory taste and sociocultural Taste by capitalizing the latter.

cultivation because it is an agreed upon social construction, is the only sure way to protect architecture from fancy." 'Fancy,' here, being a form of pure, uncontextual or even anti-contextual invention which has much more recently become many architects' calling card—exemplified in postmodernism by Charles Jencks's 'iconic building' (2005). "A crucial facet of Perrault's construct—what separates it from later developments—was his conviction that, because of its venerability, a classical language or architecture would persist indefinitely as the vehicle by which buildings would continue to communicate" (Coleman, 2005: 13).

The fixity of this notion of taste is anchored by chauvinism. It assumes that only one model of Taste: likely an upper-class European frame, is possible. It is useful for the reason of avoiding such totalizing models of 'good taste' to speak of tastes as particular to different circumstances, different cultures, and different classes. "Ethics and aesthetics reduced to rules are useless: ethical action is always singular and circumstantial," writes Alberto Péréz-Gómez (2006: 4). It is likewise useful to speak about 'architectures' instead of Architecture or knowledges instead of Knowledge. Architectures appropriate to tastes and situated knowledges might vary widely, and draw on the resources of many and variegated utopias. Hannah Arendt explains the importance of this relationality succinctly, and when she speaks of 'a culture,' she is pluralizing rather than seeing culture as unified and bounded:

> [T]aste and its ever-alert judgment of things of the world sets its own limits
> to an indiscriminate, immoderate love of the merely beautiful; into the realm
> of fabrication and of quality it introduces the personal factor, that is, gives it
> a humanistic meaning. Taste debarbarizes the world of the beautiful by not
> being overwhelmed by it; it takes care of the beautiful in its own 'personal'
> way and thus produces a 'culture.'
>
> *(1977 [1954]: 224)*

Whether our tastes are highbrow or lowbrow,[3] we still describe our sensual world in taste terms, and our lifeworlds are expressed in particular urban idioms, local and regional expressions of landscape, and are shared through foods and languages that express the local and regional. Even in a globalized world, the local is always particular. This is so because patterns of custom are played out as slowly shifting rituals that repeatedly inscribe, reinforce, and resonate with patterns of local urbanism in a dialogic way. It is important to see the customary as that which is practised, as this deeply affects the way landscapes and landscape relations are imagined. A few years

---

3 There is probably still ample room for some things or practices to be categorized as being in 'bad' taste, as the definition of bad taste is often reflective of moral judgements. For example, the possession of large sport-utility vehicles—'Chelsea tractors'—is commonly seen to be in poor taste for reasons of conspicuous waste and conspicuous consumption. A greater awareness of taste could help people to think longer and harder about making such choices and displaying those choices publicly. The 'right' to express oneself is thus tempered by the judgements of surrounding society for the benefit, ultimately, of all concerned and the ongoing health of our human habitat.

ago, I visited the Expo in Milan as a journalist (see Chapter 5). It was focused on the theme 'Feeding the Planet: Energy for Life' and amongst all the national pavilions was an installation celebrating the Slow Food movement. I had a conversation with an earnest young activist who spoke about the need to 'preserve' their home city of Genoa's food culture and protect it from outside influences. In the course of the conversation I pointed out, gently, that Genoa's food culture was explicitly the result of its cosmopolitan and outward-facing history as a port city, and that maintaining an openness to influence was the best way to value and extend a robust culinary heritage.

To see such heritage as performed, enacted, and practised in customs rather than as a given or a tradition is the key to avoiding the fixity of chauvinism. Despite the increasing tendency for people to be described as 'consumers,' a term which seems oddly drained of savour, the reality is that most people are actually 'customers' when they are in public. They act out roles and rituals repetitively, bringing repeat business to the places that enrich their everyday experience. Those urban attractors that inspire custom are each utopian fragments—dream ideals that have been realized, or at least partially realized. They can be recruited into the imagination, using "the privileges of fiction" (Shonfield, 2000: 154) to understand how they figure in people's narratives about the spaces they inhabit. These fragments of utopia help to fix the urban fabric in place and to provide loci for community and collectivity. It's the partiality of these last schemes which I find interesting, but also perhaps the utopian fragments of totalitarian regimes bear some examination as well, or perhaps the fragments of the free-market capitalist utopia, which, while it has conspired with state utopian/dystopian forms to build such horrors as the military- and prison-industrial complexes, has also contributed much fantasy architecture from Art Deco department store palaces such as Barker's or Drage's (sadly, recently demolished—sucked into a beige hole) (Figure 26.1) in London or pleasure gardens like Melbourne's Luna Park (Figure 26.2). Even dystopian fragments have importance and even allure as ruins or memorials, from the carefully maintained landscape, buildings, and artefacts at Auschwitz or Vienna's indestructible Nazi flak towers to thanatourism sites like the Atomic Research Facility at Orford Ness in Essex or Pripyat in the Chernobyl Exclusion Zone. This perhaps offers an insight into how particular buildings or sites can provide object lessons for humanity about how it ought, or ought not, to act. Religious sites and edifices, too, also act in similar ways, but the relations between religions and utopias are too complex for me to address in any reasonable way here.

Some utopian fragments are called into the world by artistic ambition and vision. It is not a stretch of the imagination to say that such exquisite masterworks such as Victor Horta's house, the Palau de la Música Catalana by Lluis Domènech i Montaner, Le Corbusier's La Tourette, or James McNeill Whistler's Peacock Room are places that provide glimpses into utopias. The park or garden is totemic in this regard as well, and is also often Arcadian. Le Nôtre's Versailles is a regicentric utopia, whereas Olmsted's Central Park is an Arcadia for the people. William Morris's house and garden at Kelmscott is emblematic of a (patrician) bucolic vision of

FIGURE 26.1 Drage's Department Store, Oxford Street. Art Deco glitz and a fragment of a capitalist retail utopia. Now sadly demolished and swallowed up by a beige hole. Credit: Tim Waterman.

utopia. But utopian fragments, crucially, appear not only in landscapes, edifices, and other buildings, but are also manifested in practices, events, and performances. Feasts and festivals are utopian manifestations that recur annually; the traditional Amish barn-raising is another vision of collective life realized; and many intentional communities around the world, both religious and secular, give testament to mutual and collective forms of utopian striving.

Utopias, with the possible exception of folk utopias such as Cockaigne or Luilekkerland, always propose a vision for collective life and public life. Almost invariably, they cannot work without systems of organization in place to ensure the smooth running of an ideal society. These may be authoritarian and very highly proscribed, as in Filarete's Sforzinda—a fifteenth-century hierarchical ideal city designed at the behest of the Duke of Milan—or they may depend more fully upon self-organization, mutual aid, and/or civil society. Often the forms that utopias take

FIGURE 26.2 Melbourne's Luna Park: A fantasy pleasure garden. Credit: Linda Robertus/ Shutterstock.

reflect the overarching political ethos quite effectively—again, witness the rigid diagram of Sforzinda (Figure 26.3), which was hierarchical in rule and also in its geometric spatial form. In the absence of any compelling justification for authoritarianism, it must be taken that any constructive utopian visions must be organized around the idea of civil society. Edward Soja sums up the idea of civil society:

> Think of the extensions we have in English for the Greek word *polis*: politics, police, policy, polite; and for its equivalent in Latin, *civitas*: civil, civic, citizen, civilization, city itself. The city, with its meeting places and public spaces, was the wellspring for thinking about democracy, equality, liberty, human rights, citizenship, cultural identity, resistance to the status quo, struggles for social and spatial justice.
>
> *(2010b: 80)*

It is difficult not to think of the end goal of civil society, civil society's horizon, as utopian in and of itself; that a polite and civilized public landscape should provide an empowering framework for free citizens. This is cast, however, against what Marx and Engels called "the idiocy of rural life" (1948 [1848]: 18). Their use of the term was not a slur against the country bumpkin, but rather denoted the isolation of rural life that existed in contrast to the rich public life of the city.[4] The term,

4 There is a very useful discussion of the term on the Monthly Review website under 'Notes from the Editors' at http://monthlyreview.org/2003/10/01/3735.

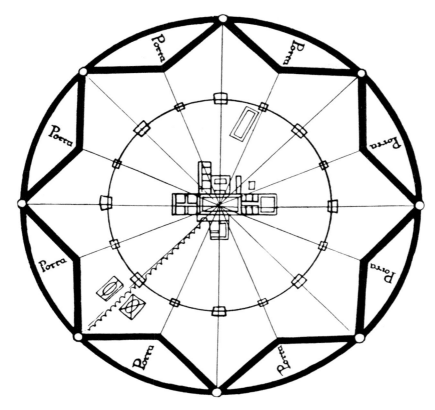

FIGURE 26.3 Diagram of Filarete's Sforzinda, 1457. Utopian geometry. (vgl. dazu eine farbige Abb. in: dtv–Atlas zur Baukunst, Bd.2, 4. Auflage, 1985, S. 432). Credit: Filarete.

from the Greek *idiotes*, denoted an inability to be public; an inability to under-stand the frameworks of polite society and to be a political actor-citizen upon the urban stage. Here is Soja again: "Living in the city defined who were the polit-ically active 'citizens' or *polites*, as opposed to everyone else: slaves, most women, barbarians, and *idiotes*, those difficult to organize nonurban folk that Karl Marx described as immersed in the apolitical and supremely individualistic 'idiocy' of rural life" (2010b: 80). An idiot, then, can be defined as someone who is not able to limit their behaviour within the terms of mutual recognition that are necessary for urbanity and civilization. They are not able to enjoy the mutually assured freedoms that result from publicity, taste, and propriety.

To the contemporary ear, it sounds odd to insist that freedoms might be dependent upon taste and propriety. Wealth enables people to separate themselves from one another and to avoid the onerous work of involvement in civil society. There is a form of independence which can be bought. Many even find it an affront to their civil liberties to be told they must behave with regard to others, but this is as the result of a dangerous conflation of the ideas of independence and of freedom. A condition is more and more developing in which many in wealthy cities can live encapsulated lives, ever suspicious and intolerant of others, ever more dependent upon various forms of regulation to guide (or avert) any interactions. A point has been reached where it is possible to speak of the idiocy of *urban* life, with all its allure and shiny surfaces. "The more the myth of empty impersonality, in popular forms, becomes the common sense of a society, the more will that populace feel morally justified in destroying the essence of urbanity, which is that men [sic] can act together, without the compulsion to be the same" (Sennett, 1974: 255).

Again, acting together asks that social and spatial practices must form the basis for understanding a utopianism as processual and engaged. "It is not so much *geometrical forms* as *forms of conduct* that concern me," writes Nathaniel Coleman (2005: 4–5, emphasis in original), in what is certainly a conceptual underpinning to *this* volume. It is crucial. If the concept of utopias in architectures is seen to be a history of formal or diagrammatic approaches to impossible perfect worlds, then this is likely to present a dry, esoteric, and primarily academic arena of study. However, if utopias as imagined modes of human–landscape engagement, which are considered through conduct, practice, process, and performance, then the questions are rich and meaningful, relational and situational. Further, they explicitly link academic and scholarly pursuits (meaning practices, vocations, activities) with pursuits (meaning the same) of paramount concern in everyday life, such as the *pursuit* of happiness or a good life. Envisioning the pursuit of happiness as a continuing activity—rather the stalking of prey—helps to show how happiness is not something *given*, *attained,* or *claimed* (or snared and subdued), but rather an ongoing affair that is *practised* in dwelling. This concept frames constitutive utopias well too: they are dynamic structures within which whole worlds of ideal associations and practices may be tested in the imagination so that elements of those ideal worlds might be brought into action in the real world. This fundamentally re-centres the practice of architecture(s), as "how architects can offer a setting able to contain the continual elaboration and invention of social action" (Coleman, 2005: 5).

This is what Karsten Harries refers to as the *ethical function* of architecture (1997: 4), and perhaps also what Alberto Pérez-Gómez describes as the "poetic representation of significant human action" (2006: 129). Harries describes 'ethos,' as containing both the practicalities and poetics of human existence: it "names the way human beings exist in the world: their way of dwelling. By the ethical function of architecture I mean its task to help articulate a common ethos" (1997: 4).

In striving for sustainability, resilience, or regenerativity, for a future for the planet, it is necessary that people recover from idiocy and learn to work together collectively once more, striving towards common ethics. Sustainable futures should be couched in terms of utopian possibilities for abundance and togetherness, and not merely the forms of austerity or martyrdom that are commonly envisioned across the political spectrum—from righteous denial on the left to righteous mockery on the right. Here, perhaps, it is possible to see that anti-utopianism is not merely a phenomenon of conservatism, shutting down possible futures with 'realism,' but that positive futures are also foreclosed at the centre, particularly as realized in the era of Blair and Clinton, and on the left. There is little point in trying to project a vision of a sustainable future that is shot through with martyrdom and deprivation. The utopia that we envision, and towards which we strive—for which we have an appetite—should also be one that is delicious in every way. It is important to try to shape public tastes and drives so that collective actions, habits, and behaviours can be supported and encouraged.

Utopias have often, in modernity, been drawn on clean slates—evoking the standard formula of modernity that complete reinvention is necessary. On this clean slate is projected an image of absolute purity—absolute synthetic purity or absolute organic purity, for example. Despite the many permutations of utopia and Arcadia, they are two hemispheres rigidly mapped and separated by a sharp and definite equator. This mapping of opposing dogmas creates two poles of irreconcilable difference that may be seen, for example, in discussions of agricultural practice that are so cleanly divided between proponents of conventional agriculture (we must continue on our chosen path or we will all starve) and organic agriculture (we must build an Eden of polycultural, permacultural practice). Utopian visions for this century must begin somewhere other than the clean slate. Stephen Toulmin, in his magisterial *Cosmopolis*, writes, "No neutral 'scratch line' exists from which to jump to a self-sustaining, tradition-free intellectual system. All of the cultural situations from which we pursue our practical and intellectual inquiries are historically conditioned. This being so, the only thing we can do is to make the best of starting with what we have got, here and now" (1990: 179). And I will echo the contemporary call for a great deal more of 'both… and' and a great deal less of 'either/or.'

Late twentieth- and early twenty-first-century anti-utopianism's manifestations in urbanism are urban forms that are largely devoid of either taste or striving, and suburban forms that are minimally inflected along a very narrow band of taste with expressions and symbols that can be easily purchased. Urban and suburban environments both have become constructs of consumerism rather than custom. This is much like the world to which H.G. Wells's Rip Van Winkle-styled protagonist, Graham, awakes in 2100; "a sophisticated corporate dystopia where people are well fed and comfortable but virtually enslaved by a business oligarchy that substitutes empty consumption for political freedom" (Belasco, 2006: 122). Marco Frascari has written, "Contemporary architecture is almost entirely tasteless. Architectural taste has been ruled out by the moral standards of the modern movement. This has, I think resulted in a meaningless architecture" (2004: 191). This exuberant and provocative statement holds particularly true for urban skylines and streetscapes populated with anodyne forms that are at best logos, and at worst, which is depressingly usual, anti-urban and instantly obsolete. Frascari indicts the international style, but to me it can still be argued that there was a strong utopian and moral underpinning to the forms generated by the style, and that really he is referring to a mis-evolved bastard form that Owen Hatherley has called 'pseudomodernism' (see Chapter 23). It expresses universalized, generic ideals that are devoid of taste or particularity. Its glazed surfaces deflect affection, affinity, dwelling, community.

It is designed to hold people separate, at a distance, and to keep them moving along. This breezy airport internationalism and monumental forms that express only monumentality create space, to be sure, but not place. If all we can do is make the best of the here and now, then it is vital to stop building this way immediately and to look hard at finding those forms that best create human habitat, which are often those forms that we have evolved with as a species. This is not a paean to neotraditionalism, but rather a plea to design and build in ways that encourage the creation of convivial urban human habitats.

We need to create utopias that are not placeless abstractions, but rather are rooted in already existing places, building upon what is there. Not to move people along, or escape from places to new blank slates, but, rather, to help existing communities to become better without changing their fundamental constitution or their established associations. Both the return of taste and the recognition of tastes that are other than our own are essential to the construction of a sustainable future public realm for which we may have an appetite. Tom Moylan helps to show how utopias can help to project alternative and more hopeful visions, to tell better stories:

> Utopian writing [...] is, at heart, rooted in the unfulfilled needs and wants of specific classes, groups, and individuals in their unique historical contexts. Produced through the fantasizing powers of the imagination, utopia opposes the affirmative culture maintained by dominant ideology. Utopia negates the contradictions in a social system by forging visions of what is not yet realized either in theory or practice. In generating such figures of hope, utopia contributes to the open space of opposition.
>
> *(1986: 1–2)*

Moylan speaks also of 'concrete utopias,' "where utopian possibilities are established in the concreteness and openness of the material of history" (ibid.: 21), giving examples such as the Paris Commune and the student protests of May 1968, and to which one now might add Occupy!. "Concrete utopia prevents the discarding of the visions of the goals ahead and calls for the living out of those visions in whatever is to be done" (ibid.: 21). Through storying that is both told and enacted, the education of desire comes to pass, and this desire allows the projection of new (educated) tastes and appetites. Ruth Levitas describes these forms of dwelling and storying as utopian method or process "which is necessarily provisional, reflexive, and dialogic. It is always suspended between the present and the future, always under revision, at the meeting point of the darkness of the lived moment and the flickering light of a better world, for the moment accessible only through an act of imagination" (2013: 149).

What, to conclude, might these collective utopian futures look like? Upon what already existing framework, what utopian fragments, might they press into service? At this last it's useful to at least give a glimpse of how desires might be educated, and how concrete utopias for the living out of visions might be employed. Visions of collective living have often been illuminated, in the West, in a very grey and Soviet light. There is little point to envision a future where long queues of identically apparelled workers wait outside soup kitchens for their ladles of gruel, nor, indeed that we should share a draughty bathhouse. There are delightful, convivial models that can be employed, each of them requiring architectures of Vitruvian firmness, commodity, and delight. Take, for example, the bathhouse. There are undeniable savings to be made by consolidating daily human bathing activities. Water can be heated all in one place and even filtered and reused on the spot. Far fewer bathroom fixtures would need manufacturing if people shared facilities, saving energy and resources. However, when I raise the subject with my students of 'collective bathing,' they instinctively recoil. When I ask, though, how many of them use a gym, large numbers of them do, and they enjoy the competition, camaraderie, and conviviality of the gym environment. Likewise for eating. The soup kitchen holds few charms, but when one is reminded that restaurants are also scenes of communal dining and consolidated modes of preparation and consumption, then it is clear that we can certainly envision utopian modes of future existence for which we can have an appetite, and which we can commence to build without a sense of penury or martyrdom, but instead with hope and with zest.

ACKNOWLEDGEMENTS

What a joy it is to contemplate all the support, friendship, and collegiality that goes into scholarship. There is also terror, too, that someone will be left out or forgotten, and of course I know there will be accidental omissions. Still, as this book represents a decade of writing and yet more years of education, friendship, and support, I wish to try to be as exhaustive here as I can. So, first thanks go to a few very special people whose influence shaped not just the ideas that went into this book, but also my life's directions for the better: Bill Bowler and Jaki Wright; Lance and Cecelia Luschnig (C.A.E. Luschnig); Bob Greene; Marsha Folks; Sandra Williams; Lynn Darroch.

A small group of scholars has provided regular feedback and pleasant conversation in meetings we call 'potlatches,' and in the tradition of the potlatch we are expected not to leave out a single contribution but to give all. Our research group comprises Oscar Brito (UAL), Christoph Lueder (Kingston University), Lara Rettondini (University of Westminster), and Ed Wall (University of Greenwich). Ed, of course, has been a close collaborator on many projects, and he and his wife Kristin and daughter Carly are treasured companions.

At Routledge, Grace Harrison has given support for many years now, and Rosie Anderson's work on this book is likewise a boon. Jen Hinchliffe has capably copyedited the text.

My colleagues at the Bartlett School of Architecture have been no less forthcoming. My ideas developed through serving as an architecture thesis tutor there for the six years prior to my full-time engagement on the new landscape architecture programme, and thus my relationships there have been significant to the last decade of my work. Of particular note are Murray Fraser, who helped host our Landscape and Critical Agency symposium in 2012, and who contributed a foreword to *Landscape and Agency: Critical Essays* (Wall and Waterman, 2017), and Matthew Gandy (now at Cambridge), Jonathan Hill, and Peg Rawes who spoke at the event.

In landscape architecture my esteemed colleagues are: Ana Abram, Nico Alexandroff, Laura Allen, Richard Beckett, Loretta Bosence, Barbara Campbell-Lange, Emma Colthurst, Tiffany Kaewen Dang, Gunther Galligioni, Elise Hunchuck, Cannon Ivers, Will Jennings, Johanna Just, Kyriaki Kasabalis, Tom Keeley, Ness Lafoy, Katya Larina, Zoe Lau, Alex Malaescu, Doug Miller, Agostino Nickl, Kyrstyn Oberholster, Aisling O'Carroll, Maj Plemenitas, Mark Smout, Harry Watkins, and Sandra Youkhana. In architecture I have had excellent, fruitful conversations with Iain Borden, Eva Branscome, Matthew Butcher, Blanche Cameron, Edward Denison, Paul Dobraszczyk, Kirti Durelle, Tom Dyckhoff, Daisy Froud, Christophe Gérard, Stelios Giamarelos, Sean Griffiths, Penelope Haralambidou, Ben Hayes, Danielle Hewitt, Steve Johnson, Chee-Kit Lai, Xiuzheng Li, Christoph Lindner, Yeoryia Manolopoulou, Emma-Kate Matthews, Claire McAndrew, Niall McLaughlin, James O'Leary, Luke Olsen, Barbara Penner, Alicia Pivaro, Sophia Psarra, Sophie Read, Guang Yu Ren, Jane Rendell, David Roberts, Diana Salazar, Tania Sengupta, Sara Shafiei, Bob Sheil, Amy Smith, Sabine Storp, Colin Thom, Nina Vollenbroker, Patrick Weber, Henrietta Williams, Robin Wilson, Oliver Wilton, and Stamatos Zografos. In planning I have enjoyed conversations and collaborations with: Elena Besussi, Camillo Boano, Michael Edwards, and William Hunter. And finally at the Institute for Global Prosperity, where I participated in their summer school for several years: Konrad Miciukiewicz, Nikolay Mintchev, Henrietta Moore, and Hannah Sender.

I spent three fruitful years at the University of Greenwich, and my colleagues there were of inestimable help. Neil Spiller and Nic Clear were at the helm there during my time, and were the source of many stimulating conversations. The other staff provided similar, and much mirth as well, an important but underrated ingredient in a robust research process. They were Mike Aling, Harry Bix, Ghislaine Boddington, Tony Clelford, Rebecca Cotton, Max Dewdney, James Fox, Duncan Goodwin, Simon Herron, Phil Hudson, Susanne Isa, Marko Jobst, Stephen Kennedy, Meaghan Kombol, Benz Kotzen, Anastasios Maragiannis, Shelley Mosco, Shaun Murray, Wouter Ombregt, Rahesh Ram, Honoré van Rijswijk, and Simon Withers.

Three other institutions have also supported me: Kingston University, where I took my first steps in teaching with the help of Pat Brown, Carine Brannan, and Bridget Snaith; and the Writtle School of Design, which I joined in 2008 after getting to know the charismatic Jeff Logsdon, then Head of School. My relationships from Writtle continue in fascinating ways, in friendship with many and in scholarship, as with Jeremy Strong, with whom a reciprocation of chapter contributions has occurred on more than a couple of edited collections, and with Saruhan Mosler and Peter Hobson who contributed an excellent chapter to my *Routledge Handbook of Landscape and Food* (2018), edited with Joshua Zeunert, then at Writtle and now at UNSW in Sydney; and in a fruitful ongoing collaboration with the radical digital arts organization Furtherfield.

I have also benefited from close association with the University of Westminster, where some of the material in this book was submitted as part of a PhD by Published Work. My amazing supervisors were Douglas Spencer, Davide Deriu, and Krystallia

Kamvasinou. Andrew Smith was also a great support. Also at the University of Westminster, those scholars involved in the Monsoon Assemblages project have expanded my (watery) horizons, amongst them Lindsay Bremner, Christina Geros, Anthony Powis (now at Central St Martins), and Éric Guibert.

Furtherfield needs a separate word, as my involvement began when I shared an office at Writtle with the luminous Ruth Catlow, co-founder of Furtherfield with Marc Garrett. Conversations in that office brought landscape worlds and digital worlds together in astonishing ways. The couple of extra chairs by the window were occupied by sparkling intellects of the sort that cast constellations of new light into what was otherwise at that time a staid and somewhat embattled agricultural college: Pryle Behrman, Charlotte Frost, and Michael Szpakowski. The discussion group, Reading the Commons, which we inaugurated at Furtherfield (and two of the products of this are included in this book) included Ele Carpenter (Goldsmiths), Anne Bottomley (Kent Law School), Joss Hands (Newcastle University), Alastair McCapra (Chief Executive at the Chartered Institute of Public Relations and board member of Wikimedia UK), Nathan Moore (Birkbeck School of Law), Christian Nold (UCL), Penny Travlou (Edinburgh School of Architecture and Landscape Architecture), and Ed Wall (University of Greenwich).

This work bears an immense debt to overlapping networks of scholars, those involved in utopian studies, in the Utopian Studies Society in Europe and the Society for Utopian Studies in the US, and landscape studies and landscape architecture, including the organizations the American Association of Geographers (AAG), The European Council of Landscape Architecture Studies (ECLAS), the Landscape Research Group (LRG), the Permanent European Conference for the Study of the Rural Landscape (PECSRL), UNISCAPE, and the International Federation of Landscape Architects (IFLA).

Notable individuals from these groups include: Jacques Abelman (University of Oregon), Simon Bell (University of Edinburgh), Laurence le du-Blayo (Université de Rennes), Vanesa Castan Broto (University of Sheffield), Sandra Costa (Birmingham City University), Kimm Curran (History of Women Religious of Britain and Ireland), Chris Dalglish (Inherit), Saskia de Wit (TU Delft), Graham Fairclough (Newcastle University), Ellen Fetzer (Kassel University), Karen Fitzsimon (University of Westminster), Steven Goossens (Erasmus University Brussels), Marouen Hehdlie (architect, Tunisia), Sarah Hobbs (LRG), Michael Jones (NSUT Trondheim), Karsten Jørgensen (NMBU), Anders Larsson (SLU Alnarp), Markus Leibenath (Leibniz Institute of Ecological Urban and Regional Development), Kent Mathewson (Louisiana State University), Gavin McGregor, Bruno Marques (Wellington School of Architecture), Lisa McKenzie (University of Edinburgh), Sophia Meeres (University College Dublin), Ian Mell (University of Manchester), Tom Mels (Uppsala University), John Stuart Murray (University of Edinburgh), Bruno Notteboom (KU Leuven), Thomas Oles (SLU), Kenneth Olwig (SLU Alnarp), Hannes Palang (Tallinn University), Susan Parham (University of Hertfordshire), Bas Pedroli (Wageningen University), Maggie Roe (Newcastle University), David Saunders (LRG), Emily Shakespeare (LRG), Amy Strecker

(University of Leiden), Paul Tabbush (Social and Economic Research Forest Research, Alice Holt Research Station), Ian H. Thompson (Newcastle University), Tiago Torres-Campos (University of Edinburgh), Marc Treib (UC Berkeley), Burcu Yigit Turan (SLU), Veerle van Eetvelde (University of Ghent), Rudi van Etteger (Wageningen), Emma Waterton (Western Sydney University), Laura Alice Watt (Sonoma State University).

At the Landscape Institute, Paul Lincoln has been a steadfast supporter of my work, and I am also grateful for my former involvement as chair of the Editorial Advisory Panel for *Landscape*: the Journal of the Landscape Institute. Also, special thanks go to George Bull, Ruth Slavid, and the designer Tim Coleman, with whom I have had the pleasure of working once again on the cover for this book.

There are a great many influences and friends, outside the institutional or con-ference circuits I attend, with whom I have close associations on several levels, often collaboration and/or rich correspondence: Ross Exo Adams (Bard College), Roo Angell, Cany Ash and Robert Sakula, Phil Askew and Nicole Collomb, Bob Bagley, Megan Blake (University of Sheffield), Isis Brook and Warwick Fox, Graeme Brooker (RCA), Pat Brown (Central), Alex Colas (Birkbeck), Steve Cole and Rebecca Bell (Middlesex University), Paul Cureton (Lancaster University), Gillian Darley, Christian Spencer Davies, Jill Desimini (Harvard), Jon Goodbun (RCA), Jason Edwards (Birkbeck), Adam Eldridge (University of Westminster), Johanna Gibbons (J&L Gibbons), Maria Giudici (RCA), David Haney (Kent School of Architecture), Sophie Hope (Birkbeck), Jane Hutton (University of Waterloo), Joern Langhorst (University of Colorado Denver), Katya Larina (Gustafson, Porter + Bowman), Patrick Lynch, Ewa Majewska (ICI Berlin Institute for Cultural Inquiry), Doreen Massey, Anna Minton, Don Mitchell (Uppsala University), Joni Palmer (University of Colorado Boulder), Elspeth Probyn (University of Sydney), Alex Rook, David Grahame Shane (Columbia), Michael Sorkin (City University), Carolyn Steel, Jon Thomson and Alison Craighead (UCL/Goldsmiths/Westminster), Karma Waltonen (UC Davis), Allen S. Weiss (NYU), Jane Wolff (University of Toronto).

And in the community I have found in the Utopian Studies Society: Siân Adiseshiah (Loughborough University), Heather Alberro (Nottingham Trent University), Emrah Atasoy (Cappadocia University), Raffaella Baccolini (University of Bologna), Antonis Balasopoulos (University of Cyprus), David Bell (Loughborough University), James Block and Ruth Fuerst (DePaul University), Emile Bojesen (University of Winchester), Verity Burgmann (Monash University), Gregory Claeys (Royal Holloway), Nathaniel Coleman (Newcastle University), Zsolt Czigányik (Central European University), Lorna Davidson (New Lanark), Laurence Davis (University of Cork), Edson Luiz André de Sousa (Universidade Federal do Rio Grande do Sul), Jacqueline Dutton (University of Melbourne), Rhiannon Firth (University of Essex), Justyna Galant (UMCS), Lisa Garforth (Newcastle University), Joseph Giacomelli (NYU), Kenneth Hanshew (Universität Regensburg), Richard Howells (King's College London), Céline Keller, Michał Kłosiński (University of Silesia in Katowice), Ruth Levitas (University of Bristol), James McIntyre (Loughborough University), Heather McKnight (University of Sussex), Etta

Madden (Missouri State University), Annette Magid, Krzysztof Maj (Facta Ficta), Timothy Miller (University of Kansas), Andrew Milner (Monash University), Diane Morgan (University of Leeds), Tom Moylan (University of Limerick), Eglé Paçkauskaité, Nicole Pohl (Oxford Brookes University), Liz Russell (Universitat Rovira i Virgili), Peter Sands (University of Wisconsin), David Sergeant (University of Plymouth), Simon Spiegel (University of Zurich), Adam Stock (York St John University), Judith Suissa (UCL), Elida Tessler, Fatima Vieira (University of Porto), Darren Webb (University of Sheffield).

Individuals and institutions that hosted me for lectures, symposia, and other events, and which were hugely useful for trying out ideas included: Richard Anderson, Elinor Scarth, Penny Travlou, Lisa McKenzie, Francisca Lima, and Ross McLean, Edinburgh University; Luca Csepely-Knorr, Manchester School of Architecture; José Alfredo Ramirez, Architecture Association; Idrees Rasouli and Paulo Zaide, Ravensbourne University; The New Anarchist Research Group; Ingrid Sarlöv-Herlin, SLU Alnarp; SLU Ultuna; Jonathan Beaver, Portland Design Week; Gary Austin and David Giese, University of Idaho; David Drake and Jolie Kaytes, Washington State University; Ceylan Belek Ombregt, Martha Schwartz Partners; David Haney, University of Kent; Nayla Al-Akl and Jala Makhzoumi, American University of Beirut; Salma Samaha, Lebanese University, Beirut; Jens Haendeler, Al-Quds Bard College for Arts and Sciences, Jerusalem and Palestinian Territories; Emile Bojesen, University of Winchester; Megan Blake and Kamni Gill, University of Sheffield; Shelley Egoz, NMBU Norway; Landscape Institute Northeast; London Festival of Architecture; Oliver Wainwright, Fundamentals series at UAL; Ele Carpenter, Goldsmiths; Frequency Festival Lincoln; Ian Thompson, Newcastle University; Birkbeck Institute of Social Research; Christopher Woodward, Garden Museum; Jane Wolff and Alissa North, University of Toronto; Pratt Institute; Lynda Schneekloth, University of Buffalo; Peter Trowbridge, Cornell University; Colgate Searle, Rhode Island School of Design; Linda Corkery, University of New South Wales; Victoria University of Wellington; University of Pennsylvania; Boston Architectural College; Giovanni Santamaria, NYIT; Noël van Dooren, Van Hall Larenstein University of Applied Sciences; Jeroen de Vries, Wageningen University; Antonio Colchete, Universidade Federal de Juiz de Fora, Juiz de Fora, Brazil; Patricia Maya, Universidade Federal do Rio de Janeiro; and the Australian Institute of Landscape Architects.

Many of the ideas which have resulted in published work arose from my Master's degree in landscape architecture from the Rhode Island School of Design. I am, of course, in debt to all my teachers there, but most particularly to my thesis supervisors Derek Bradford, Brian Goldberg, and Elizabeth Grossman.

More than anything I am grateful for the love, support, and understanding of my husband, Jason Tong. My other immediate family, too, have provided not just love but intellect and critique: my parents, Larry and Judy, my brother David, and my brother Alex, his wife Elisa, and their wonderful boys Eliot and Alasdair.

Finally, it's crucially important to thank my students, who have so often been invaluable contributors to the formation of these ideas.

WORKS CITED

Waterman, Tim (2020, Chapter 21) "During and after the pandemic, our streets need more democracy," *Landscape Exchange* (website), June. Landscape Research Group. https://lex.landscaperesearch.org/content/covid-thoughts-during-and-after-the-pandemic-our-streets-need-more-democracy/. Accessed 11 December 2020.

Waterman, Tim (2020, Chapter 26) "The Tasty City: Democratic Life and the Fulfilment of Desire," in Nathaniel Coleman, Ed., *Architecture and Utopia, Vol 2*. New York: Peter Lang.

Waterman, Tim (2018, Chapter 16) "Democracy and Trespass: Political Dimensions of Landscape Access," in Shelley Egoz, Deni Ruggeri, and Karsten Jørgensen, Eds., *Defining Landscape Democracy: A Path to Spatial Justice*. London: Edward Elgar, 143–152.

Waterman, Tim (2018, Chapter 14) "Making Meaning: Utopian Method for Minds, Bodies, and Media in Architectural Design," *Open Library of Humanities*, 4(1), 4.

Waterman, Tim (2018, Chapter 25) "National Progress," *Eleven 2018: National Reserve*. London: Bartlett School of Architecture, n.p.

Waterman, Tim (2018, Chapter 2) "Thailand, Highland, and Secret Island: Landscape and Power in Bond Films," in Jeremy Strong, Ed., *Bond Uncovered*. Cham, Switzerland: Palgrave Macmillan, 185–202.

Waterman, Tim (2018, Chapter 7) "Feasting is a Project," in David Sergeant, Ed., *Imagining Alternatives with Feasts for the Future* [University of Plymouth, website]. http://blogs.plymouth.ac.uk/imaginingalternatives/2018/09/30/feasting-is-a-project-tim-waterman/. Accessed 15 August 2021.

Waterman, Tim (2018, Chapter 23) "Two London Squares and a Theory of the Beige Hole," *Landscape Architecture Magazine*, 108(7), 96–109. Washington, DC: The American Society of Landscape Architects.

Waterman, Tim (2017, Chapter 19) "Despot, Martyr, and Fool: An Obituary for the Garden Bridge," *Landscape Architecture Magazine* [website] 12 May. https://landscapearchitecturemagazine.org/2017/05/12/despot-martyr-and-fool/. Accessed 15 August 2021.

Waterman, Tim (2017, Chapter 18) "It's About Time: The Genius Temporum of Martí Franch's Girona Landscapes," *Landscape Architecture Magazine*, 107(1), 98–103. Washington, DC: The American Society of Landscape Architects.

Waterman, Tim (2016, Chapter 9) "A Word … 'Profession,'" in *Landscape*, Spring. London: The Landscape Institute, 66.

Waterman, Tim (2016, Chapter 24) "A Word … 'Storytelling,'" in *Landscape*, Winter. London: The Landscape Institute, 72.

Waterman, Tim (2016, Chapter 15) "Other Stranger's Paths," *Testing Ground*. London: University of Greenwich, 42–45.

Waterman, Tim (2015, Chapter 3) "A Word … 'Blang,'" in *Landscape*, Spring. London: The Landscape Institute, 66.

Waterman, Tim (2015, Chapter 22) "A Word … 'Inevitable,'" in *Landscape*, Summer. London: The Landscape Institute, 66.

Waterman, Tim (2015, Chapter 5) "The Global Cucumber," in *Landscape Architecture Magazine*, 105(7), 50–56. Washington, DC: The American Society of Landscape Architects.

Waterman, Tim (2014, Chapter 6) "A Word … 'Theatre,'" in *Landscape*, Spring. London: The Landscape Institute, 48.

Waterman, Tim (2014, Chapter 8) "At Liberty," in *Landscape Architecture Magazine*, 104(4), 112–127. Washington, DC: The American Society of Landscape Architects.

Waterman, Tim (2013, Chapter 17) "A Word … 'Habitat,'" in *Landscape*, Winter. London: The Landscape Institute, 74.

Waterman, Tim (2011, Chapter 13) "A Word … 'Vast,'" in *Landscape*, Summer. London: The Landscape Institute, 48.

Waterman, Tim (2011, Chapter 4) "The Flavor of the Place: Eating and Drinking in Payottenland," in Jeremy Strong, Ed., *Educated Tastes: Food, Drink, and Connoisseur Culture*. Lincoln, NE: University of Nebraska Press, 58–80.

Waterman, Tim and Ruth Catlow (2015, Chapter 10) "Situating the Digital Commons: A Conversation Between Tim Waterman and Ruth Catlow," Furtherfield (website), 28 October. www.furtherfield.org/situating-the-digital-commons-a-conversation-between-ruth-catlow-and-tim-waterman/. Accessed 20 November 2020.

REFERENCES

Abensour, Miguel (2011) *Democracy Against the State: Marx and the Machiavellian Moment.* Cambridge and Malden, MA: Polity Press.

Abram, David (1996) *The Spell of the Sensuous: Perception and Language in a More-Than-Human World.* New York: Vintage Books.

Anderson, Benedict (1991 [1983]) *Imagined Communities: Reflections on the Origin and Spread of Nationalism.* London: Verso.

Appadurai, Arjun (1996) *Modernity At Large: Cultural Dimensions of Globalization.* Minneapolis, MN: University of Minnesota Press.

Arendt, Hannah (1977 [1954]) *Between Past and Future: Eight Exercises in Political Thought.* Harmondsworth: Penguin Books.

Arruda, Angela (2015) "Image, Social Imaginary and Social Representations," in *The Cambridge Handbook of Social Representations.* Cambridge: Cambridge University Press, 128–142.

Augé, Marc (1995) *Non-Places: Introduction to an Anthropology of Supermodernity.* Trans. John Howe. London and New York: Verso.

Bachelard, Gaston (1964) *The Psychoanalysis of Fire.* Boston, MA: Beacon Press.

Bachelard, Gaston (1964 [1958]) *The Poetics of Space.* Trans. Maria Jolas. Boston, MA: Beacon Press.

Bailey, Nick (1981) *Fitzrovia.* New Barnet: Historical Publications.

Bakhtin, Mikhail (1981) *The Dialogic Imagination: Four Essays.* Trans. Caryl Emerson and Michael Holquist. Edited by Michael Holquist. Austin, TX: University of Texas Press.

Baldwin, James (2014) *Jimmy's Blues & Other Poems.* Boston, MA: Beacon Press.

Barnes, Barry (2001) "Practice as Collective Action," in Theodore R. Schatzki, Karin Knorr-Cetina, and Eike von Savigny, Eds., *The Practice Turn in Contemporary Theory.* London and New York: Routledge, 1–14.

Baron, Cynthia (2009) "*Doctor No*: Bonding Britishness to Racial Sovereignty," in Christoph Lindner, Ed., *The James Bond Phenomenon: A Critical Reader.* Manchester: Manchester University Press. 153–168.

Barrell, John (1980) *The Dark Side of the Landscape: The Rural Poor in English Painting 1730–1840.* Cambridge: Cambridge University Press.

Bateson, Gregory (2000) *Steps to an Ecology of Mind: Collected Essays in Anthropology, Psychiatry, Evolution, and Epistemology*. Chicago, IL: University of Chicago Press.

Bauman, Zygmunt (2011) *Culture in a Liquid Modern World*. Cambridge and Malden, MA: Polity Press.

Bauman, Zygmunt (2010) "Culture: Liquid-Modern Adventures of an Idea," in John R. Hall, Laura Grindstaff, and Ming-Cheng Lo, Eds., *Handbook of Cultural Sociology*. London and New York: Routledge, 326–334.

Bauman, Zygmunt (2006) *Liquid Fear*. Cambridge and Malden, MA: Polity Press.

Bauman, Zygmunt (2003) *City of Fears, City of Hopes*, Critical Urban Studies, Occasional Papers, London: Goldsmith's College. www.gold.ac.uk/media/documents-by-section/departments/…/city.pdf. Accessed 23 April 2018.

Bauman, Zygmunt (2000) *Liquid Modernity*. Cambridge and Malden, MA: Polity Press.

Bauman, Zygmunt (1994) *Life in Fragments: Essays in Postmodern Morality*. Oxford: Blackwell.

BBC News (2021) "Elon Musk changes job title to 'Technoking of Tesla,'" *BBC News*, 15 March. www.bbc.co.uk/news/technology-56404583. Accessed 14 July 2021.

Beckert, Jens (2016) *Imagined Futures: Fictional Expectations and Capitalist Dynamics*. London and Cambridge, MA: Harvard University Press.

Belasco, Warren (2006) *Meals to Come: A History of the Future of Food*. Berkeley, CA: University of California Press.

Benjamin, Walter and Asja Lacis (1996 [1925]) "Naples," in Walter Benjamin (ed.), *Selected Writings Volume 1: 1913–1916*. London and Cambridge, MA: Harvard University Press, 414–421.

Berman, Marshall (2010 [1982]) *All That Is Solid Melts Into Air: The Experience of Modernity*. London and New York: Verso.

Bermingham, Ann (1987) *Landscape and Ideology: The English Rustic Tradition, 1740–1860*. London and New York: Thames and Hudson.

Betancourt, Sarah (2021) "Richard Branson Flies to the Edge of Space in Virgin Galactic Passenger Rocket Plane," *The Guardian*, 11 July. www.theguardian.com/science/2021/jul/11/richard-branson-virgin-galactic-space. Accessed 12 July 2021.

Bhabha, Homi K. (1994) *The Location of Culture*. London and New York: Routledge.

Biesta, Gert J.J. (2014) The Beautiful Risk of Education. London and Boulder, CO: Paradigm Publishers.

Bloch, Ernst (1986) The Principle of Hope. Trans. Nevill Plaice, Stephen Plaice, and Paul Knight. Oxford: Basil Blackwell.

Bookchin, Murray (2005) *The Ecology of Freedom: The Emergence and Dissolution of Hierarchy*. Oakland, CA: AK Press.

Bottici, Chiara (2014) *Imaginal Politics: Images Beyond Imagination and the Imaginary*. New York: Columbia University Press.

Bourdieu, Pierre (2000) "For a Scholarship of Commitment," in *Profession*, 40–45.

Bourdieu, Pierre (1979) *Distinction: A Social Critique of the Judgement of Taste*. Trans. Richard Nice. New York and London: Routledge.

Bourdieu, Pierre (1977) *Outline of a Theory of Practice*. Trans. Richard Nice. Cambridge: Cambridge University Press.

Carruthers, Peter (2006) "Why Pretend?" Shaun Nichols, Ed., *The Architecture of the Imagination: New Essays on Pretence, Possibility, and Fiction*. Oxford: Oxford University Press, 89–109.

Casid, Jill H. (2005) *Sowing Empire: Landscape and Colonization*. London and Minneapolis, MN: University of Minnesota Press.

Castells, Manuel (1997) *The Power of Identity*. Malden, MA: Blackwell Publishing.

Castells, Manuel (1989) *The Informational City: Information Technology, Economic Restructuring, and the Urban Regional Process.* Oxford and Cambridge, MA: Blackwell.

Castoriadis, Cornelius (1987 [1975]) *The Imaginary Institution of Society.* Trans. Kathleen Blamey. Cambridge: Polity Press.

Catlow, Ruth (2011) "12.6.11 Ruth Catlow's Response to TDP," *6Months: Telematic Dinner Party* (website). https://web.archive.org/web/20160628180736/http://www.6months.shadiblue.org/2011/06/12/12-6-11-ruth-catlows-response-to-tdp/. Accessed 11 July 2021.

Catlow, Ruth and Marc Garrett (2012) "Do It With Others: No Ecology without Social Ecology," in Simon Biggs, Ed., *Remediating the Social 2012.* Edinburgh: University of Edinburgh, 69–74.

Chancellor, E. Beresford (1930) *London's Old Latin Quarter.* London: Jonathan Cape.

Charlesworth, J.J. (2014) "The Ego-Centric Art World is Killing Art," *Artnet News*, 30 December. https://news.artnet.com/art-world/the-ego-centric-art-world-is-killing-art-197530. Accessed 3 November 2015.

Choi, Jaz Hee-jeong (2014) "Introduction," in Jaz Hee-jeong Choi, Marcus Foth, and Greg Hearn, Eds., *Eat, Cook, Grow: Mixing Human-Computer Interactions with Human-Food Interactions.* Cambridge, MA and New York: MIT Press, 1–8.

Chomsky, Noam (2012) *Occupy.* London and New York: Penguin.

Churchill, Chris (2020) "SpaceX, Blue Origin, Virgin Galactic and the Overview Effect," *Las Cruces Sun News* https://eu.lcsun-news.com/story/life/sunlife/2020/06/07/spacex-blue-origin-virgin-galactic-and-overview-effect/3141774001/. Accessed 12 July 2021.

Clément, Gilles (2015) *The Planetary Garden and Other Writings.* Trans. Sandra Morris. Philadelphia, PA: University of Pennsylvania Press.

Code, Lorraine (2006) *Ecological Thinking: The Politics of Epistemic Location.* Oxford and New York: Oxford University Press.

Coleman, Nathaniel (2005) *Utopias and Architecture.* London and New York: Routledge.

Collini, Stefan (2017) *Speaking of Universities.* London and New York: Verso.

Comber, Robert, Pollie Barden, Nick Bryan-Kinns, and Patrick Olivier (2014) "Not Sharing Sushi: Exploring Social Presence and Connectedness at the Telematic Dinner Party," in Jaz Hee-jeong Choi, Marcus Foth, and Greg Hearn, Eds., *Eat, Cook, Grow: Mixing Human-Computer Interactions with Human-Food Interactions.* Cambridge, MA and New York: MIT Press, 65–79.

Corner, James, Ed. (1999) *Recovering Landscape: Essays in Contemporary Landscape Architecture.* New York: Princeton Architectural Press.

Cosgrove, Denis (1998 [1984]) *Social Formation and Symbolic Landscape.* Madison, WI: The University of Wisconsin Press.

Council of Europe (2000) *The European Landscape Convention* [Leaflet]: Florence, 20 October. https://rm.coe.int/CoERMPublicCommonSearchServices/DisplayDCTMContent?documentId=09000016802f28a4. Accessed 27 September 2016.

Cox, Kenneth J. (1998 [1987]) "Foreword to the Second Edition," in Frank White, Ed., *The Overview Effect: Space Exploration and Human Evolution*, 2nd edition. Reston, VA: American Institute of Aeronautics and Astronautics.

Cresswell, Tim (2003) "Landscape and the Obliteration of Practice," in Kay Anderson, Mona Domosh, Steve Pile, and Nigel Thrift, Eds., *Handbook of Cultural Geography.* London: Sage Publications, 269–281.

Cresswell, Tim (1996) *In Place/Out of Place: Geography, Ideology, and Transgression.* London and Minneapolis, MN: University of Minnesota Press.

Cronon, William (1996) *Uncommon Ground: Rethinking the Human Place in Nature*. New York: W.W. Norton.

Curtis, Neal (2013) *Idiotism: Capitalism and the Privatisation of Life*. London: Pluto Press.

Daniels, Stephen (1993) *Fields of Vision: Landscape Imagery and National Identity in England and the United States*. Cambridge: Polity Press.

Daub, Adrian and Charles Kronengold (2015) *The James Bond Songs: Pop Anthems of Late Capitalism*. Oxford and New York: Oxford University Press.

de Certeau, Michel, Luce Giard, and Pierre Mayol (1998) *The Practice of Everyday Life Vol. 2: Living and Cooking*. Trans. Timothy J. Tomasik. Minneapolis, MN: University of Minnesota Press, 205.

de Certeau, Michel (1984) *The Practice of Everyday Life*. Trans. Steven Rendall. Berkeley, CA: University of California Press.

Defoe, Daniel (1995 [1722]) *Journal of the Plague Year*. Project Gutenberg. www.gutenberg. org/files/376/376-h/376-h.htm. Accessed 7 July 2021.

Denning, Michael (1987) "Licensed to Look: James Bond and the Heroism of Consumption," in Francis Mulhern, Ed., (1992) *Contemporary Marxist Literary Criticism*. Harlow, Essex and New York: Longman Publishing. 211–229.

Department for Transport (2007) *The Official Highway Code*, revised 2007 edition. London: The Stationery Office.

Deutsche, Rosalyn (1991) "Boys Town," *Environment and Planning D: Society and Space* 9: 5–30. Quoted in Tim Cresswell and Deborah Dixon, Eds. (2002) "Introduction: Engaging Film," in *Engaging Film: Geographies of Mobility and Identity*. Lanham, MD: Rowman & Littlefield Publishers, Inc. 1–10.

Dissanayake, Ellen (1992) *Homo Aestheticus: Where Art Comes From and Why*. New York: The Free Press.

Douzinas, Costas (2014) "From Greece to Ukraine: Welcome to the New Age of Resistance," *Open Democracy, The Guardian*, 4 March. www.theguardian.com/commentisfree/2014/mar/04/greece-ukraine-welcome-new-age-resistance. Accessed 22 September 2014.

Driskill, Qwo-Li, Chris Finley, Brian Joseph Gilley, and Scott Lauria Morgensen, Eds. (2011) *Queer Indigenous Studies: Critical Interventions in Theory, Politics, and Literature*. Tucson, AZ: University of Arizona Press.

Eno, Brian (n.d.) "Scenius," n.d. *P2P Foundation*. http://p2pfoundation.net/Scenius. Accessed 30 April 2016.

Fisher, M.F.K. (2004 [1943]) "The Gastronomical Me," in *The Art of Eating*. Hoboken, NJ: Wiley, 351–572.

Fitch, Robert (1993) *The Assassination of New York*. London and New York: Verso.

Frascari, Marco (2004) "*Semiotica ab Edendo*: Taste in Architecture," in Jamie Horwitz and Paulette Singley, Eds., *Eating Architecture*. London and Cambridge, MA: MIT Press.

Freire, Paulo (2007 [1968]) *Pedagogy of the Oppressed, 30th Anniversary Edition*. Trans. Myra Bergman Ramos. New York: Continuum.

Furtherfield (2015) "Beyond the Interface," (exhibition) at Furtherfield Gallery May–June 2015, *furtherfield.org*. www.furtherfield.org/beyond-the-interface-london/. Accessed 2 July 2021.

Furtherfield (2014) "Piratbyrån and Friends," (exhibition) at Furtherfield Gallery May–June 2014, *furtherfield.org*. www.furtherfield.org/piratbyran-and-friends/. Accessed 2 July 2021.

Furtherfield (2012) "We Won't Fly For Art: Media Art Ecologies," *furtherfield.org*. www.furtherfield.org/we-wont-fly-for-art-media-art-ecologies/. Accessed 8 July 2021.

Furtherfield (Ruth Catlow, Marc Garrett, Charlotte Frost, and Rob Myers) (2011) *Collaboration and Freedom—The World of Free and Open Source Art*. https://wiki.p2pfoundation.net/World_of_Free_and_Open_Source_Art. Accessed 2 July 2021.

Furtherfield (2009) "Feral Trade Café," (exhibition) at HTTP Gallery, June–August 2009, *furtherfield.org*. www.furtherfield.org/feral-trade-cafe-2/. Accessed 8 July 2021.

Furtherfield (2006) "DIWO: Do It With Others Resource," *furtherfield.org*. www.furtherfield.org/diwo-do-it-with-others-resource/. Accessed 2 July 2021.

Furtherfield (n.d.) "Rich Networking," *furtherfield.org*. www.furtherfield.org/rich-networking/. Accessed 8 July 2021.

Gardiner, Michael E. (2000) *Critiques of Everyday Life*. London and New York: Routledge.

Garrett, Marc (2014) "We Need to Talk About Networked Disruption and Business: An interview with Tatiana Bazzichelli," *furtherfield.org*. www.furtherfield.org/we-need-to-talk-about-networked-disruption-and-business-an-interview-with-tatiana-bazzichelli/. Accessed 2 July 2021.

Gayah, Vikash V. (2012) "Analytical Capacity Comparison of One-Way and Two-Way Signalized Street Networks," *Transportation Research Record*, No. 2301, 76–85.

Geddes, Patrick (1885) *An Analysis of the Principles of Economics (Part I)*. London and Edinburgh: Williams and Norgate.

Gilbert, Jeremy (2014) *Common Ground: Democracy and Collectivity in an Age of Individualism*. London: Pluto Press.

Giroux, Henry A. (2007) "Utopian Thinking in Dangerous Times: Critical Pedagogy and the Project of Educated Hope," in Mark Coté, Richard J.F. Day, and Greig de Peuter, Eds., *Utopian Pedagogy: Radical Experiments Against Neoliberal Globalization*. Toronto: University of Toronto Press, 25–42.

Goldman, Emma (1931) *Living My Life*. New York: Alfred A. Knopf.

Gould, Stephen Jay (1997) "Kropotkin was no Crackpot," Marxists.org. www.marxists.org/subject/science/essays/kropotkin.htm. Accessed 23 August 2018. Originally published in 1988 in *Natural History*, vol. 97, issue no. 7.

Graeber, David (2013) *The Democracy Project: A History, A Crisis, A Movement*. London and New York: Penguin.

Gudeman, Stephen (2001) *The Anthropology of Economy: Community, Market, and Culture*. Oxford and Malden, MA: Blackwell Publishers.

Hall, Stuart (2007) "Universities, Intellectuals, and Multitudes: An Interview with Stuart Hall," in Mark Coté, Richard J.F. Day, and Greig de Peuter, Eds., Utopian *Pedagogy: Radical Experiments Against Neoliberal Globalization*. (Interviewed by Greig de Peuter). Toronto: University of Toronto Press, 108–128.

Hall, Stuart (1992) "The West and the Rest: Discourse and Power," in Stuart Hall and Gieben, Bram, Eds., *Formations of Modernity*. Cambridge: Polity Press and Open University, 276–320.

Hallward, Peter (2012) "People and Power: Four Notes on Democracy and Dictatorship," in Federico Campagna and Emanuele Campiglio, Eds., *What We Are Fighting For: A Radical Collective Manifesto*. London: Pluto Press, 61–72.

Haraway, Donna J. (2016) *Staying with the Trouble: Making Kin in the Chthulucene*. London and Durham, NC: Duke University Press.

Haraway, Donna J. (1991) *Simians, Cyborgs, and Women: The Reinvention of Nature*. London: Free Association Books.

Haraway, Donna J. (1988) "Situated Knowledges: The Science Question in Feminism and the Privilege of Partial Perspective," *Feminist Studies*, 14(3), 575–599.

Hardin, Garrett (1968) "The Tragedy of the Commons," *Science*, 13 December, 1243–1248.

Harries, Karsten (1997) *The Ethical Function of Architecture*. London and Cambridge, MA: MIT Press.

Harris, John (2014) "London has become a Citadel, Sealed off from the rest of Britain," *The Guardian*, 14 April. www.theguardian.com/commentisfree/2014/apr/14/london-oligarch-city-capital-cost-of-living. Accessed 7 July 2021.

Harrison, Ann (2006) "LSD: The Geek's Wonder Drug?" *Wired*, 16 January. www.wired. com/2006/01/lsd-the-geeks-wonder-drug/?currentPage=2. Accessed 12 July 2021.

Harvey, David (2013) *Rebel Cities: From the Right to the City to the Urban Revolution*. London and New York: Verso.

Harvey, David (2005) *A Brief History of Neoliberalism*. Oxford and New York: Oxford University Press.

Hatherley, Owen (2010) *A Guide to the New Ruins of Great Britain*. London and New York: Verso.

Hayden, Dolores (1997) "Urban Landscape History: The Sense of Place and the Politics of Space," in Groth, Paul and Todd W. Bressi, *Understanding Ordinary Landscapes*. London and New Haven, CT: Yale University Press, 114.

Heatherwick, Thomas (2017) "One Day I Hope London Gets its Garden Bridge," *Evening Standard*, 2 May. www.standard.co.uk/comment/comment/thomas-heatherwick-one-day-i-hope-london-gets-its-garden-bridge-a3528321.html. Accessed 7 July 2021.

Helsinger, Elizabeth (2002) "Turner and the Representation of England," in W.J.T. Mitchell, Ed., *Landscape and Power*, 2nd edition. London and Chicago, IL: University of Chicago Press, 103–125.

Hobbes, Thomas (1782 [1642]) *Elementa Philosophica de Cive*. Lausanne: François Grasset & Socios.

Hofmann, Albert (1997 [1979]) *LSD: My Problem Child* (website). https://web.archive.org/web/19970618092810/www.lycaeum.org/books/books/my_problem_child/. Accessed 12 July 2021.

hooks, bell (2000) *Feminist Theory: From Margin to Center*, 2nd edition. Cambridge, MA: South End Press.

Hope, Sophie (n.d.) *1984 Dinners* (website). https://1984dinners.sophiehope.org.uk/. Accessed 8 July 2021.

Howells, Richard (2015) A Critical Theory of Creativity: Utopia, Aesthetics, Atheism and Design. Basingstoke and New York: Palgrave Macmillan.

Hunchuck, Elise Misao, Marco Ferrari, and Jingru (Cyan) Chen (2021) "Prologue to the Sky River," *The Avery Review*, Issue No. 53, June. http://averyreview.com/issues/53/prologue-to-the-sky-river. Accessed 14 July 2021.

Ingold, Tim (2007) *Lines: A Brief History*. Abingdon, Oxon. and New York: Routledge.

Ingold, Tim (2000) *The Perception of the Environment*. London and New York: Routledge.

Jackson, John Brinckerhoff (1997 [1957]) "The Stranger's Path," in Helen Lefkowitz Horowitz, Ed., *Landscape in Sight: Looking at America*. London and New Haven, CT: Yale University Press, 18–29.

Jackson, John Brinckerhoff (1984) *Discovering the Vernacular Landscape*. London and New Haven, CT: Yale University Press, xii.

Jacobs, Jane (1970) *The Economy of Cities*. New York: Vintage.

Jamie, Kathleen (2008) "A Lone Enraptured Male," London Review of Books, Vol. 30, No. 5, 6 March. https://www.lrb.co.uk/the-paper/v30/n05/kathleen-jamie/a-lone-enraptured-male. Accessed 13 July 2021.

Jencks, Charles (2005) *The Iconic Building: The Power of Enigma*. London: Frances Lincoln.

Johnson, Mark (2007) *The Meaning of the Body: Aesthetics of Human Understanding*. London and Chicago, IL: University of Chicago Press.

Kern, Sim (2021) "No, Billionaires Won't 'Escape' to Space While the World Burns," *Salon* (website), 7 July. www.salon.com/2021/07/07/no-billionaires-wont-escape-to-space-while-the-world-burns/. Accessed 13 July 2021.

Khaleeli, Homa (2015) "A Body Language Lesson Gone Wrong: Why is George Osborne Standing Like Beyoncé?" in *The Guardian*, 7 October. www.theguardian.com/politics/shortcuts/2015/oct/07/who-told. Accessed 1 November 2016.

Klein, Naomi (2001) *No Logo*. London and New York: Harper Collins.

Knorr-Cetina, Karin (1999) *Epistemic Cultures: How the Sciences Make Knowledge*. London and Cambridge, MA: Harvard University Press.

Kockel, Ullrich (2014) "Towards an Ethnology Beyond Self, Other and Third: Toposophical Explorations," *Tradicija ir dabartis*, 9: 19–40.

Korsmeyer, Carolyn (1999) *Making Sense of Taste: Food and Philosophy*. Ithaca, NY: Cornell University Press.

Kostof, Spiro (1991) *The City Shaped: Urban Patterns and Meanings Through History*. London and New York: Thames and Hudson.

Kropotkin, Peter (1987 [1902]) *Mutual Aid: A Factor of Evolution*. London: Freedom Press.

Kropotkin, Peter (1985 [1912]) *Fields, Factories and Workshops Tomorrow*. Edited by Colin Ward. London: Freedom Press.

Lakoff, George and Mark Johnson (1999) *Philosophy in the Flesh: The Embodied Mind and Its Challenge to Western Thought*. New York: Basic Books.

Lefebvre, Henri (2014) *Toward an Architecture of Enjoyment*. Edited by Łukasz Stanek. Trans. Robert Bononno. Minneapolis, MN: University of Minnesota Press.

Lefebvre, Henri (2008 [1947]) *Critique of Everyday Life Volume 1*. Trans. John Moore. London: Verso.

Lefebvre, Henri (2005 [1981]) *Critique of Everyday Life, Volume 3: From Modernity to Modernism*. Trans. John Moore. London: Verso.

Lefebvre, Henri (2002 [1961]) *Critique of Everyday Life, Volume 2: Foundations for a Sociology of the Everyday*. Trans. John Moore. London: Verso.

Lefebvre, Henri (2000 [1968]) *Everyday Life in the Modern World*. Trans. Sacha Rabinovitch. London: The Athlone Press.

Lefebvre, Henri (1991 [1974]) *The Production of Space*. Trans. Donald Nicholson-Smith. Malden, MA: Blackwell Publishing.

Leopold, Aldo (1966 [1949]) *A Sand County Almanac*. New York: Ballantine.

Leski, Kyna (2015) *The Storm of Creativity*. Cambridge, MA: MIT Press.

Levitas, Ruth (2013) *Utopia as Method: The Imaginary Reconstitution of Society*. Basingstoke and New York: Palgrave Macmillan.

Linebaugh, Peter (2014) *Stop Thief! The Commons, Enclosures, and Resistance*. Oakland, CA: PM Press.

Linebaugh, Peter and Rediker, Marcus (2000) *The Many-Headed Hydra: Sailors, Slaves, Commoners, and the Hidden History of the Revolutionary Atlantic*. London: Verso.

Makdisi, Saree (1998) *Romantic Imperialism: Universal Empire and the Culture of Modernity*. Cambridge and New York: Cambridge University Press.

Malm, Andreas (2016) *Fossil Capital: The Rise of Steam Power and the Roots of Global Warming*. London: Verso.

Marx, Karl and Frederick Engels (1948 [1848]) *The Communist Manifesto*, Centenary edition. London: Lawrence and Wishart.

Mbembe, Achille (2019) *Necropolitics*. Trans. Steven Corcoran. London and Durham, NC: Duke University Press.

McHarg, Ian (1992 [1969]) *Design with Nature*. New York: John Wiley & Sons.

Meinig, D.W. (1979) "The Beholding Eye: Ten Versions of the Same Scene," in D.W. Meinig, Ed., *The Interpretation of Ordinary Landscapes: Geographical Essays*. Oxford and New York: Oxford University Press.

Mexico City News Daily (2016) "CDMX Parade Attracts Crowds—and Criticism," 1 November. http://mexiconewsdaily.com/news/cdmx-parade-attracts-crowds-and-critic ism/. Accessed 2 November 2016.

Meyer, Elizabeth K. (2000) "The Post-Earth Day Conundrum: Translating Environmental Values into Landscape Design," in Michel Conan, Ed., *Environmentalism in Landscape Architecture—Dumbarton Oaks Colloquium on the History of Landscape Architecture XXII.* Washington, DC: Dumbarton Oaks.

Minton, Anna (2017) *Big Capital: Who is London For?* London and New York: Penguin.

Minton, Anna (2009) *Ground Control: Fear and Happiness in the Twenty-First Century City.* London and New York: Penguin.

Mitchell, W.J.T., Ed. (2002 [1994]) *Landscape and Power*, 2nd edition. London and Chicago, IL: University of Chicago Press.

Morell-Hart, Shanti (2012) "Foodways and Resilience under Apocalyptic Conditions," in *Culture, Agriculture, Food and Environment*, 34(2), 161–171.

Morris, William (1993 [1890]) *News from Nowhere and Other Writings.* London and New York: Penguin.

Morris, William (1882) "The Beauty of Life," in Hopes and Fears for Art. www.marxists.org/archive/morris/works/1882/hopes/chapters/chapter3.htm. Accessed 11 May 2018.

Morrison, Jonathan (2017) "Joanna Lumley Fights On for Her Fabulous Bridge," *The Times*, 29 April. www.thetimes.co.uk/article/lumley-fights-on-for-her-fabulous-bridge-5mt70xmqm. Accessed 7 July 2021.

Moylan, Tom (1986) *Demand the Impossible: Science Fiction and the Utopian Imagination.* London and New York: Methuen.

Murphy, Douglas (2017) *Nincompoopopolis: The Follies of Boris Johnson.* London: Repeater.

Neimanis, Astrida (2017) *Bodies of Water: Posthuman Feminist Phenomenology.* London and New York: Bloomsbury.

Nichols, Shaun and Stich, Stephen (2000) "A Cognitive Theory of Pretense," *Cognition*, 74(2), 115–147.

Norton, Peter D. (2011) *Fighting Traffic: The Dawn of the Motor Age in the American City.* Cambridge, MA: MIT Press.

Olwig, Kenneth R. (2019) *The Meanings of Landscape: Essays on Place, Space, Environment and Justice.* London and New York: Routledge.

Olwig, Kenneth R. (2011) "The Right Rights to the Right Landscape?" in Egoz, Shelley, Jala Makhzoumi, and Gloria Pungetti. *The Right to Landscape: Contesting Landscape and Human Rights.* Farnham and Burlington, VT: Ashgate, 39–50.

Olwig, Kenneth (2005) "Representation and Alienation in the Political Land-*scape*," *Cultural Geographies*, 12, 19–40. London: Edward Arnold.

Olwig, Kenneth (2002) *Landscape, Nature, and the Body Politic: From Britain's Renaissance to America's New World.* Madison, WI: University of Wisconsin Press.

Olwig, Kenneth (1996) "Recovering the Substantive Nature of Landscape," *Annals of the Association of American Geographers*, 86(4) (December), 630–653. www.jstor.org/stable/2564345. Accessed 31 October 2021.

Olwig, Kenneth R. and Don Mitchell, Eds. (2009) *Justice, Power and the Political Landscape.* Abingdon and New York: Routledge.

Omaze (n.d.) *Omaze* (website). www.omaze.com/products/virgin-galactic-2021?ref=space. Accessed 12 July 2021.

Ong, Walter J. (1982) *Orality and Literacy: The Technologizing of the Word.* London and New York: Routledge.

Ortner, Sherry (2006) *Anthropology and Social Theory: Culture, Power, and the Acting Subject.* London and Durham, NC: Duke University Press.

Ostrom, Elinor (1990) *Governing the Commons: The Evolution of Institutions for Collective Action.* Cambridge: Cambridge University Press.

Pérez, Santiago R. (2012) "Towards an Ecology of Making," in Gail Peter Borden and Michael Meredith, Eds., *Matter: Material Processes in Architectural Education*. Abingdon and New York: Routledge, 379–395.

Péréz-Gómez, Alberto (2006) *Built upon Love: Architectural Longing after Ethics and Aesthetics*. London and Cambridge, MA: The MIT Press.

Poulain, Jean-Pierre (2017) *The Sociology of Food: Eating and the Place of Food in Society*. Trans. Augusta Dörr. London and New York: Bloomsbury Academic.

Probyn, Elspeth (2016) *Eating the Ocean*. London and Durham, NC: Duke University Press.

Proctor, Robert N. and Londa Schiebinger (2008) *Agnotology: The Making and Unmaking of Ignorance*. Stanford, CA: Stanford University Press.

Rancière, Jacques (1991) *The Ignorant Schoolmaster: Five Lessons in Intellectual Emancipation*. Trans. Kristin Ross. Stanford, CA: Stanford University Press.

Raqs Media Collective (Jeebesh Bagchi, Monica Narula, and Shuddhabrata Sengupta) (2003) "A Concise Lexicon Of / For the Digital Commons," *Sarai Reader 3: Shaping Technologies*. Delhi: Centre for the Study of Developing Cities, 357–365.

Ravetz, Joe (2000) "Recasting the Urban Fringe," *The Journal of Landscape Design*, 294(10), 13–16.

Reed, Chris and Nina-Marie Lister, Eds. (2014) *Projective Ecologies*. New York: Actar Publishers.

Rich, Kate (n.d.) *Feral Trade (Import/Export)* (website) https://feraltrade.org/cgi-bin/cour ier/courier.pl. Accessed 8 July 2021.

Ricoeur, Paul (1979) "The Function of Fiction in Shaping Reality," *Man and World*, 12, 123–141.

Robin Hood Asset Management Cooperative (n.d.) *Robin Hood Coop* (website) www. robinhoodcoop.org/. Accessed 2 July 2021.

Robinson, Joan (1971) *Economic Heresies: Some Old-Fashioned Questions in Economic Theory*. New York: Basic Books.

Robinson, Kim Stanley (2018) "Enough Is as Good as a Feast," in David Sergeant, Ed., *Imagine with Plymouth University: Imagining Alternatives with Feasts for the Future* (blog). http://blogs.plymouth.ac.uk/imaginingalternatives/2018/08/15/enough-is-as-good-as-a-feast-by-kim-stanley-robinson/. Accessed 25 April 2021.

Ross, Kristin (1991) "Translator's Introduction," in Jacques Rancière, *The Ignorant Schoolmaster: Five Lessons in Intellectual Emancipation*. Trans. Kristin Ross. Stanford, CA: Stanford University Press, vii–xxiii.

Rothman, Benny (2012 [1982]) *The Battle for Kinder Scout Including the 1932 Mass Trespass*. Timperley, Cheshire: Willow Publishing.

Ruskin, John (1921 [1860]) *Unto This Last*. Library of Congress. https://archive.org/details/ untothislast00rusk. Accessed 18 August 2017.

Rybczynski, Witold (2014) "The Franchising of Architecture," *The New York Times*, 11 June. www.nytimes.com/2014/06/11/t-magazine/gehry-norman-foster-moshe-safdie-starchitects-locatects-franchising-of-architecture.html. Accessed 7 July 2021.

Rykwert, Joseph (1976) *The Idea of a Town: The Anthropology of Urban Form in Rome, Italy and the Ancient World*. London: Faber and Faber.

Ryley, Peter (2013) *Making Another World Possible: Anarchism, Anti-Capitalism and Ecology in Late 19th and Early 20th Century Britain*. New York and London: Bloomsbury.

Sargent, Lyman Tower (1994) "Three Faces of Utopianism Revisited," *Utopian Studies*, 5(1): 1–37.

Sargisson, Lucy (2012) *Fool's Gold? Utopianism in the Twenty-First Century*. Basingstoke and New York: Palgrave Macmillan.

Sargisson, Lucy (2000) *Utopian Bodies and the Politics of Transgression*. London and New York: Routledge.

Scarry, Elaine (2000) *On Beauty and Being Just*. London: Gerald Duckworth and Co.

Schatzki, Theodore R. (2010) *The Timespace of Human Activity: On Performance, Society, and History as Indeterminate Teleological Events*. Lanham, MD: Lexington Books.

Schatzki, Theodore R., Karin Knorr-Cetina, and Eike von Savigny, Eds. (2000) *The Practice Turn in Contemporary Theory*. London and New York: Routledge.

Schatzki, Theodore R. (1996) *Social Practices: A Wittgensteinian Approach to Human Activity and the Social*. Cambridge: Cambridge University Press.

Scott, James C. (1998) *Seeing Like a State: How Certain Schemes to Improve the Human Condition Have Failed*. London and New Haven, CT: Yale University Press.

Seamon, David (1980) "Body-Subject, Time-Space Routines, and Place-Ballets," in Anne Buttimer and David Seamon, Eds., *The Human Experience of Space and Place*. London: Croom Helm, 148–165.

Sedgwick, Eve Kosofsky (2003) *Touching Feeling: Affect, Pedagogy, Performativity*. London and Durham, NC: Duke University Press.

Sennett, Richard (1974) *The Fall of Public Man*. London and New York: Penguin Books.

Shonfield, Katherine (2000) *Walls Have Feelings: Architecture, Film and the City*. London and New York: Routledge.

Simons, Maarten and Jan Masschelein, Eds. (2011) Rancière, Public Education and the Taming of Democracy. Malden, MA and Oxford: Wiley Blackwell.

Simons, Maarten and Jan Masschelein (2007) "The Learning Society and Governmentality: An Introduction," in Jan Masschelein et al., Eds., *The Learning Society from the Perspective of Governmentality*. Oxford and Malden, MA: Blackwell Publishing, 3–16.

Smith, Linda Tuhiwai (2012) *Decolonizing Methodologies: Research and Indigenous Peoples*, 2nd edition. London and New York: Zed Books.

Snyder, Gary (1974) "I Went into the Maverick Bar," *Turtle Island*. New York: New Directions, 9.

Snyder, Gary (1969) "For the Children," *Turtle Island*. New York: New Directions, 86.

Soja, Edward (2010a) "Six Discourses on the Postmetropolis," in Gary Bridge and Sophie Watson, Eds., *The Blackwell City Reader*, 2nd edition. Chichester and Malden, MA: Wiley-Blackwell. 374–381.

Soja, Edward (2010b) *Seeking Spatial Justice*. Minneapolis, MN: University of Minnesota Press.

Soja, Edward (1996) *Thirdspace: Journeys to Los Angeles and Other Real-and-Imagined Places*. Oxford and Malden, MA: Blackwell Publishing.

Soper, Kate (2020) *Post-Growth Living: For an Alternative Hedonism*. London and New York: Verso.

Soper, Kate, Martin Ryle and Lyn Thomas, Eds. (2009) *The Politics and Pleasures of Consuming Differently*. Basingstoke and New York: Palgrave Macmillan.

Spencer, Douglas (2016) *The Architecture of Neoliberalism: How Contemporary Architecture Became an Instrument of Control and Compliance*. London and New York: Bloomsbury.

Stalder, Felix (2010) "Digital Commons: A Dictionary Entry," *Notes & Nodes on Society, Technology and the Space of the Possible*. http://felix.openflows.com/node/137. Accessed 2 July 2021.

Stallman, Richard (2005) "Bill Gates and Other Communists," *Gnu Operating System*. www.gnu.org/philosophy/bill-gates-and-other-communists.en.html. Accessed 7 April 2017.

Stanek, Łukasz (2014) "A Manuscript Found in Saragossa: Toward an Architecture," in Lefebvre, Henri *Toward an Architecture of Enjoyment*. Edited by Łukasz Stanek. Trans. Robert Bononno. Minneapolis, MN: University of Minnesota Press, xi–lxi.

Stanek, Lukasz (2011) *Henri Lefebvre on Space: Architecture, Urban Research, and the Production of Theory*. Minneapolis, MN: University of Minnesota Press.

Steel, Carolyn (2008) *Hungry City: How Food Shapes Our Lives*. London: Chatto and Windus.

Stengers, Isabelle (2010) *Cosmopolitics I*. Trans. Robert Bononno. London and Minneapolis, MN: University of Minnesota Press.

Stewart, Kathleen (2007) *Ordinary Affects*. London and Durham, NC: Duke University Press.

Stoppard, Tom (1993) *Arcadia: A Play*. London: Samuel French.

Storr, Cait (2020) "Could corporations control territory in space? Under new US rules, it might be possible," *The Conversation*, 2 June 2020. https://theconversation.com/could-corporations-control-territory-in-space-under-new-us-rules-it-might-be-possible-138 939. Accessed 12 July 2021.

Thompson, E.P. (2013) *Whigs and Hunters: The Origin of the Black Act*. London: Breviary Stuff Publications.

Thrift, Nigel (2010) "Understanding the Material Practices of Glamour," in Melissa Gregg and Gregory J. Seigworth, Eds., *The Affect Theory Reader*. London and Durham, NC: Duke University Press, 289–308.

Tomasello, Michael (1999) *The Cultural Origins of Human Cognition*. London and Cambridge, MA: Harvard University Press.

Toulmin, Stephen (1990) *Cosmopolis: The Hidden Agenda of Modernity*. Chicago, IL: University of Chicago Press.

Toussaint-Samat, Maguelonne (2009 [1987]) *A History of Food*, 2nd edition. Trans. Anthea Bell. Malden, MA and Oxford: Wiley-Blackwell.

Tsing, Anna Lowenhaupt (2015) *The Mushroom at the End of the World: On the Possibility of Life in Capitalist Ruins*. Princeton, NJ: Princeton University Press.

Tuan, Yi-Fu (1990 [1974]) *Topophilia: A Study of Environmental Perceptions, Attitudes, and Values*. New York, Columbia University Press.

Turkle, Sherry (2011) *Alone Together: Why We Expect More from Technology and Less from Each Other*. New York: Basic Books.

UNESCO World Heritage Commission (n.d.) "Cultural Landscape, History and Terminology," *UNESCO.ORG* http://whc.unesco.org/en/culturallandscape/. Accessed 17 January 2009.

UNOOSA (United Nations Office for Outer Space Affairs) (n.d.) *Treaty on Principles Governing the Activities of States in the Exploration and Use of Outer Space, including the Moon and Other Celestial Bodies* (website). www.unoosa.org/oosa/en/ourwork/spacelaw/treaties/introouterspacetreaty.html. Accessed 12 July 2021.

van Eijk, Cristian (2020) "Sorry, Elon: Mars is not a legal vacuum—and it's not yours, either," *Völkerrechtsblog*, 5 November. https://voelkerrechtsblog.org/sorry-elon-mars-is-not-a-legal-vacuum-and-its-not-yours-either/. Accessed 12 July 2021.

von Osten, Marion (2009) "Architecture Without Architects: Another Anarchist Approach," *e-flux*, Vol. 6 (May) www.e-flux.com/journal/06/61401/architecture-without-architects-another-anarchist-approach/. Accessed 29 August 2018.

Wainwright, Oliver (2014) "London's Garden Bridge: 'It feels like we're trying to pull off a crime,'" *The Guardian*, 24 June. www.theguardian.com/artanddesign/2014/jun/24/garden-bridge-london-thomas-heatherwick-joanna-lumley. Accessed 7 July 2021.

Walker, Peter (2017) "Thames Garden Bridge Scrapped by Sadiq Khan," *The Guardian*, 28 April. www.theguardian.com/uk-news/2017/apr/28/garden-bridge-across-thames-scrapped-by-sadiq-khan-london. Accessed 7 July 2021.

Wall, Ed and Tim Waterman, Eds. (2017) *Landscape and Agency: Critical Essays*. London and New York: Routledge.

Walzer, Michael (1992) "The Civil Society Argument," in Chantal Mouffe, Ed., *Dimensions of Radical Democracy: Pluralism, Citizenship, Community*. London and New York: Verso, 89–107.

Ward, Colin (1982 [1973]) *Anarchy in Action*. London: Freedom Press.

Warde, Alan (2016) *The Practice of Eating*. Cambridge and Malden, MA: Polity Press.

Waterman, Tim (2019) "Introducing Hope: Landscape Architecture and Utopian Pedagogy," in Richard Stiles, Elke Mertens, Nilgül Karadeniz, and Karsten Jørgensen, Eds., *Routledge Handbook of Teaching Landscape*. London and New York: Routledge.

Waterman, Tim (2018) "Taste, Foodways, and Everyday Life," in Josh Zeunert and Tim Waterman, Eds., *Routledge Handbook of Landscape and Food*. London and New York: Routledge, 517–530.

Waterman, Tim (2017) "Publicity and Propriety: Democracy and Manners in Britain's Public Landscape," in Ed Wall and Tim Waterman, Eds., *Landscape and Agency: Critical Essays*. London and New York: Routledge, 117–130.

Waterman, Tim (2014) "Pedestrian Etiquette, Gormless Phone Users, and the Rise of the Meanderthal,'" 8 August, on *The Conversation UK* website: https://theconversation.com/pedestrian-etiquette-gormless-phone-users-and-the-rise-of-the-meanderthal-30282. Accessed 31 December 2015.

Waterman, Tim and Ruth Catlow (2015a) Sophie Hope (interview), 30 April.

Waterman, Tim and Ruth Catlow (2015b) "Situating the Digital Commons: A Conversation Between Tim Waterman and Ruth Catlow," Furtherfield (website), 28 October. www.furtherfield.org/situating-the-digital-commons-a-conversation-between-ruth-catlow-and-tim-waterman/. Accessed 20 November 2020.

Waterman, Tim, Ed Wall, and Jane Wolff, Eds. (2021) *Landscape Citizenships*. London and New York: Routledge.

Watt, Laura Alice (2016) *The Paradox of Preservation: Wilderness and Working Landscapes at Point Reyes National Seashore*. Berkeley, CA: University of California Press.

Webb, Tim, Chris Pollard, and Joris Pattyn (2004) *Lambicland: The World's Most Complex Beers and Simplest Cafés*. Cambridge: Cogan and Mater.

White, Frank (1998 [1987]) *The Overview Effect: Space Exploration and Human Evolution*, 2nd edition. Reston, VA: American Institute of Aeronautics and Astronautics.

Williams, Matt (2021) "Richard Branson and Friends Reach the Edge of Space, and Lived to Tell About it!" *Universe Today* (website), 11 July. www.universetoday.com/151806/richard-branson-and-friends-reach-the-edge-of-space-and-lived-to-tell-about-it/. Accessed 12 July 2021.

Williams, Raymond (2011 [1973]) *The Country and the City*. Nottingham: Spokesman.

Willis, Carol (1995) *Form Follows Finance: Skyscrapers and Skylines in New York and Chicago*. New York: Princeton Architectural Press.

Wilson, Edward O. (1990 [1984]) *Biophilia: The Human Bond with Other Species*. Cambridge, MA: Harvard University Press.

Wroe, Nicholas (2012) "Thomas Heatherwick: The New Leonardo of Design," *The Guardian*, 18 May. www.theguardian.com/artanddesign/2012/may/18/thomas-heatherwick-da-vinci-design. Accessed 7 July 2021.

Zeunert, Josh, and Tim Waterman, Eds. (2018) *Routledge Handbook of Landscape and Food*. London and New York: Routledge.

INDEX